Praise for *Grant's Final Victory*

"A moving account of a hero's last heroic deeds"
—William C. Davis, author of *Battle at Bull Run*

"Charles Bracelen Flood has combined his talents as a novelist and historian to create an irresistible book."
—Thomas Fleming, author of *The Secret Trial of Robert E. Lee*

"Charles Bracelen Flood writes . . . with an elegance and insight no previous author has mustered."
—John F. Marszalek, Executive Director,
Ulysses S. Grant Association, Mississippi State University

"Anyone with as much as a grain of interest in the nation's history will derive both profit and pleasure from Flood's work."
—Charles P. Roland, author of *An American Iliad*

"[A] winning book . . . [a] sensitive telling of Ulysses S. Grant's last campaign."
—Frank J. Williams, president of the Ulysses S. Grant Association

"[A] vivid portrait. . . . a grand achievement"
—Sidney Offit, president of the Author's Guild Foundation

"[An] exhilarating and heroic story" *—Houston Chronicle*

"Vivid . . . not easily put down" *—Richmond Register*

"A compelling read" *—Deseret News*

"Poignant . . . inspiring" *—Washington Times*

"Inspiring" *—Minneapolis Star Tribune*

"So well told, I could not put it down." *—New York Journal of Books*

"A lucid . . . swiftly moving narrative" *—Kirkus Reviews*

"[A] compelling portrait" *—Library Journal*

GRANT'S FINAL VICTORY

Ulysses S. Grant's Heroic Last Year

CHARLES BRACELEN FLOOD

DA CAPO PRESS
A Member of the Perseus Books Group

Designed by Brent Wilcox
Set in 11.5 point Janson Text by The Perseus Books Group

Library of Congress Cataloging-in-Publication Data
Flood, Charles Bracelen.
    Grant's final victory : Ulysses S. Grant's heroic last year / Charles
Bracelen Flood. — 1st Da Capo Press ed.
       p.   cm.
    Includes bibliographical references and index.
    ISBN 978-0-306-82028-1 (hardcover : alk. paper) —
    ISBN 978-0-306-82056-4 (e-book)
    1. Grant, Ulysses S. (Ulysses Simpson), 1822–1885—Last years.
2. Presidents—United States—Biography.   3. Generals—United States—
Biography.   4. United States. Army—Biography.   I. Title.
    E672.F56 2011
    973.8'2092—dc23
    [B]
                                                        2011020263
    ISBN 978-0-306-82151-6 (paperback)

First Da Capo Press edition 2011
First Da Capo Press paperback edition 2012

Published by Da Capo Press
A Member of the Perseus Books Group
www.dacapopress.com

Da Capo Press books are available at special discounts for bulk purchases in the U.S. by corporations, institutions, and other organizations. For more information, please contact the Special Markets Department at the Perseus Books Group, 2300 Chestnut Street, Suite 200, Philadelphia, PA 19103, or call (800) 810-4145, ext. 5000, or e-mail special.markets@perseusbooks.com.

10 9 8 7 6 5 4 3 2 1

To

THOMAS FLEMING

SIDNEY OFFIT

EDWARD PULLIAM

DWIGHT TAYLOR

*Valued Companions in This and Our
Other Voyages Through the
Life of the Mind*

CONTENTS

"I know two tunes. One is 'Yankee Doodle,' and the other isn't."

———————

GRANT
describing his tone-deafness.

"He worked on and on in his labor of love, his health gradually failing."

———————

GRANT'S WIDOW, JULIA DENT GRANT
describing the months in which her husband worked on his personal memoirs in his race with cancer to finish the book that would provide money for her after his death.

"It will be a thousand years before Grant's character is fully appreciated."

———————

GENERAL WILLIAM TECUMSEH SHERMAN
speaking of Grant in September 1885,
two months after his death.

"As we look back with keener wisdom into the nation's past, mightiest among the mighty dead loom the figures of Washington, Lincoln, and Grant . . . these three greatest men have taken their place among the great men of all nations, the great men of all time. They stood supreme in the two greatest crises of our history, on the two great occasions when we stood in the van of humanity and struck the two most effective blows that have ever been struck for human freedom under the law."

THEODORE ROOSEVELT, 1900

"I, his wife, rested in and was warmed in the sunlight of his loyal love and great fame, and now, even though his beautiful life has gone out, it is as if when some far-off planet disappears from the heavens; the light of his glorious fame still reaches out to me, falls upon me, and warms me."

JULIA DENT GRANT

ACKNOWLEDGMENTS

Of the many persons I have to thank, foremost is my wife, Kathy. She has stood by me in every way, often using her own excellent knowledge of history and feeling for language in reading many passages in the manuscript phase. My daughter Lucy, herself a writer, has added many pertinent suggestions, as has my sister, Mary Ellen Reese, the author of several books, who sketched out for me an improved approach to opening this book. My son Caperton, a business consultant, clarified certain nineteenth century financial business practices, and my son Curtis was immensely helpful during a research trip to the Grant Cottage at Mt. McGregor, New York.

Before turning to the many other sources from which I have received help, I wish to single out the constant efficient assistance and encouragement I have received from Carol Tudor Thomas, of the Government Documents division of the Crabbe Library at Eastern Kentucky University. For the third book in a row, she has kept track of the myriad odds and ends involved in a project of this nature, taking home hundreds of hours of work she has done on her own time. She also keeps me in touch with the library when I am away from it on research trips or on vacation. I will have much to say about the contributions made by other members of the staff of this really splendid, patron-friendly library, but this kind of assistance was begun several years ago by Linda Sizemore, the team leader of Government Documents, who remains supportive of my efforts.

For many years I have relied on the judgment and encyclopedic knowledge of my friend Thomas Fleming, author of some forty books of history and biography. As I developed this book, he pointed out a number of facts about the later life of Ulysses S. Grant that added greatly to my understanding of this often underrated figure. His efforts have been paralleled by those of Professor John Marszalek, the W. L. Giles Distinguished Professor Emeritus of History at Mississippi State University, who has succeeded the late John Y. Simon as editor of the monumental *Papers of Ulysses S. Grant*. I feel that Professor Simon would be well pleased with the way in which his marvelous life work has been continued since his untimely death.

Once again, my manuscript has profited by a reading from Edward Pulliam, who combines his instinct for proportion and accuracy in matters large and small with his knowledge of local history, particularly that of the Washington area.

I have taken great pleasure in my longstanding friendship and collegial relationship with Dwight Taylor, who entered my life when I was a freshman at Harvard and he was a dormitory proctor who lived next to me in Matthews Hall. Dwight, returning to complete law school after service in the South Pacific during World War II, had no responsibility for my indifferent grades, but he saw that I was a storyteller. and took an interest in my writing, which at that point consisted of required weekly themes and my fledgling efforts on the *Harvard Lampoon*. Now here I am, returning to Harvard for my sixtieth reunion, with Dwight, who went on to be a successful corporate lawyer, still sending me important suggestions from his home in San Francisco.

When I moved to Richmond, Kentucky, in 1975, I soon met the late Ernest E. Weyhrauch, Dean of Libraries. Rising from behind his desk in the Crabbe Library, which now houses 800,000 volumes, he greeted me with, "We'd like to help you in every way that we can." Ernie was true to his word; we became close friends and his gifted successors have continued a policy of giving me every possible form of cooperation. Now, thirty-six years later, the present dean, Carrie Cooper, is leaving to become Dean of Libraries at William and Mary, a position that speaks for itself. Betina Gardner, the able and experienced Coordinator of Public Services, has been named as Interim Dean.

In a large building that is open seven days a week and has more than sixty people working in it at various hours, there are some individuals I never see, but I know that they also contribute to this extremely efficient library's success. For the sake of simplicity, I will mention a number of Team Leaders and specialists, and then single out a few of these dedicated staff members, other than those already mentioned, who have been of particular help to me. Julie George, as Reference Team Leader, was able to direct me to many useful volumes, a practice continued by Interim Leader Kevin Jones, who also worked out for me a good analysis and chronology of Church-State relations in the United States, emphasizing Ulysses S. Grant's views on the subject. Once again I am indebted to Pat New, whose work in charge of Interlibrary Loan remains remarkable in my eyes: always ahead of me, seeing when I am going to need something more and asking me when I want it to arrive. Pat's work is ably supported by her assistant Ashley Wray. My friend Kari Martin, Director of Library Advancement, has promoted this institution admirably, and has been the moving spirit in re-energizing our Friends of the EKU Libraries organization. Her assistant Krista Rhodus has carried out her part in this with admirable energy. In past efforts, I have had much help from Cindi Trainor, Coordinator of Data and Technology, and Todd King, Library Systems Administrator.

Other members of the library staff have stepped forward to solve specific problems or needs. Emily Aldridge managed to pull from cyberspace an obscure citation hidden within another citation. Kelly Smith produced a detailed record of weather conditions in

Manhattan during May and June of 1885. Other information was provided by Sarah Cooper, Rob Sica, and Victoria Koger. Before Julia Turpin went on to work at the Henry County Library as Adult Services Coordinator, she handled my queries swiftly and accurately. Particularly on weekends, when the library is under the overall supervision of Michelle Scarberry, I have had the help of Savannah Marlow (I have told Savannah that with a name like that, she should be writing romantic novels, rather than working at the circulation desk.) Trenia Napier serves as the Research Coordinator in the new Noel Studio for Academic Creativity.

Among those who seem to be almost everywhere at once, I think of Dean Cooper's assistant Anna Collister, who I refer to as "The Go-To-Girl." When I was facing a number of deadlines in this book's transition from manuscript to printed pages, she stepped in; twenty minutes later she had devised a software shortcut that saved me hours of frustrating work.

What keeps me from staring at a computer for longer than I want to, is a kind standing invitation from "The Lunch Bunch," a group of staffers who gather daily for a brief but often entertaining session involving food and conversation. Largely consisting of employees under the leadership of Circulation Services Manager Jeremy Turner, the group includes Jens Arneson, Leah Banks, Stefanie Brooks, Eric Hall, Brad Marcum and Judy Warren, They are often joined by Beverly Hisel, who is the Stacks and Library Facilities Specialist.

Many hundreds of students and other patrons use the Crabbe Library every day, and Catherine Robertson, the Custodial Services Manager, is to be praised for maintaining the big building in its remarkably clean and neat condition. One of her workers whom I have gotten to know well is Sandra Blanton, who works hard in one of the most frequently used areas. No matter what the weather conditions, she greets me with a pleasant smile and a few words that encourage me to face even the most complicated workday ahead.

A final word is to be said for the cheerful staff of the Java City Café located in the entrance atrium of the library. *Everyone* shows up there sooner or later, with some students impatiently looking at their watches as they see if they can get the complicated coffee drink they have ordered at the last minute, and still make it on time to their next class. The unflappable workers behind the counter, led by Supervisor Ashley Obergfell and including Cari Huntziger and Brenda Lesson, smilingly dish out hundreds of these concoctions, and swiftly get them on their way. Although he is not a member of the library staff, my friend Professor Carroll Hale of the Department of Art and Design brought to my attention some favorable mention of my past work that will be useful in publicizing *Grant's Final Victory*.

Among my friends who have been helpful to me in this or my work on related past books are Thomas Parrish, an author living in Berea, Kentucky, and Gerald Toner, an attorney in Louisville who has written both juvenile and adult books and stories about Christmas. The writer Sidney Offit, who I first met when we were working in the Frederick Lewis Allen Room of the New York Public Library in 1959, has remained a constant source of encouragement for me, as well as being a force for fostering and rewarding worthwhile literary work. Barbara Pluff, a dear family friend from many summers in Brooksville, Maine, took the photograph of me that appears on this book's jacket. Dr. Paul M. Denoncourt, an orthopedic surgeon in Ellsworth, Maine, furnished me with a copy of the medical journal article dealing with Ulysses S. Grant's injuries and general condition in early 1885. I thank my friend Jim Lowenstein for his first-hand knowledge of the Grant's summer cottage at Long Branch, which Jim's grandfather bought, and in which Jim spent some childhood summers.

During my research trip to the Grant Cottage at Mt. McGregor, New York, a few miles from Saratoga, I had the great good fortune to meet Cynthia Finger, who spends many hours at the

Grant Cottage as an interpretive guide. This has led to frequent e-mail exchanges that have clarified and amplified the physical details of both the Cottage, and of the last five weeks of Grant's life, which he spent there.

When it came time to offer the manuscript of this book to publishers, my literary agent John Taylor ("Ike") Williams once again came up with an extremely satisfactory result: this book is being published by Da Capo Press and Perseus Books Group. My editor there, Bob Pigeon, shares many of my interests: in our first conversation after agreeing on some details of publication, I remarked that there was a place in the current shelf of books about Civil War figures for a first-rate biography of Philip Sheridan. Bob paused, and said in a bemused way, "I just signed up a biography of Sheridan today."

In the matter of my having "Ike" Williams as my agent, this is due to my half-century friendship with Alfred Donovan, who died in the summer of 2010 after a long and gallant battle with cancer, during which both he and his wife Melinda displayed magnificent courage and devotion. It was Alfred who brought me together with Ike, whose friendly staff includes his invaluable assistant Hope Denekamp, and Katherine Flynn, a fine acquisitions editor.

As the progress to publication continues, at Perseus I have had the able additional editorial assistance of Cisca Schreefel. Senior Publicist Lissa Warren has for some time been producing speaking engagements and signing parties for *Grant's Final Victory*, in some cases scheduled a year in advance.

All in all, I have every reason to be grateful to those who have been so helpful to me—family, friends, colleagues, and those strangers who write me what used to be five "fan letters." They keep me going, and herewith I thank them all.

A Change in Fortune

O N Friday, May 2, 1884, a carriage drawn by a team of two fine grey horses pulled up in front of the United Bank Building at 2 Wall Street in Manhattan. A coachman dismounted; with some difficulty, he helped his employer, a beefy man with a short grey beard, arrange a pair of crutches and step down to the sidewalk. Moving painfully as the result of an accident that occurred four months previously, the man approached a door that led to the offices of the investment banking firm of Grant & Ward. Men tipped their hats as he passed, paying their respects to sixty-two-year-old Ulysses S. Grant, the general to whom Robert E. Lee surrendered at Appomattox Court House nineteen years before, and the man who subsequently served two terms as president. At this moment Grant was the most famous man in the United States and was on his way to being the most photographed person of the nineteenth century.

That Friday in May Grant stayed busy at 2 Wall Street in his usual fashion. Although a full partner in Grant & Ward, he came in only three days a week and worked in a separate small office upstairs, primarily in his additional capacity as president of the Mexican Southern Railroad Company. (He reached this second floor by means of a hydraulically operated elevator, an invention coming into use in the downtown office buildings.) The objective of this venture was to build a line south from Mexico City to Guatemala; despite his best efforts for this Mexican partnership, including two trips to Mexico, Grant never succeeded in bringing the enterprise to fruition. He did, however, come to admire Mexico, whose soldiers he had fought against during the Mexican War, and whose beautiful landscapes he had ridden through at that war's end.

Grant's progression from the presidency to this office in Wall Street was far from predictable. In March of 1877, at the end of his two terms in the White House, Grant and his wife, Julia, set off on a trip around the world that would last for two years. Grant was a fundamentally shy man despite his years in the American public eye. The Grants thought of themselves as sightseers—private citizens taking an extended vacation after his many years of military and civilian public service. Yet in nation after nation, they found themselves the focus of enormous interest. Wherever they went, crowds gathered to see them. It became clear that Grant, although an unofficial ambassador, was one of the most popular representatives of the United States ever to travel abroad. Although the crowds who flocked to see him knew nothing about his background, they seemed to sense that this son of the successful operator of a small tannery was a man of the people.

At the same time, throughout Europe the Grants were honored and entertained by royalty and other prominent personages. In England, they spent a weekend with Queen Victoria at Windsor Palace. In Rome, they met with the newly installed pope, Leo XIII. During their visit to Berlin, Prince Otto von Bismarck—Germany's "Iron Chancellor" of whom Grant said, "He is no doubt the greatest statesman of the present time"—spent two hours in his office at the Radziwill Palace discussing world affairs with Grant, treating him with great respect as a military and national leader who possessed firsthand knowledge he was eager to acquire. Bismarck knew a highly organized and compartmentalized mind when he encountered one; describing the way Grant handled the topics that arose at their meeting, he said, "I saw at once that he knew his subject thoroughly, or else he avoided it completely."

Eventually the Grants continued on from Europe to Egypt, India, and the Far East. After visits to China and Japan, during which Grant so impressed the leadership of both nations that they entrusted him with what proved to be the successful settlement of a boundary dispute involving the Ryukyu Islands, the Grants crossed the Pacific on the liner *City of Tokio* to return to the United States. As they came ashore in San Francisco in September of 1879, they received an immensely enthusiastic welcome, but as was so often the case with the Grant family, a unique personal story hid behind the headlines. As reported by their twenty-one-year-old son, Jesse, who had come west to be reunited with them:

> Father and mother were at the Palace Hotel when I rejoined them, and mother was the first to hasten to greet me. "If your father asks if there is anything peculiar about his articulation, pretend not to notice it," she urged, after the first breathless greeting. And then mother went on to explain that father's Japanese servant [shipboard steward] had accidentally thrown overboard his [dental] plate with two teeth attached, and since this loss he frequently whistled in his speech.
>
> True enough, father almost at once asked me if I noticed anything peculiar about his speech, and I promptly answered no, to his evident relief.

Grant and Julia then began some months of traveling and living in various places in the United States. This period of Grant's life ended in June of 1880, when his backers at the Republican National

Convention in Chicago failed in their clumsy, complacent attempt to make him their party's presidential candidate for a third time. (At this point in his life, Grant was ambivalent concerning a third term, but Julia would have enjoyed returning to the White House.) That resulted in the nomination and subsequent election of Republican James A. Garfield, a man Grant characterized as "not possessed of the backbone of an angleworm." (However Garfield might have turned out as a president, he was assassinated ninety days after his inauguration and was succeeded by his vice president, Chester A. Arthur.)

Ulysses and Julia were then drawn to New York City by its magnet of money and success. Grant was a man who knew real poverty during his pre–Civil War years—at one point, having resigned from the Regular Army to avoid a court martial for being drunk on duty, he peddled firewood from a wagon on the streets of St. Louis. In Manhattan, however, he found that he had powerful friends who remembered and revered him as the victor of Shiloh, Vicksburg, and Chattanooga, and as the man who set new standards of military honor by his simple, gracious, generous treatment of Robert E. Lee and his men at Appomattox Court House. (For the rest of his life, Lee never allowed a word against Grant to be spoken in his presence.) Grant's rich admirers, including J. P. Morgan, raised $100,000 to help the couple settle in New York. In addition, they were supposed to receive $15,000 a year from a $250,000 trust that a group of his supporters had raised for him in the autumn of 1880, when it became clear that the botched attempt to make him the Republican nominee had ended his political career. The money was invested for the Grants in the Wabash Mainline Railroad, but the Grants received only $18,000 from the entire arrangement, because that company went into default in 1883.

The Grants' second son, Buck—thirty-year-old Ulysses S. Grant, Jr.—was already in New York. Educated at Exeter, Harvard, and the

Columbia Law School, he began working in New York several years before his parents arrived there. He spent part of his time in a New York law practice with the well-known attorney Stanley Elkins. Three years before this, Buck had also begun to work in Wall Street with two men of finance, Ferdinand Ward and James D. Fish, the latter no relation to Grant's secretary of state Hamilton Fish.

On November 2, 1880, Buck married Fanny Chaffee, the daughter of United States Senator Jerome B. Chaffee of Colorado, who had made a fortune in mining, banking, and speculation in western lands and now had two houses in New York. The wedding was in one of those houses; six days after that, Grant and Julia rented Chaffee's other house, and Buck and his bride, Fanny, moved in with them.

About the middle of 1881, the Grants decided to settle permanently in New York and sought a house of their own. For $98,000, they bought a townhouse at 3 East Sixty-sixth Street, a spacious four-story reddish-brown limestone structure with big bay windows, just east of the great Fifth Avenue mansions that overlooked Central Park. Julia later wrote, "It was a much larger and a more expensive house than we had intended (or had the means) to buy, but it was so new and sweet and large that this quite outweighed our more prudential scruples." With it came a life that included household servants, a carriage, horses, and a coachman.

Grant would not have become a partner in the firm of Grant and Ward had it not been for his son Buck, whose connection with Ward and Fish gave Grant the opportunity to make significant amounts of money. Despite his having been president, Grant had emerged from his two terms in the White House in March of 1877 with relatively little money saved from his army pay and presidential salary, that salary being $25,000 a year until his last year in office, when it became $50,000. In that era, despite the many great fortunes being made and spent, presidents did not receive pensions for their service. (Grant's parsimonious father, Jesse, was reportedly furious when Grant ran for president because a civilian office holder could not receive a military pension.) Much of Grant and Julia's modest net worth consisted of a few small houses and parcels of land in places where they had lived, and they had an income of $10,000 a year from rental properties.

Grant had little understanding of money. On their trip around the world, he had miscalculated the cost of their months of first-class travel through Europe. They ran out of money in Venice and were able to continue on to the East only because of $60,000 sent to them by Buck, who was making far more than his father ever had.

To become a partner with Ward and Fish, each of whom had put up securities they valued at $100,000, Ulysses S. Grant placed $100,000 into their then-small investment firm. Buck's father-in-law, Senator Chaffee, gave Buck $100,000 so that he could also become a partner, and he followed that with another $400,000 as an investment for himself. Thus Ulysses S. Grant's name became linked with the financial reputation of thirty-year-old Ferdinand Ward, a handsome, charming man known as the "Young Napoleon of Wall Street."

Ward's meteoric rise in that moneyed world, and the people he met on the way up, demonstrated the possibilities of the nineteenth-century American business scene. It all began for Ward when he came to Manhattan from the small town of Geneseo near Rochester in upstate New York and met and married Henriette Green, whose father was an officer in New York City's Marine Bank. Through that connection, Ward met the respected president of the bank, James D. Fish, a sixty-five-year-old man who had begun his business career on Manhattan's waterfront at the age of twenty-two. With a partner, Fish had rented an empty store and started what became one of the Port of New York's largest dealers in ship's supplies, selling everything from candles for lanterns to anchors and chains. As a service to ship captains, who often arrived in port with considerable amounts of cash, Fish would give them receipts for their money, lock it in a safe, and use it as his business needed it. "These deposits," he later wrote, "amounted in the aggregate to thousands of dollars, and although left with us for safe keeping, were a convenience to us, as they obviated the necessity of our borrowing money to carry on our business."

For the next thirty-two years, Fish was in effect both a merchant and a banker; in 1873 he withdrew from the shipping supply firm and started what he appropriately named the Marine Bank. When Fish met the up-and-coming Ferdinand Ward, he loaned Ward the money to buy two seats on the city's produce exchange. Ward made a profit on that and also successfully speculated in the stocks of elevated railway companies, the predecessors to subways. When these four men—Ulysses S. Grant, his son Buck, Ward, and Fish—became the four equal partners in Grant & Ward, this combination of fame and financial reputation attracted hundreds of investors, including many sophisticated ones. (Henry Clews, a prominent stock exchange figure who knew both success and failure on Wall Street, observed that Ward attracted "some of the richest financiers," who were "chiefly induced by promises of high rates of interest and large profits in various ventures.") At a time when stock dividends averaged 5.5 percent, the dividends of 40 percent or more that Grant & Ward began to pay out were remarkable, all the more so because the Bradstreet rating service annually gave the firm its highest ranking for financial security.

Despite his being at Grant and Ward, Ulysses S. Grant remained naïve about matters of money, and his principal contribution to the business boiled down to his partners having the use of the immense prestige his name conferred upon the firm. Thus he had time on his hands in his upstairs office. His friends often dropped in to see him: occasionally, using a small room behind his own office as a dining room, Grant would have a restaurant send in a meal. Among his companions were famous soldiers such as his flamboyant Civil War subordinate General Philip Sheridan, who since the autumn of 1883 had been the general in chief of the United States Army, replacing Grant's principal Civil War subordinate William Tecumseh Sherman. Among the political operatives often to be found in his inner circle was his lawyer Roscoe Conkling, the former United States Senator from New York who had botched the effort to make Grant the Republican nominee in 1880. Samuel Clemens, known by his pen name Mark Twain and nationally famous for his *Tom Sawyer* and other books, was also a frequent visitor. Eleven years earlier, with a collaborator named Charles Dudley Warner, Twain had published a satirical novel, *The Gilded Age*, which portrayed the dramatic economic fluctuation and rampant political corruption by which this dynamic era in American life became known.

Ulysses S. Grant knew little of what happened to the money that poured in—Ward would later say that Grant was in the habit of signing papers without paying much attention to what they were. Nonetheless, while Grant understood that he was not one of Manhattan's financial titans, the ledgers of Grant & Ward showed that in three years his initial investment of $100,000 had grown to $750,000 in his personal account. Other members of his family had entrusted their money to the firm, and Grant had reason to feel that the 25 percent share he held in a partnership that now recorded an overall capitalization of $16 million probably made him worth "well nigh to a million," as he put it, at a time when a household servant earned twenty dollars a month.

Ward, who left twenty-five Havana cigars on Grant's desk every morning that he came in—the same number that Grant had smoked every day for many years—said of the little gatherings that took place in Grant's office, "The topics of the day were discussed and the most intimate social relations existed. The General seemed to enjoy . . . [himself] as he sat in his familiar chair and smoked his cigar. He was so hearty and genial in his manner that no one could fail to like him and feel drawn toward him. And not only did he show this side of his character to men of influence and promise, but even to those more lowly in station he was ever polite and pleasant." At other times, Grant was to be found in his office penning letters to friends and associates from his days in the army and in Washington, and he was always available to sign anything endorsing the operations of the firm. Every three or four hours Ward would come in with papers for his signature; George Spencer, the firm's young cashier, said that on Fridays Grant would sign as many as fifty assorted letters and other documents.

In the world outside his office, Grant enjoyed being among New York's rich men, who saw in his military victory for the Union the same kind of vision and determination that had brought them success in their different fields. His friend William H. Vanderbilt, president of the New York Central Railroad and the son of the legendary railway entrepreneur "Commodore" Cornelius Vanderbilt, said of Grant, "He is one of us." Julia loved Manhattan's social life and remarked on "how regally New York entertains." Of the many dinners and receptions they attended, she observed, "In our journey around the world I saw nothing that excelled them in magnificence or elegance."

Seeing the millions of dollars now recorded in the ledgers of Grant & Ward, Grant began to mellow. Although those closest to him had always known him as a warm but reserved man, people in general now saw less of the grave, resolute public figure of earlier years. He had been trained in adversity. After he left the pre–Civil War army Grant had failed as a farmer and realtor before losing a job as a surveyor for lack of the right political connections. On December 23, 1857, he had pawned his gold watch for twenty-two dollars to buy Christmas presents for Julia and their children. Now, even though the stock market was having a bad year, he was able to give Julia $1,000 a month to spend as she pleased and asked for no accounting of it. He felt sufficiently affluent to contribute $5,000 to a fund to begin building the pedestal on which the Statue of Liberty was to stand when that gift from France to the United States would be shipped across the Atlantic in sections to be assembled and erected on Bedloes Island in New York Harbor. Always devoted to those closest to him, he gave each of his four young granddaughters bonds worth $2,500 as presents at Christmas of 1883. According to the memoirs Julia later wrote, this family prosperity caused Grant to tell her this, in her description of a conversation they had just before these days in early May of 1884.

> Julia, you need not trouble to save for our children. Ward is making us all rich—them as well as ourselves—and I have been thinking how pleasant it would be for us to make our impecunious friends (several of whom we were then helping) independent, get them comfortable little homes, and make them allowances. I would like to, and I am sure it would be a great pleasure to you.

* * *

AS GRANT ENTERED and left the office during these spring days, he was on crutches because of a severe accident that had occurred some four months before, on Christmas Eve of 1883. Starting to enter his carriage on the way to make a holiday call, he reached up to give his coachman a present in the form of a roll of bills. As he did, he slipped, crashed to the icy pavement, and thereafter was confined to bed. In a time of uncertain orthopedic diagnoses—the X-ray would not be invented for another ten years—he may have suffered from a fractured hip. Another possibility, expressed by a man who knew him well and said that a surgeon was called in for consultation, was that "the injury was thought to be a rupture of a muscle in the upper part of the thigh . . . any quick or sudden movement of the limb was so painful that the General was unable to move in his bed without assistance: he did not leave it for weeks." Grant gave his own estimate of his condition in letters: on January 21, 1884, less than a month after the accident, he dictated a letter to a friend in which he told him, "I have not been able to leave my room since, nor to dress myself"; and on February 27, two months after the accident, he said in another dictated letter, "I think the injury that I received from my fall has been well this last six weeks, but we have had a very horrid winter here, and it has given me what I never had before in my life— the rheumatism, and it has settled in the injured leg . . . and is very painful and prevents my being able to walk except with crutches." Occasionally he would use only one crutch, or a cane. During that winter he also came down with what he described as being the inflammation of the chest cavity known as pleurisy.

So, late in the afternoon of Friday, May 2, 1884, Grant left his office and went home in his carriage as a man still feeling some physical pain, but nonetheless a man at peace with the world.

* * *

HALFWAY THROUGH the following Sunday morning, May 4, Ferdinand Ward came to see Grant at his house. Ward passed through rooms that he described as being "laden with curios and rich gifts— the spoils of the Grants' tour around the world—which practically converted them into a museum." Grant greeted his young partner pleasantly; he thought of him as his son Buck's contemporary and friend and as the gifted financier who was steadily increasing the Grant family's assets.

Ward quickly revealed the purpose of his visit. He told Grant that the treasury of the city of New York had withdrawn so much of its money from the Marine Bank over the weekend that, unless $400,000 could be raised on this Sunday, the Marine Bank would not be able to open its doors for business on Monday morning.

Grant knew that city treasuries were sometimes suddenly faced with unexpected large expenditures, and he knew that his and Ward's partner, James D. Fish, was president of the Marine Bank—but he thought of that bank as being an entirely different repository of funds. "Why are you concerned about the Marine Bank?" Grant asked.

"We have six hundred and sixty thousand dollars on deposit there," Ward answered. "It would embarrass us very much if the bank should close its doors." He went on to say that he had been able to round up commitments for $250,000, but if Grant could not come up with an additional $150,000 before the following morning, Grant & Ward would be in trouble.

Grant digested this news and soon left his house, telling Ward he would come back with whatever funds he could raise. In his carriage, he began going to the mansions of his rich friends, trying to find someone who on this Sunday would write a check to Grant & Ward for $150,000 because he asked him to do so. After calling on several men who received him politely but declined to help, he arrived at the home of his friend William Vanderbilt—a palatial house that extended the entire block of Fifth Avenue between Fifty-first and Fifty-second Streets.

As anyone who ever read one of Grant's wartime orders knew, he could explain a situation with great clarity and brevity, leaving no doubt about his expectations. Vanderbilt had the same ability. As soon as Grant set forth the state of affairs, he replied: "I care nothing about the Marine Bank. To tell the truth, I care very little about Grant and Ward. But to accommodate you personally, I will draw my check for the amount you ask. I consider it a personal loan to you, and not to any other party."

Asking for nothing as collateral, Vanderbilt wrote the check, and Grant returned to his house, where a grateful Ward thanked him, took the check, and left. Grant believed that when the word went through Wall Street the next morning that Vanderbilt, a man with an estimated worth of $200 million, had given him $150,000 to cover a shortfall, everything would be all right.

On Monday, May 5, that assumption seemed to be correct. Ward told him that he had deposited Vanderbilt's check at Fish's Marine Bank. Grant spent the day uneventfully, and went home in the afternoon.

Tuesday, May 6, was different. When Grant arrived at 2 Wall Street late on that sunny morning, he saw a group of angry men milling about the doors of Grant & Ward. Inside he found his son Buck, who was in his shirtsleeves and vest, trying to talk to several people at once. Buck turned to him and said, "The Marine Bank closed this morning. Ward has fled. We cannot find our securities." (Buck said soon thereafter that his first words actually were, or included, "Father, everything is bursted and we cannot get a cent out of the concern.")

Without a word, Grant entered the elevator and went up to his office. He stayed there, alone, waiting to learn the extent of this emergency. The firm's cashier, George Spencer, caught a glimpse of him as he sat with his hands gripping the arms of a chair, his face expressionless.

The Man Waiting for More Bad News

FORTY-FIVE YEARS BEFORE this startling situation, Grant had been traveling from his home in Georgetown, Ohio, to begin his plebe year at West Point. During a squad drill early in that first year, a big, swaggering cadet named Jack Lindsay looked at Grant, who was then seventeen, stood only five foot one, and weighed 117 pounds, and shoved him out of line. Grant asked him to stop. Lindsay disdainfully pushed him again. Grant knocked him to the ground with one punch.

The Grant of Civil War days had many strengths, both mental and physical. Since his days as a slender West Point cadet, he had become deceptively muscular. Sometimes referred to in the family as "The Captain"—his rank when he resigned from the army in 1854—his sister-in-law Mrs. Orvil Grant compared his strength to that of her husband, and of Grant's other brother, Simpson. She said this of an aspect of his prewar work in his father's tannery:

Ulysses Grant had what was then called "the thrower's forearms;"
in a leather and saddlery business there is always the strongest one

15

who would throw the frozen hides down the chute for them to be cleaned and distributed. The Captain could take a hide with a weight of 200 pounds and throw it with a fling of his arm, whereas Orvil could not, nor could Simpson when he was in the business.

Grant came back into the army for the Civil War in 1861, and by early May of 1864, when he had risen to command the entire army, his men of the Army of the Potomac suffered the ghastly total of 17,000 casualties during their first two days of fighting Robert E. Lee's Army of Northern Virginia in the Battle of the Wilderness. When they marched away from those sixty-four square miles— thousands of its acres now a tangle of bloody bodies and burning trees—they thought that their new commander was, like all his predecessors, leading the Union's Army of the Potomac back to the north to reorganize and recover from its severe wounds. They dispiritedly trudged up to the crossroads where they were certain they would turn right to retreat across the Rapidan River. Instead the troops saw that their long columns were turning to the left— south, toward the enemy, toward Lee, toward the Confederate capital of Richmond. Grant was not giving an inch; he was taking them south. "Our spirits rose," a soldier from Pennsylvania said. "We marched free, and men began to sing." Regimental bands that had been carrying their instruments broke them out and started to play rousing tunes. As darkness fell, Ulysses S. Grant came up the road beside the marching columns, mounted on his big bay horse, Cincinnati, passing regiment after regiment as he headed right for the front with a calm, intent expression on his face. Grant's aide Horace Porter described the scene.

Wild cheers echoed through the forest. Men swung their hats, tossed up their arms [muskets], and pressed forward to within touch of their chief, clapping their hands, and speaking to him with the familiarity of comrades. Pine-knots and leaves were set on fire, and lighted the scene with their weird flickering glare. The night march had become a triumphal procession.

That was an entirely accurate picture of Ulysses S. Grant, but a Confederate prisoner captured after days of desperate fighting on the slopes and ridges of Chattanooga in November of 1863 saw Grant at an altogether different moment, one that prefigured the respect Grant later showed for a vanquished foe at Appomattox Court House. As this man and his fellow prisoners were being herded to the rear, all of them in wretched condition and some limping from wounds, his group was halted beside a road to make way for several Union generals and their staffs who were crossing a bridge on horseback. "When General Grant reached the line of ragged, bloody, starveling, despairing prisoners strung out on each side of the bridge," the Confederate later wrote, "he lifted his hat and held it over his head until he passed the last man of that living funeral cortege. He was the only officer . . . who recognized us as being on the face of the earth."

As for Grant's famous tenacity in his wartime campaigns, Lincoln said of him, "When Grant once gets possession of a place, he holds on to it as if he had inherited it."

~ II ~

By late afternoon of Tuesday, May 6, 1884, the man sitting at his desk at 2 Wall Street had learned a lot, all of it bad. His son Buck was able to tell him much of what had happened. Buck had been present on Sunday when Ward came and asked his father to raise $150,000 immediately. Buck had felt for some time that Ward and Fish tended to play fast and loose with money, but when his father secured the $150,000 loan from William H. Vanderbilt, Buck thought that the firm was "all right." Then on Monday, May 5, at a time when both father and son felt that Vanderbilt's check had averted a serious problem, Ward sent a memorandum to Buck telling him that he needed another $500,000. He wrote, "I am very much afraid that the end has come, and that unless something is done to-night, everything will be over to-morrow." That shocked Buck, but he did not want to trouble his father until he learned more. Buck, who left all the mechanics of Grant & Ward's investments to his partners Fish and Ward, gathered up a list of the firm's current holdings, and walked over to the Wall Street office of the multimillionaire investor Jay Gould.

Gould was one of the era's fiscal freebooters. In the tempestuous post–Civil War financial scene, soon after Grant began his first presidential term in 1869, Gould had attempted to corner the nation's gold supply, a maneuver that Grant had thwarted with the help of his secretary of the treasury George Boutwell. That was in the past; with the aid of skillful lawyers, Gould had escaped federal legal action, made more millions in other investments, and was considered to have as good a grasp of financial matters as anyone in the nation. Mark Twain said of Gould's role in the Gilded Age, "The people had *desired* money before his day, but *he* taught them to fall down and worship it." Buck had no hesitation in seeking his advice. Gould quickly studied the portfolio of securities held by Grant & Ward and said that most of them were not worth the paper on which they were printed.

Fearfully, Buck went to see his law partner Stanley Elkins, who was also the attorney for Buck's father-in-law, Senator Jerome Chaffee. Elkins told him they needed to confront Ward immediately. Not seeing him at the Grant & Ward office, they made their way to Ward's handsome house in Brooklyn, where his pregnant wife, Henriette, told them that he was not there, and that she did not know just when to expect him. Buck and Elkins came in and sat down, and waited, and waited. After five hours Ward appeared, and assured them that the firm's finances were in order; any difficulties would soon be solved. Elkins said that was good to hear, but he would feel better if Ward would write a check for $400,000 to his client Senator Jerome Chaffee. This annoyed Ward, but he said that if they insisted he would comply, and would deposit a check for $400,000 with the Marine Bank in the morning.

With that, Buck and Elkins said a polite good night, and left. As soon as they were outside, Elkins told Buck, "The whole thing is suspicious. Did you observe Ward had his slippers on? He was in the house the whole time and was afraid to come down and see us."

Thus, while Grant prepared to come down to Wall Street on that fateful Tuesday morning of May 6, his son Buck wrote a check for $400,000 in the name of the firm and sent it over to the Marine Bank to recover Senator Chaffee's investment in Grant & Ward. The Marine Bank refused to cash it, and with that the whole house of cards began to collapse. Ward had never deposited Vanderbilt's check for $150,000, and there was no evidence that Ward had raised a penny of the $250,000 he said he had when he went to Grant's house on Sunday. By noon on Tuesday, May 6, the nearby First National Bank had refused payment on three checks totaling $190,000 that Ward drew on his personal account there, because there was only $1,000 in that account. About that time, the Marine Bank closed its doors—permanently, as it turned out—taking Grant & Ward down with it.

The picture was still murky, but, coupled with what he was learning of Buck's experiences in the past twenty-four hours, Grant knew that his and Julia's money was lost. Other members of the Grant family had also entrusted their money to Grant & Ward. Among them was Grant's thirty-four-year-old first son, Colonel Frederick Dent Grant, a West Point graduate like his father who had resigned from the army three years before; since then he had been involved in running a furniture company in New Jersey. Frederick had turned over $57,000 to his brother Buck to put into Grant & Ward. Grant's beloved only daughter, Nellie, a married woman aged twenty-eight who lived in England with her husband, Algernon Sartoris, and their three children, invested what was for her the major sum of $12,000. His youngest son, Jesse, by now twenty-six and trying to make his own fortune in a mining venture in the West, had sent in $95,000; when Jesse finished counting up that loss and the personal bills he still had to pay, he had forty dollars to his name. Further complicating the tangled family crisis, Frederick owed $25,000 to his aunt, Grant's sister Virginia Grant Corbin, and $7,300 to another of Grant's sisters, Mary Grant Cramer.

The last man to see Grant in his office that afternoon was the firm's cashier, George Spencer, who had been duped along with Grant's son Buck and everyone else but Ward's accomplice, the hitherto respected Marine Bank president James D. Fish. When Spencer came in carrying some ledgers that recorded sums of money that no longer existed and perhaps never had, Grant, the muscles of his face working, said of Ward, "Spencer, how is it that man has deceived us all in this way?"

Spencer had no answer for that and remained silent. After a time Grant added, "I have made it the rule of my life to trust a man long after other people gave him up. But I don't see how I can ever trust any human being again." As Spencer backed out, still holding the useless ledgers, he saw Grant bury his head in his hands.

What Grant had just said about trust went to the essence of his being. He had always wanted to believe the best of people. When he began his rise in the earlier phases of the Civil War, he learned that a fellow West Pointer, General Henry Halleck, his superior in the western theater of operations, was undercutting him by taking credit for his successes. Halleck followed this by sidelining him after

Grant's immensely important victory at Shiloh; the only thing that kept Grant from leaving the army then and there was a personal appeal that he should stay for his own good and the good of the service, a plea made to him by General William Tecumseh Sherman, who stood to be advanced if Grant resigned.

When Grant became president, his second term in the White House, from 1873 to 1877, was particularly marked by scandals. He was surrounded by corruption in which he was not personally involved, such as the Whiskey Ring, a scheme wherein federal agents in St. Louis were caught embezzling more than a million dollars collected in taxes on sales of whiskey, rather than sending the money on to the Treasury Department in Washington. Some of the frauds involved groups conspiring to accept bribes in awarding government contracts, while other officials engaged in individual freelancing: George M. Robeson, Grant's Secretary of the Navy for seven years, was paid $8,000 a year, and in that time managed to deposit $320,000 in his bank accounts. During this second term, Democrats in Congress initiated an unprecedented thirty-seven investigations into allegations of corruption in his Republican administration. None of those hearings implicated Grant in any of the often massive bribery and kickbacks, but man after man who he had appointed or approved was shown to have abused the public trust. Grant became so wary of possible disloyalty that late in his second term he installed his sons Frederick and Buck in the White House as his personal secretaries. Despite the clamor for scapegoats caused by corruption in his administration, Grant's popularity survived it all. Crowds in the North and the West continued to think of him primarily as the general who saved the Union; indeed, other than during the time he served as president, he was universally referred to as "General Grant."

And now, seven years after he left the White House, there was this, a personal betrayal that bankrupted him and his family, committed by Ward, a young man who was a friend of his son, a man whom he liked and had made welcome in his house.

After a time, Grant stood up from his desk, arranged his crutches, and made his way out of his little office. At the age of sixty-two, five foot eight, and weighing 186 pounds—forty pounds more than he had at the end of the war—he was in poor health. This was no longer the tireless general who twenty years before had led to victory the largest army the world had seen. This man, whom the people of the United States had twice elected to serve as the nation's president, had to go home and discuss his day at the office with his wife. She had always been his closest friend, the individual he trusted implicitly. And now he had to go home and tell her this.

The Lady at
3 East Sixty-sixth Street

WHILE ULYSSES S. GRANT was a cadet at West Point, he made friends with a classmate named Frederick Dent, who came from St. Louis. After Grant graduated in the spring of 1843, now five foot seven inches tall but still weighing not much above 117 pounds, he was assigned to the Fourth Infantry Regiment, stationed at Jefferson Barracks, a post beside the Mississippi River ten miles south of St. Louis. Dent urged him to call on his family, who had a large farm called White Haven just five miles from there, and eventually Grant did.

Little Emma Dent was six years old at the time, and her eighteen-year-old sister, Julia, was away on a months-long visit to St. Louis. Emma described the moment that she met Grant.

I was nearing my seventh birthday, that bright . . . afternoon . . . This day, I remember, we were out in front of the turnstile and I had my arms full of birds' nests and was clutching a tiny un-fledged birdling in one hand when a young stranger rode up to the stile.

In answer to this stranger on horseback's "How do you do? Does Mister Dent live here?" Emma was speechless.

> I thought him the handsomest person I had ever seen, this strange young man. He was riding a splendid horse, and oh, he sat it so gracefully! . . . His cheeks were round and plump and rosy; his hair was fine and brown, very thick and wavy. His eyes were a clear blue . . . full of light. His features were regular, pleasingly molded and attractive, and his figure so slender, well formed and graceful that it was like that of a young prince to my eye.

Grant came to call several times, but when Emma's vivacious older sister, Julia, returned from St. Louis in the spring of 1844 he began to appear every day after he finished his military duties. "She was not exactly a beauty," Emma said of Julia, mentioning that one of Julia's eyes would go out of focus in a cross-eyed condition known as strabismus, "but she was possessed of a lively and pleasing countenance." There was more to Julia than that: high-hearted, charming, generous, and very intelligent, she was invariably at the center of every social gathering, the favorite of girls and young men alike. Having grown up on this big farm with three older brothers as well as her three younger sisters, Julia loved the outdoors. She and Grant would go fishing for perch along the banks of the broad pebbly Gravois Creek that ran through White Haven. Her impression of her new friend Lieutenant Grant was that she had met "a darling little lieutenant." Among their innocent occupations was that of riding their horses across the 925 acres of the family farm. Watching them, Emma did not know that in a jumping event at West Point Grant and a horse named York had set an academy record that would stand for twenty-five years, but she recalled that "Lieutenant Grant was one of the best horsemen I ever saw, and he rode a fine blooded animal." Julia would ride her spirited Kentucky mare; Emma said, "Many a sharp race they used to have in the fine mornings before breakfast or through the sunset and twilight after supper."

It seemed not to occur to this young couple that they were falling in love until Grant's regiment received orders to go to Mexico in September of 1845 in the prelude to the Mexican War. Then he realized that there was something "serious the matter with me . . . I mustered up the courage to make known, in the most awkward manner imaginable, the discovery I had made . . . Before separating it was definitely understood that at a convenient time we would join our fortunes."

That convenient time did not come for four years. In Mexico Grant fought in most of the major engagements, often performing with distinction, and received successive battlefield promotions for the bravery and skill he displayed at the American victories at Molino del Rey and Chapultepec. He wrote Julia frequently; in a letter he sent after the American victory at Matamoras, he said, "In the thickest of it I thought of Julia. How I should love to see you." They were married in St. Louis on August 28, 1848, with Julia's cousin Lieutenant James Longstreet, Grant's West Point friend and future opponent in the Civil War, acting as his best man. Then they began their honeymoon aboard what Julia called "one of those beautiful great steamboats," going up the Ohio. She recalled this:

> Our honeymoon was a delight. We had waited four long years for this event and we adjusted to one another like hand to glove . . . I enjoyed sitting alone with Ulys . . . He asked me to sing to him, something low and sweet, and I did as he requested. I do not remember any of the passengers on that trip. It was like a dream to me.

* * *

THAT YOUNG BRIDE experienced so much in the years that followed. By the Civil War year of 1863, when she was thirty-eight and the mother of three boys and a girl, her "Ulys" had become the Union Army's rising star, the general commanding the western theater of operations. Whenever she could, Julia visited him wherever his forward headquarters happened to be. After his victory at Shiloh in 1862, she joined him at nearby Corinth, Mississippi. In 1863 she was aboard a vessel just upstream from Vicksburg on the night that he took the greatest gamble of the war, moving thousands of men on makeshift transports past the array of Confederate cannon commanding the bluffs above the Mississippi to land south of the city and set the stage for his successful siege. The following year, when Abraham Lincoln brought Grant east to assume the double role of general in chief of the entire Union Army and to oppose General Lee in Northern Virginia, Grant asked Julia to join him at his headquarters at City Point, Virginia, on a bluff above the James River. They shared a cabin, a small structure that combined his office and their bedroom, and she frequently heard enemy fire along the river south of Richmond. On one occasion, after they had gone to sleep, Julia said this occurred:

> . . . a sharp, quick, nervous rap was heard at our cabin door. The General at once called: "Hello! Enter." Captain [William M.] Dunn entered the office door and said hurriedly: "General, the rebel rams [armored warships] are coming down the river and have passed the obstructions."
>
> The General at once arose, drew on his long boots and his coat over his pajamas. He lighted a cigar and seated himself, writing one dispatch after another. All this time, the only expression of excitement was the rapid and sharp puffs of his cigar. I remember it was like a little steam engine. I quickly dressed, entered the office room, and asked: "Will the ram shell the bluff?" "Yes, of

course." "Then what shall I do?" The General looked up and for the first time thought of me. He simply said: "You have no business to be here." And he had sent for me, mind you!

. . . The [leading] rebel ram did pass the obstruction[s], but was so crippled in doing so that it lay utterly helpless.

Whenever Julia came to visit Grant, she would visit wounded men in hospitals; she sewed missing buttons on the uniforms of the young officers of his staff, who adored her. And always there was that loving bond between Grant and Julia. His aide Horace Porter wrote this:

> They would seek a quiet corner of his quarters of an evening, and sit with her hand in his, manifesting the most ardent devotion; and if a staff-officer came upon them, they would look as bashful as two young lovers spied upon in the scenes of their courtship. In speaking of the general to others, his wife referred to him as "Mr. Grant," from force of habit formed from before the war. In addressing him she said "Ulyss," [she sometimes spelled it with one "s"] and when they were alone . . . she applied a pet name that she had adopted after the capture of Vicksburg, and called him "Victor."

In his letters to Julia, Grant frequently demonstrated the compartmentalized mind that had impressed Bismarck. Writing her on May 13, 1864, near the end of the Wilderness/Spotsylvania Court House campaign, he told her this:

> The ninth day of battle is closing with victory so far on our side. But the enemy are fighting with great desperation entrenching themselves in every position they take up. We have lost many thousand men killed and wounded and the enemy have no doubt lost more . . .

The world has never seen so bloody or protracted a battle as the one being fought and I hope never will again. As bad as it [the Confederate cause] is they have fought for it with a gallantry worthy of a better.

Near the end of this gory recital, Grant added, "Kisses for yourself and for the children." And to a friend who paraphrased his words, he wrote, "We have taken in battle over four thousand prisoners & I should think killed & wounded at least twenty thousand of the enemy. I never felt better in my life."

It was at this point in Grant's dramatic Civil War career, when he was being spoken of as a future presidential candidate, that he and Julia had a revealing conversation. Realizing that she had become something of a public figure herself, Julia consulted a specialist to see if surgery could correct her cross-eyed condition. The expert told her that surgery might have succeeded if tried sooner, but now it was, in Julia's words, "too late, too late."

I told the General and expressed my regret. He replied, "What in the world put such a thought in your head, Julia?"

I said: "Why you are getting to be such a great man and I am such a plain little wife. I thought if my eyes were as others are I might not be so very plain, Ulys; who knows?"

He drew me to him and said: "Did I not see you and fall in love with you with these same eyes? I like them just as they are, and now, remember, you are not to interfere with them. They are mine, and let me tell you, Mrs. Grant, you had better not make any experiments, as I might not like you half as well with other eyes."

Julia never doubted that her "Ulys"—she also sometimes fondly called him "Dudy"—was a man of destiny. Even in the seven lean years between the time he resigned from the army in 1854 and the outbreak of the Civil War, years when he was an obscure former captain who had to scrape for a living, Julia knew his hour would come. At one point she said, to the amusement of some friends, "Just wait until Dudy is president."

Then his hour began: Grant started the Civil War leading a regiment of less than a thousand men and ended it commanding an army of a million. His astonishing ascent was marked by innovation: more than any general in either army, he saw that the rivers of the South were an integral part of a vast battlefield area and could be used as avenues for invading and cutting up the Confederacy. Swiftly developing enormous administrative skills, he became a transitional figure in the history of warfare. At Shiloh in 1862 he rode a horse back and forth a few yards behind the Union infantrymen who were firing at the enemy; by the time of the siege of Petersburg in 1864, he was communicating with his corps commanders by telegraph from his headquarters miles behind the lines. In his military philosophy, Julia's Dudy was characteristically straightforward. "The art of war is simple enough," he said. "Find out where your enemy is. Strike him as hard as you can, and keep moving on."

After the war, life continued to unfold for Julia in a remarkable way. She lived in the White House for eight years as First Lady. During their world tour, in addition to their staying overnight with Queen Victoria at Windsor Palace, the Prince of Wales gave a dinner in their honor at Marlborough House in London. At one of several receptions in London she met the author Anthony Trollope, the poet Robert Browning, and the composer Arthur Sullivan, who was then collaborating with the lyricist William S. Gilbert on their operetta *HMS Pinafore*.

In Berlin, Julia received as gallant a compliment as any woman could. On an evening after the day he conferred privately with Grant for two hours, the tall, imposing Bismarck gave a dinner in their honor at the Radziwill Palace. Julia wrote of how that party ended.

When I gave my hand to Prince von Bismarck to say farewell, he bent low over my hand and kissed it. I said, laughing, "If that were known in America, Prince Bismarck, every German there would want to be kissing *my* hand."

The Prince, still holding my hand in his great palm, looked down admiringly upon it and said: "I would not wonder at all at them." I was, of course, enchanted with Prince Bismarck.

Julia had come a long way from her family's peaceful farm on the Gravois Creek, and every day of that journey she quietly demonstrated her devotion to her man. Occasionally that love expressed itself impulsively. On May 22, 1875, during her husband's second term in the White House, at an hour when she knew he was busy in his office with affairs of state, she nonetheless had one of the staff carry in to him a message she marked, "The President, immediate." Grant stopped his work and read this:

Dear Ulys
How many years ago to day is [it] that we were engaged: Just such a day as this too was it not?
Julia

Grant quickly penned a reply.

Thirty-one years ago. I was so frightened however that I do not remember whether it was warm or snowing.
Ulys

Julia brought the great events of life to the White House. The Grants' daughter, Nellie, was married there to an Englishman named Algernon Sartoris. During the wedding service, Grant wiped tears from his eyes. Julia's granddaughter Julia, daughter of the

Grants' oldest son Colonel Frederick Dent Grant and his wife, the socially well-connected Ida Marie Honore of Chicago, was born in the White House in 1876. (The timing of granddaughter Julia's birth saved her father's life: as a Regular Army officer serving with General George Armstrong Custer in the Black Hills of South Dakota, he received leave to travel to Washington for her birth; if he had remained there on duty, in late June he would have been killed at the Battle of the Little Big Horn, along with Custer and the troopers of the United States Seventh Cavalry Regiment.)

Writing many years later, Julia's namesake had these memories of a visit to her grandparents when she was three, after their post-presidential trip around the world.

> Grandmama was delightful; she let me come to see her dress; allowed me to touch all her dainty clothes, and even to try on a ribbon now and then—while in a special corner I found there was a little box or jar kept always half-hidden. Only she and I knew this secret, she said, and somehow the supply of goodies to be found there was inexhaustible and varied—cookies, dried prunes, small apples, peppermints, and so on . . . always leaving me eager for tomorrow's surprise. Grandmama was gay, knew poetry and stories, and was a human, sunny friend, and a sympathizer to little people.

> And then there was Ulysses S. Grant.

> With my grandfather my relations were quite different. He wasn't exactly gay, and I do not remember his laughing ever, but the talk between us was very interesting. He always took me seriously. I felt promoted and inclined to live up to my new position as his companion . . . We walked together hand in hand . . . I was not at all afraid of him, and though his face was generally grave, now

and then a sudden gleam lighted up the eyes and made them seem
to smile in answer to my chatter.

~ II ~

On this evening of financial disaster, when Grant came through the
door of 3 East Sixty-sixth Street he came right to the point. Julia
took it matter-of-factly, but later wrote, "The failure of Grant and
Ward came like a thunderclap."

Ulysses and Julia sat down and began to count what cash they
had. Grant had eighty dollars in his pocket; after looking through
her purse and going over to a cookie jar, Julia produced a hundred
and thirty. They could not cash a check because their bank accounts
had been frozen. Remembering these first days of crisis, Julia later
wrote: "Imagine the shock to us, who thought we were independ-
ently wealthy! . . . My sons had already ordered their summer supplies of groceries, wine, cigars, etc., and at once ordered them
returned as they could not pay for them. They had not enough to
pay for carfare."

Julia did not exaggerate the family crisis. In addition to the financial damage, during the next five weeks an avalanche of newspaper stories descended on them, twenty-one in the *New York
Times* alone. (The *Times* had reporters covering Grant on a constant basis from this point on.) Day after day, details emerged that
kept changing the picture from one of suspicious financial
bungling to that of alleged criminal activity. Wall Street veterans
and the general public became avid readers of this developing saga
of an unprecedented scandal. It had elements of mystery and
celebrity. New telephones that could carry local calls were coming into use on Wall Street; presumably those were already abuzz
with gossip on the Tuesday that Fish's Marine Bank closed its
doors, but the first story to break into print came two days later,

on May 8, when the column-wide headline and subhead on page
one of the *New York Times* read:

GIVING NO EXPLANATIONS
THE PECULIAR BUSINESS METHODS OF
FERDINAND WARD.

At this point, the reporter had found only the tip of the iceberg;
in smaller type, the subhead continued, DRAWING CHECKS FOR
$215,000 WITH NO FUNDS TO MEET THEM—THE MARINE
BANK AFFAIRS STILL UNRAVELED. The story presented far
more questions than answers. "Ferdinand Ward, who was so con-
spicuous by his absence on Tuesday, appeared in the vicinity of his
office about 9 o'clock yesterday morning. He spent most of his time
in consultation with his counsel [lawyers], and, acting under their
advice, it was said, declined to make any statement whatever. The
door of Grant & Ward's office was guarded by a zealous small boy,
who assured all inquirers that the members of the firm were not
prepared to give any information."

The figure of greatest interest appeared later in the day.

Gen. Grant's coach drove up to the Broadway entrance of the
United Bank Building about 2:30 yesterday afternoon. It contained the ex-president and ex-senator Roscoe Conkling. The last
named gentleman stepped out of the carriage, bade his illustrious
friend good-bye, and hurried into the building. Gen. Grant
glanced at the darkened windows of Grant & Ward, and settling
back in his seat, bade his coachman to drive up town.

An eager crowd of 40 or 50 persons surrounded the carriage, and
as it moved rapidly away, several persons pursued the ex-Senator
to ask how seriously Gen. Grant had been affected by the financial disaster that had swamped the firm of Grant & Ward and the

Marine National Bank. Mr. Conkling was as dumb as "the deeps" on this subject. Another intimate friend of the ex-president said, however, after careful deliberation: "If the firm of Grant & Ward goes under completely, Gen. Grant will probably lose all of his available possessions."

This initial story concluded with the observation that a bank failure could affect the behavior of the stock market as a whole. "The feeling among Wall-street men yesterday was decidedly nervous and panicky. In the early part of the day the market was very feverish. Rumors started on the slightest provocation, and within two hours the names of half a dozen well-known [financial] houses unwarrantably mentioned as being in trouble."

The next day, Friday, May 9, the *Times* offered its readers a darker picture. "Gen. Grant reached the building at 10 o'clock, and after passing a few minutes in the office of the firm went up the stairs to the room of Roscoe Conkling, his private counsel, with whom he was closeted for a long time. The General looked weary and troubled, and declined to see anybody but the most intimate friends. He left the office after 2 o'clock, and entering a carriage was driven up town."

By Friday evening, as Wall Street insiders began to learn more about what Ward and Fish had been doing, it became easier for that *Times* reporter to get quotes to expand his story. A man identified only as "a prominent bank official" came out with this:

Ward by his persuasions induced his friends and those easily gulled by the tempting bait of large interest to place their money with him . . . The victims, in drawing their principal profits, were simply drawing on the principal . . . In the whole business Gen. Grant and his family have been used as decoys, while reaping none of the advantages . . . I was told today by a man conversant with their affairs that Grant & Ward admit to owing at least $8,000,000.

In twenty-four hours, from Thursday to Friday, the picture given to the public had changed from, "Drawing checks for $215,000 with no funds to meet them," to an $8 million loss for those who had invested with Grant & Ward. Two days later, on May 11, a director of the Marine Bank who evidently had been kept in the dark about its devious operations agreed with the statement that it was "hopelessly insolvent," and added that "the transactions of Grant & Ward constituted the most colossal swindle of the age." During the days to come, a team headed by a bank examiner and a court-appointed receiver delved into a mass of paperwork, an effort that led the *Times* to report: "One of the expert accountants employed on the books of the firm said yesterday: 'I don't believe we shall ever get to the bottom of matters, as everything apparently has been deliberately complicated . . . the statement, at best, will be an approximation.'"

Approximation or not, the figures involved in the bankruptcy continued to climb, first to $10 million, and then to $14.5 million. The final accounting, no longer an approximation, showed that Grant & Ward owed its investors $16,792,647, against which it had assets of $67,174.30. At the time, $16 million would finance the cost of constructing 730 miles of railroad track—the distance from Salt Lake City to San Francisco—or build four major warships.

The fraud was stunning. From the outset, Ferdinand Ward and Marine Bank president Fish had been cheating the Grants and Senator Chaffee. The securities that Ward and Fish valued at $200,000 as their initial investment in the firm had been close to worthless. Beyond that, they had been cheating all their investors by making entries in two sets of books. The set kept for the official record, the one setting Grant & Ward's capitalization at $16 million, was a financial fairy tale. What had taken place was a variation on what a later generation knew as a Ponzi scheme. One part of it had been a complete misrepresentation: unbeknownst to Grant, Ward had been telling prospective investors that the former president was influencing the awarding of government contracts, and that Grant & Ward was using that insider information to great advantage. The *Times* said: "WARD invented the mythical Government contracts, and began to draw in the money of millionaires and old speculators by promising enormous interest and enormous profits." For example, Ward would take $100,000 in stocks put in his hand by an eager investor, and use those stocks as collateral for loans with which the investor could buy more stocks. That procedure was legal, and common practice. What he did then, however, was to "re-hypothecate," and, without the investor's permission, use the same stocks as collateral against multiple loans for far more than their worth, all the loans to other investors being made by his co-conspirator Fish at the Marine Bank. Out of the continuing stream of money coming in, Ward would hand out some of it to those who had put in their money first and thought that these bountiful payments were from profits earned by Grant & Ward's exceptionally shrewd investments. In fact, the majority of investors never saw anything approaching the total amount they paid in, and they never owned a share of anything.

* * *

DEVASTATING BEHIND-THE-SCENES encounters took place during these tempestuous days. This description of what Buck had to say appeared in a summary of his testimony before a court-appointed referee examining the collapse.

He said that he had a talk with Ward the day after the failure. At the time the phenomenal financier was in a state of intense nervous excitement, weeping and wringing his hands in his distress. He admitted to Mr. Grant that he had been a wicked thief and a great rascal, robbing, cheating, and deceiving him and the other members of his family from first to last. He was humble and penitent. Mr. Grant said that he then told his crushed partner that the least he could do would be to tell the truth in the matter. Ward promised to do so . . .

Ward's co-conspirator Fish claimed that, despite the evidence against him, he, too, had been duped by Ward. In scrambling to distance himself from his partner, Fish came up with this fanciful statement in his own testimony:

It was three or four days after the crash that Ward came to my private apartments on the second floor of the [Marine] bank building. He said that he wanted to explain about matters. He said that he could not help what he had done. He admitted that he had ruined me and my family by his deception and roguery. He had broken the bank . . .

I told him that if he wasn't the most ungrateful, contemptible and black-hearted villain that ever lived and a miserable, dirty reptile I would kill him. When I said that I caught up a chair and raised it over him. He crouched down on the floor at my feet and whined like a puppy . . . he admitted everything that I charged him with—deception, hypocrisy, treachery and ingratitude. . . . I advised him to go and commit suicide—drown himself, hang himself, or anything else.

In the meantime the law began to close in on Ward and Fish. On May 24, sixteen days after the first disclosures, Ferdinand Ward was arrested and housed in Manhattan's downtown Ludlow Street jail. He was allowed to go out occasionally, in the custody of a jailor or deputy sheriff, on one occasion going to Grant's house to try to see him. After eventually being tried and convicted for grand larceny, Ward was sentenced to serve ten years at Sing Sing and was paroled after six and a half. Fish, convicted of bank embezzlement, received seven years' imprisonment in the state prison at Auburn, New York, and served four.

Not everyone saw Ulysses S. Grant as an innocent victim: there were those who found it hard to believe that he had no idea of what had been going on within yards of where he sat every day. Others went further. A week after the Marine Bank failed, the *New York Sun,* a Democratic Party–affiliated paper with a long history of attacking Grant, headlined an editorial with the words, "Is Grant Guilty?" The paper quoted from a letter, one of the many documents that Ward had put in front of Grant that he routinely signed, which said in part, "I think the investments are safe, and I am willing that Mr. Ward should derive what profit for the firm that the use of my name and influence may bring." The paper said that Fish relied on this letter in good faith when he dealt with Ward's investors—a completely inaccurate description of what had occurred. Portraying Fish as Grant's victim, the editorial stated that Fish was "misled by the written word of a man who has been twice chosen President of the United States, and whose name is one of the most famous in the military history of modern times . . . For the love of money the greatest military reputation of our time has been dimmed." This denunciation was reinforced by an editorial in the *New York Post,* which told its readers, "The conclusion is irresistible that a large number of persons were drawn into the maelstrom by a belief that General Grant's influence was used in some highly improper way to the detriment of the government and the benefit of Grant and Ward."

In addition, some felt that Grant, while intending no harm, had been so negligent that he could not escape a measure of responsibility. C. W. Moulton, who worked on Wall Street, wrote to his uncle, the now-retired General William Tecumseh Sherman. Giving Sherman his views about the kind of juggling done by Ward and Fish, Moulton said: "The opinion on the Street is very unfriendly not only to . . . [them], but to the General . . . The practice of *rehypothecation* is looked upon here as an offense against the law and the ethics of mercantile dealing. No man or firm who have [sic] engaged in it have ever survived the condemnation that is placed upon it." He added, "There is much sympathy for the General, but it is mingled with much fault finding." As for Sherman, who was then in St. Louis, he had already written to his brother, United States Senator John Sherman of Ohio, who was in Washington. Usually loyal to Grant despite some immediate postwar quarrels about the scope of his authority as Grant's successor as general-in-chief, on this occasion Sherman changed his attitude.

> Look at *Grant* now—His experience in the White House poisoned his mind and tempted his family to yearn for that Sort of honor—he is now bankrupt . . . [by] coming into Competition with trained & experienced dealers in money—I fear he has lost Every thing—and 'more in reputation' . . .

That was not Sherman's core view of Grant's involvement in the collapse. Within three months, speaking to a reunion of veterans in Minnesota, he told them "no soldier ever believed that General Grant personally was in the least responsible or censurable."

* * *

OTHERS RALLIED to Grant's support as soon as they heard of his financial ruin. Long distance telephone service had not yet been established between New York and Washington, but telegraph lines carried the first news overnight to the nation's capital. The next day a bill was introduced in the Senate that would authorize President Chester Arthur to restore Grant's highest rank, that of General of the Army, and then retire him with full pay. In addition to the pension of $19,000 a year, there would be "commutations for forage, rations, the care of horses, &c., that would probably foot up between $4,000 and $5,000."

This was the reintroduction of a bill that had failed to pass three years previously. At that time, the man bringing it to the floor of the House was Congressman Joseph E. Johnston, the former Confederate general who fought skillfully against Grant and Sherman in the Vicksburg campaign. The bill ran into powerful opposition that defeated it. This time it met with approval in the Senate. The *New York Times* swiftly and eloquently endorsed that sentiment in an editorial that placed Grant's military strategy and victories above Lincoln's leadership in terms of what had defeated the Confederacy and brought about the reunification of the nation: "The plain fact is that it [the country] was saved by him, and that, humanly speaking, this great people owes its existence, with its vast achievements and wonderful possibilities as a united nation, to him more than any one man."

That was not the way the bill to benefit Grant was seen in the House of Representatives. According to the *Times*, "Mr. [Representative William] Springer, of Illinois, took occasion to speak in strong condemnation of the bill to retire Gen. Grant, and to give him a pension . . . simply because he had been unfortunate in Wall-street. It was said that Gen. Grant has not been aware of the dealings of his partners, but the fact remained that he had associated himself with speculators who were involved in the most disreputable practices which had ever been heard of in this country, and were only paralleled in other countries by the South Sea Bubble . . ."

The future of that bill remained in doubt, but other entities and individuals began coming to Grant's aid. Five days after Grant's bankruptcy became known, there was this, from upstate New York.

ITHACA, N.Y., MAY 13—A subscription was started to-day in this village for the benefit of Gen. Grant, to be known as Grant's Fund of Honor. . . . It is intended that everyone in Ithaca shall subscribe $1 and no more. A snug little sum is expected to be reached by this means for the hero of Appomattox . . .

Individuals across the country also felt moved to help Ulysses S. Grant. The first to do so was a man unknown to him. Charles Wood of Lansingburgh, New York, who had fought in Grant's ranks in Virginia against Robert E. Lee, sent him $500, "on account of my share for [your] services ended April, 1865." (As Julia remembered it, his words were, "General, I owe you this for Appomattox.") When Grant wrote to thank Wood, telling him, as Julia put it, "that his timely thoughtfulness had been a great relief to him," Julia recounted that, "The gentleman then sent a cheque for a thousand dollars, telling the General to consider it a loan to be repaid at his convenience." The next to help was Matias Romero, Mexico's minister (ambassador) to the United States; in addition to his vital role as a diplomat, he had served his nation as a senator and as secretary of the treasury. Romero had worked closely with Grant in the effort to authorize and organize the proposed railroad line south from Mexico City to Guatemala; although that had not materialized, they remained good friends. Now he paid a call on Grant, chatting with no mention of money; on his way out of the house Romero placed a check for a thousand dollars on a table near the door.

That total of $2,500 gave Ulysses and Julia a few days during which she arranged to sell two small houses that she owned in

Washington, a transaction that would make slightly less than $6,000. Even that payment would not reach her for several weeks, and in any case they knew this was only a stopgap. Their family world was threatened. Within a week of the first word of the Grant & Ward crisis, creditors repossessed their oldest son Frederick's house in Morristown, New Jersey; he, his wife, and their two children came into the city to stay with Ulysses and Julia at 3 East Sixty-sixth Street. Their son Buck was suddenly the most unemployable man in New York's financial district; with no remaining money of his own and worried about legal action against him (which did not take place), he and his wife Fanny went to live in a house owned by his father-in-law Senator Chaffee in Purdy's Station, a hamlet in New Salem, New York, forty-six miles from Manhattan in the northeast part of Westchester County. Grant wrote to his widowed sister Virginia (Jennie) Corbin, who had lost $25,000 his son Frederick had borrowed from her earlier.

> Dear Jennie: I presume Fred has written to you—or will write— of the great disaster to the firm of Grant & Ward. He and I will endeavor to keep you from harm . . . We are all well, and are trying to be happy. Do not be the slightest uneasy.

To his niece, his sister Mary's daughter Clara Cramer, Grant wrote:

> Financially the Grant family is ruined for the present, and by the most stupendous frauds ever perpetrated. But your Aunt Jennie must not fret over it. I still have a house and as long as I live she shall enjoy it as a matter of right; at least until she recovers what she has lost. Fred. is yong [sic] active, honest and intelligent and will work with a vim to recuperate his looses [sic]. Of course his first effort will be to repay his Aunts.

Ulysses and Julia had to give up the life of rich New Yorkers. She paid the servants their final wages and a severance bonus, sadly sending them off with letters of recommendation; he sold horses and carriages that he owned and regretfully paid off his coachman. He kept in his service "Faithful Harrison," a black valet named Harrison Terrell who had been with the family for three years

Grant was determined to pay all his debts, something that appeared impossible to do. William H. Vanderbilt swiftly dispatched his lawyer to call on the Grants and reassure them that his "personal loan" of $150,000, swept away in the Grant & Ward debacle, should not be a matter of concern. Grant considered repaying this debt to be a matter of honor, as did Julia, and he quickly set about selling the small pieces of property he owned in Missouri, in Chicago, in Philadelphia, and Galena, Illinois. To lessen the financial pressure on his friend Grant, Vanderbilt started the novel process of trying to find legal ways of delaying any attempt to repay him.

When the Grants remained adamant, Vanderbilt came up with the idea of taking title to their handsome house on Sixty-sixth Street, although he made it clear that they could continue living there. Then Vanderbilt and the Grants discovered that the Grants did not in fact own their house, which they thought that they had bought for $98,000 three years before. The man to whom they and their son Buck had entrusted that transaction was Ferdinand Ward. He had not bought it. Taking the $98,000 the Grants had given him to buy the house, Ward had managed to assume a mortgage for $48,000 that left the house still in the hands of the original owners, and then deposited the remaining $50,000 in one of his own accounts at Grant & Ward. Confronted by this additional theft on Ward's part, Vanderbilt took title to the contents of the house, including Grant's collection of Civil War and presidential memorabilia, along with the gifts showered upon him by heads of state during his trip around the world. With Vanderbilt's approval, Julia would later give all these objects, and Grant's large collection of books, five thousand of them a gift from the citizens of Boston, to the federal government. For the time being, no one else wanted to occupy the big house on Sixty-sixth Street.

While Grant kept up a dignified outer appearance, he was inwardly furious. Buck's father-in-law, Senator Jerome Chaffee, saw Grant frequently at this time and later spoke of the conversations in which he commiserated with him.

> No one will ever know the extent of his anguish, not even his own family, for he was the bravest in their presence. I was with him after the exposure of Ward. The General would suffer for hours in his large armchair, clutching nervously with his hands at the arm-rests, driving his fingers into the hard wood. One day he said to me; "Chaffee I would kill Ward, as I would a snake. I believe I should do it, too, but I do not wish to be hanged for killing such a wretch."

The reality of the moment remained: Ulysses and Julia had to have more money, just to live simply, let alone pay off their debts. Neither of them had any idea of how he could make any money at all.

Retreat to New Jersey

As the Grants took stock of their situation, they considered a property they still owned. Julia called it "my little villa," but it was actually a twenty-eight-room four-story summerhouse at the seaside resort of Long Branch, New Jersey, thirty miles south of New York City and two hundred miles north of Washington. The Grants had spent their first summer at Long Branch in 1869, soon after he became president; since then, Long Branch had provided them with a comfortable refuge from the heat of Washington and New York. There they would sit on a porch—Julia called it a "piazza"—that overlooked the Atlantic, and chat with family and friends. Below them was their private beach; among pine trees near the house was their little family playground, complete with swings, where their six oldest grandchildren, ranging in age from two to eight, could play with their friends. The grandchildren also had garden patches in which they grew vegetables and flowers.

A little girl who was one of the grandchildren's friends remembered this Long Branch haven, and Grant before he was on crutches.

At Elberon, New Jersey, General Grant's summer place was not a half-mile from ours, and I frequently played there with his grandchildren . . .

Occasionally the General came down and watched the fun. When one child climbed [a tree] too adventurously, he or she was peremptorily ordered to a lower branch. We were not to swing too high or seesaw too hard. He always looked out for the little ones of the party.

As for the man issuing these orders, she described him in these words.

If asked to-day how tall he was or whether his hair was turning gray, I could not answer; I know only that his hair was still thick and grew well on his forehead. What I remember distinctly are his eyes, his voice, and his hands. He had a way of suddenly look-ing up and fixing his eyes upon you. They were the finest fea-ture he had, true and searching but never hard; they were of a deep gray-blue, and had sometimes a questioning look almost like a boy's. His voice had a clear, carrying quality which was agreeable to hear; it was never loud . . . I used to watch his hands; they were well-shaped, with fingers somewhat long and taper-ing, and he had an expressive way of using the index finger of his right hand.

Even in this summer of 1884, despite his being either on crutches or leaning heavily on a cane, Grant, who always loved horses and had a seemingly intuitive relationship with and mas-tery of them, would still get up at seven in the morning at Long Branch and drive his horse and buggy for many miles along the ocean front and the inland roads. When Julia later wrote of the be-wildering days after Grant & Ward collapsed, she said of the house at Long Branch, "We decided at first to rent it," but they found that what people were willing to pay "was so small that we decided to occupy it ourselves and have some of our family with us, a very happy arrangement for all." "Some of our family" included the Grants' oldest son, Fred, and his wife, Ida, and their two children.

After the financial calamity struck the Grants in early May, they closed the big house in Manhattan and by mid-June were living modestly at Long Branch. Julia, who as First Lady had the White House kitchen staff at her disposal for eight years, now did all the cooking. Grant worried about being bankrupt and continued to feel wounded, betrayed, and humiliated by the way it had happened and by the questions that many people continued to have concerning his role in it.

~ II ~

During these weeks when Grant knew he was being seen as a failure and even as an accessory to the theft of investors' money, three events occurred that placed him back among the veterans of the war in which he led them. The first was the city of Brooklyn's massive celebration of Decoration Day, later to be known as Memorial Day. Grant and General Philip Sheridan, the latter now the commanding general of the United States Army, were the guests of honor. By eight on that morning of May 31, 1884, thousands of people had crowded around the ferry terminal at the foot of Brooklyn's Broadway, waiting for the big commuter ferry that would bring Grant and Sheridan across the harbor from the Battery at the southern tip of Manhattan. At nine thirty cannon began booming from that side of the water; on the Brooklyn side, salutes from rapid-firing Gatling guns greeted the great Civil War figures as the ferry arrived. The *New York Times* described it all:

A few minutes later the ferry gates swung back and an open carriage was driven out on Broadway containing Gens. Grant and Sheridan side by side on the back seat . . . A salvo of cheers that for a time almost rendered inaudible the booming of the cannon burst from the thousands who thronged the streets . . . [which] were lined with veterans of the war in the uniform of the Grand Army of the Republic, [and] United States soldiers and sailors and marines.

The excited crowd was paying tribute to the two most aggressive Union generals. At Chattanooga, where Grant had arrived to save the day after the Confederate victory at Chickamauga, he was struck by Sheridan's military skill and fiery fighting spirit. For Sheridan, as for Grant, the battle was never over. While Grant's other subordinate generals halted after driving the Confederates off Chattanooga's Missionary Ridge, Sheridan had his men chasing the enemy through the darkness until two thirty in the morning. With Grant promoting him, Sheridan had gone on to win dramatic victories over Jubal Early in the Shenandoah Valley. And here the two of them were, Grant now with a grey beard and short "Little Phil" Sheridan, broad-shouldered and barrel-chested, still with the same flushed olive face, black moustache and flashing brown eyes, coming up a street in Brooklyn in an open carriage to a reception for them at the house of a prominent citizen named Joseph Knapp. The *Times* portrayed the scene.

It was a triumphal progress. All the houses along the route were decorated with flags, and the cheering was continuous. Gens. Grant and Sheridan returned the welcome of the people by lifting their hats and bowing on all sides. The front of Mr. Knapp's house was a mass of silken flags and streamers . . . When Gen. Grant, looking well but moving rather feebly, was helped down from his carriage, and with the aid of a crutch walked up the steps of Mr. Knapp's residence, the cheering was simply deafening.

After a reception, a lunch, and a lengthy parade, Grant and Sheridan stopped at yet another reception. Here, the newspaper account said, "Gen. Grant was unable to leave his carriage, but Gen. Sheridan entered the building and was received with the wildest enthusiasm. 'Little Phil's' face beamed with good nature, and he shook hands with old soldiers until his arm must have been nearly wrenched from its socket." There was yet one more ceremony, a memorial service in a cemetery, after which the two generals returned across the water to Manhattan.

Twelve days later Grant was back in Brooklyn for an event that drew even larger crowds. On June 11 the city played host for the annual meeting of the Society of the Army of the Potomac. That army, although it had been under the day-to-day management of George Gordon Meade, was the one the Union Army's commanding general Grant had led in battle against Lee in Northern Virginia during the last year of the war. Some four thousand veterans of that force, a thousand of them belonging to the Society, were converging on Brooklyn; some brought with them tattered and faded regimental banners, a few with wartime bullet holes in them. The *New York Times* spoke of the event as drawing the largest crowds since May 24 of the previous year, when 150,300 people had paid a penny apiece to cross the Brooklyn Bridge on the day it was opened to the public. The paper reported that Brooklyn's streets were "one spectacle of flags and streamers, the buildings in many instances being almost completely hidden by the many-colored bunting which hung from its [sic] walls." Montague Street, down which the veterans were to parade, "seemed to be one continuous bank of red, white, and blue."

Grant was to be elected as the next president of this veterans' organization. Before the parade, in which he had declined to participate because of his health, the Society held its annual meeting in
the large auditorium of the Brooklyn Academy of Music. As they
entered, those thousand veterans and their wives saw not only scores
of flags and many yards of red-white-and-blue bunting decorating
the walls and balconies, but also this: "The stage was set to repre-
sent a camp scene. It was a clearing in a wood, in which stood five
tents, two on either side and one to the rear. To the right and left
stood a brass cannon, with a number of muskets stacked . . . Over
the stage a series of gas jets had been arranged as a greeting, 'Welcome to the Army of the Potomac,' from which depended a fine picture of Lincoln, the head encircled with flowers."

Among the famous Civil War figures sitting in the first rows was
Joshua Chamberlain, commander of the legendary Twentieth Maine
during the heroic defense of Little Round Top at the Battle of Gettysburg. Chosen to command the Union regiments that received
the Confederate surrender at Appomattox, Chamberlain had ordered his troops to raise their thousands of muskets to present arms
in a final salute to the hungry, exhausted survivors of Lee's forces as
they marched up to lay down their arms—an act that reduced many
hardened warriors on both sides to tears.

After some welcoming speeches and the completion of much
of the organization's business, the annual meeting turned to the
foreordained election of Grant, who was having lunch with General Henry Slocum at the nearby Brooklyn Club. When General
Martin T. McMahon, representing the famous Sixth Corps of
which he had been chief of staff, rose to put Grant's name in nomination, "the name of Grant had scarcely passed his lips when a
loud shout went up that seemed to shake the massive building.
Then a sudden inspiration seemed to seize upon everyone in the

great hall, and the soldiers jumped on their seats waving hats and hand-kerchiefs wildly in the air, and cheering themselves hoarse in their enthusiasm. It was more than two minutes before order was restored."

A delegation was dispatched from the meeting to inform Grant of his election and escort him back to the hall, and the meeting continued. Grant entered the back of the building as General Winfield Scott Hancock, who had thrown back Pickett's Charge at Gettysburg, was coming to the end of a speech of thanks for the "royal hospitality" that Brooklyn was extending to them all. Hancock had just finished "when a great shout arose, and every member of the society was on his feet, yelling as lustily as lungs would permit." The crowd had caught sight of Ulysses S. Grant, hobbling forward on crutches from the back of the stage through the scene of tents and cannons and stacked muskets. He came to the front of the stage and stood quietly until the long ovation subsided. Despite the speeches he had given as part of his presidential duties, Grant was no public speaker. He frequently blushed when applauded and always kept his remarks brief.

The cheers stopped, but the entire audience, the thousand men and the many hundreds of women, remained on their feet, silently gazing at Grant. They finally sat down, and he began: "Comrades of the Society of the Army of the Potomac. I accept the trust put in me today, and feel highly flattered that you have selected me, one who has never been more than an honorary member of your society, to preside over you." Then he added: "But after all, twenty years ago, our relations were intimate and close." This unleashed a torrent of appreciative shouts. After a few more remarks, during which he told these veterans that under his command they had fought "so nobly," Grant concluded with, "I shall not be able to join you to-day and tomorrow in your festival, but if I may secure my health again, as I hope I shall, I will be with you next year wherever you go."

With that, "there was another burst of enthusiasm, which continued for nearly a minute." Then,

> Gen. McMahon stepped to the front and shouted:
>
> "Now, to prove that the hearts of all soldiers are with our great commander, get up and give three more cheers!" Again the society jumped to its feet, and nine cheers instead of three were given, while hats darted into the air and the ladies present converted their handkerchiefs into flags and waved them furiously. Gen. Grant remained in the hall only a short time longer, and as he hobbled out on his crutches he was met with another ovation from the dense crowd which now filled the street.

Some days after that Grant attended an event that touched him more visibly. It was an unusual reunion, a convention of those who had worked during the Civil War for the United States Christian Commission. Established by the YMCA to assist Protestant chaplains, it had distributed medical supplies and comforts to soldiers in hospitals, prison camps, army posts, and even to men right on the battlefields, as well as conducting activities such as evenings of song to raise morale. Held in Ocean Grove, six miles from Long Branch, this gathering attracted ten thousand people to the Ocean Grove auditorium, a structure covered by a roof made of an enormous expanse of tenting and filled with folding chairs. Those who made their way down its sloping aisles to find seats included many women who had been among the five thousand volunteers who served in the Christian Commission during the war.

Grant came limping onto the stage, using one crutch and leaning on the arm of one of his friends, millionaire George H. Stuart of Philadelphia, an abolitionist and evangelical Christian who had been one of this organization's founders. As Stuart helped Grant settle into a chair on the stage, facing what one account described as the "vast congregation," the ten thousand people there stood and "cheered with a vigor and unanimity very uncommon in a religious assemblage." There was "tumultuous cheering and waving of handkerchiefs, which lasted several minutes." Everyone joined in prayer, and then sang a hymn.

The man who introduced Grant was a Methodist minister, the Reverend A. J. Palmer, who had been a private in the Union Army. He began by saying, "I was one of a million of your soldiers," and concluded his introduction by meeting the recent questions about Grant's integrity head on. "No combination of Wall Street sharpers," he said, "shall tarnish the fame of my old commander for me." As he said this, with Stuart helping Grant to rise and come forward to speak, the ten thousand people present rose again, cheering for several minutes.

In a voice that could barely be heard by those in the front row, Grant thanked Palmer for his words. The rich and influential George W. Childs, publisher of the *Philadelphia Public Ledger* newspaper and the man who occupied the house next to the Grants in Long Branch, was sitting near him, and saw what a *New York Times* reporter said happened next. Grant, leaning on his crutch, said that, an hour before, he could have "told you the good these agencies did, for I had especial opportunities to know of the services they rendered, the consolation they administered by the side of deathbeds, and their patient, unswerving attention to the sick, but"—referring to the way these memories were affecting him—"now I can't."

Here the General's voice, which was on the point of breaking several times, sank almost into a sob, and, with tears flowing from his eyes, he turned and sank into his seat. Tears were flowing from the eyes of the delegates and many others in the audience, besides those of the old veterans who sat in front.

Grant understood what had just happened. That afternoon, ten thousand citizens dedicated to good works, including hundreds of chaplains who had conducted religious services during the war, conveyed a redemptive message: they still believed in him.

5

An Opportunity

BEING AMONG THE MEN he had led and crowds that so clearly admired him may have been why Grant now reconsidered doing something he had declined to do when he thought himself a millionaire. He knew that the American public had a great appetite for articles and books about the Civil War. Many appeared in the years immediately after the war: in 1875, ten years after Appomattox, at a time when Grant was serving his second term in the White House, Sherman had successfully published his two-volume *Memoirs of General William T. Sherman.*

In November of 1883 Alfred D. Worthington, a publisher in Hartford, Connecticut, wrote Grant a letter offering him "at least twenty five thousand dollars" if "you will write for us a book as we shall propose, to consist of personal recollections & reminiscences mainly, to make a volume of say 600 to 700 . . . [pages.]" Two days after receiving that letter, Grant responded with, "I feel much complimented by your proposition, but I schrinck [sic] from such a task." When Worthington made another overture on May 25, less than three weeks after the news of the Grant & Ward failure became generally known, Grant replied, "I would have no objection to seeing you at any time that might be convenient to you, and talk about the subject you write about. But I do not feel equal to the task of collecting all the data necessary to write a book upon the War, or of my travels."

That ended the communications with Worthington, but another and more prestigious publishing enterprise was also interested in what Grant might be willing to write. As early as January, four months before the collapse of Grant & Ward, he had been approached by the widely read and well-regarded *Century Magazine*, which was planning a series of articles on the Civil War by men who had fought in it. The concept was to put before the public the best things yet written about the war. The magazine's editor in chief, Richard Gilder, and his two junior associate editors felt that the ideal person to write the first article would be Grant. With Lincoln's assassination and Lee's death five years after the war, Grant was by far the most prominent survivor of that convulsive event. Grant had no interest in even discussing the idea. "It is all in Badeau," he told them, speaking of a work published two years before, the three-volume *Military History of Ulysses S. Grant* written by General Adam Badeau, who had joined his staff as a lieutenant colonel during the final year of the war and continued to serve him while Grant commanded the postwar peacetime army. Emphasizing his views at that moment, Grant wrote Badeau on January 21 of 1884, "I have no idea of undertaking the task of writing any of the articles the Century requests."

The magazine's gifted young associate editor Robert Underwood Johnson later said of Grant's rejection of the overture, "His declination was so decisive that it left us without hope." They had been thinking of starting the series in the fall of 1884, but after Grant's refusal they felt they might have to postpone the entire project for a year. Then, with the news of Grant's financial plight, they renewed their efforts through Adam Badeau, arming him with a letter written by Johnson that said in part, "The country looks with so much regret and sympathy upon General Grant's misfortune that it would gladly welcome . . . the publication of material relating to him or by him concerning a part of his career in which every one takes pride." Grant soon replied, saying that if the editors were still interested in his writing about his wartime experiences, he would welcome the chance to discuss it.

This was received with "surprise and joy" at the *Century* office; within days, associate editor Johnson arrived at Long Branch to meet with Grant. Now thirty-one, Johnson had begun working for the magazine ten years before, when it was known as *Scribner's Monthly*, and he had quickly established himself as one of the best editors in American magazine publishing. Johnson could develop a variety of ideas for articles and make them interesting to a well-educated audience. For Johnson, this was a priceless opportunity to meet the greatest living figure of the Civil War. And here, welcoming Johnson to his house by the sea, was Grant himself. When he greeted Grant, Johnson paid little attention to the fact that on this warm June day Grant wore a heavy cape and had a white silk scarf around his neck because he had a sore throat. The two men began to talk; Johnson's account of his first meeting with Grant provides what is by far the clearest picture of how Grant felt about what had recently gone on in his life. After some discussion about the *Century's* overall plans for a Civil War series, Grant "began to open his heart to me as to the situation in which he found himself as the result of the failure of Grant & Ward. In his direct and simple fashion he reviewed the *debacle* of his fortunes without restraint, showing deep feeling, even bitterness, as to his betrayal."

Johnson added that Grant, who owed him no explanations, spent fifteen minutes setting forth the details of his being swindled, "to clear the slate."

In all this he gave me the impression of a wounded lion. He had been hurt to the quick in his proud name and in his honor, and the man who, we had been told, was stolid and reserved showed himself to me as a person of the most sensitive nature and the most human expression of feeling . . .

At last, with an air of relief, the General turned to the subject of the war, saying that his changed financial condition had compelled him to consider what resources might be afforded him by his pen. He told me, frankly and simply, that he had arrived at Long Branch almost penniless.

"[Grant] asked me how many articles we could use if it should prove that he could write at all . . . I replied that we could use as many as he could write, but that our first impression was that he could perhaps cover the ground in four articles." Johnson then mentioned the Battle of Shiloh, the bitter battle in April of 1862 in which Grant's victory prompted the Confederate soldier and writer George Washington Cable to write, "The South never smiled again after Shiloh." Next he spoke of the desirability of having an article on Grant's great success at Vicksburg in 1863, the victory that moved Lincoln to say, "Grant is my man, and I am his, to the end of the war." Johnson then added Grant's first tremendous clash with Lee in Virginia's Wilderness area in May of 1864. Finally he suggested that Grant write about his acceptance of Lee's surrender at Appomattox Court House—an idea that would be changed to having Grant write an account of the Battle of Chattanooga.

> He agreed, and said he would try the Shiloh first, and at once. I told him that we should be glad to pay him five hundred dollars for each article . . . and he said that it was entirely satisfactory. I left him with a deep impression of his dignified sorrow, his courage, and his greatness. I was overjoyed that our important historical enterprise was to have his cooperation.

* * *

THAT EUPHORIA in the *Century* office in Manhattan lasted for two weeks. On July 1, when Johnson eagerly opened an envelope from Grant containing the article about Shiloh that he had written so quickly, the editor found that it was "substantially a copy of his dry official report of that engagement, as printed in the 'Rebellion Records,' with which we had already made ourselves familiar."

For a young editor who felt that he was involved in the most important project of his career to date, this was distressing. The mood at the magazine was one of "dismay." Johnson began to demonstrate what made him the editor he was. He sensed that Grant might be able to write the most important reflections anyone ever wrote on the Civil War, and that Grant's recollections, and the conclusions he could draw from them, might be some of the greatest writing a president ever left to the nation. Of that moment of "dismay," Johnson said this:

> The General, of course, did not realize the requirements of a popular publication on the war, and it was for me to turn this new disaster of Shiloh into a signal success. This required all the tact that I could muster, that he should not be discouraged, and at the same time our project should be saved from the blight of the deadly official report . . . which is lacking in the personal touch that makes a great battle a vital and interesting human event.

Johnson went to see Grant again at Long Branch, this time carrying the lifeless article in an inside pocket. He recalled that, without conveying any of the disappointment he and his colleagues felt, he "managed to draw him into a description of the engagement. I then discovered that General Grant, instead of being a silent man, was positively loquacious. He spoke rapidly and long of the two days' battle [of Shiloh]." Among other things, "he revealed the human side of his experience, saying . . . that in the pouring rain that succeeded the first day he had gone for shelter into an improvised military hospital. 'But,' he said, 'I couldn't stand the amputations, and had to go out in the rain and sit for the most of the night against a tree.'"

Before he left Long Branch, Johnson gave Grant some instructions that Grant took as if they were marching orders.

> I told him that what was desirable for the success of the paper [article] was to approximate such a talk as he would make to friends after dinner, some of which would know all about the battle and some nothing at all, and that the public . . . was particularly interested in his point of view, in everything that concerned him, in what he planned, thought, saw, and did.
>
> This was a new idea to him, and when I told him that I was convinced that he could do what was desired if he would not try too hard, he said that he would begin again.

Grant set to work. Johnson said, "no one ever had an apter pupil. He got out of the writing not only diversion from his troubles but the happiness of finding that he could do something new. He said to me once: 'Why, I am positively enjoying the work. I am keeping at it every night and day, and Sundays.'"

Writing about the war seemed to revive the immense energy that Grant had brought to his military campaigns. On July 1 Johnson had opened the unacceptable manuscript that occasioned dismay; by July 15 Grant submitted the Shiloh article in a revised form that Johnson found "admirable," although it required more work. As if he were back in the middle of that battle, Grant recalled his experiences in passages such as one that started off as a quiet moment early on the afternoon of the second day at Shiloh, when he and two members of his staff, then-colonel James B. McPherson and a Major Hawkins, were riding along a clearing above the Tennessee River.

> There did not appear to be an enemy to our right, until suddenly a battery with musketry opened upon us from the edge of the woods on the other side of the clearing. The shells and balls whistled about our ears very fast for about a minute. I do not think it took longer than that for us to get out of range and out of sight. In the sudden start we made, Major Hawkins lost his hat. He did not stop to pick it up.
>
> When we arrived at a perfectly safe position we halted to take account of damages. McPherson's horse was panting as if ready to drop. On examination it was found that a ball had struck him forward of the flank just back of the saddle, and gone entirely through. In a few minutes the poor beast dropped dead; he had given no sign of injury until we came to a stop. A ball had struck the metal scabbard of my sword, just below the hilt, and broken it nearly off: before the battle was over it had broken off entirely. There were three of us: One had lost a horse, killed; one a hat and one a sword-scabbard. All were thankful that it was no worse.

* * *

AS THE SUMMER of 1884 unfolded, the *Century*'s senior editor, Richard Watson Gilder, worried that other publishers were learning that Grant was at work on articles that could be the basis of a book, and that his company had no contract for that book. Prodding the Century Company's president, Roswell Smith, the executive who authorized all its publishing contracts, Gilder urged him to make Grant a definite offer for a book. "We have never had such a card before as Grant," he said, adding that Grant had an international reputation, and that a book by him would have international sales possibilities.

"If we take it, it would be good for the book to announce its appearance in England, France, & Germany—simultaneously."

Gilder's concern led Johnson to visit Grant at Long Branch in early September, this time accompanied by Century president Smith. In due course, Smith raised the subject of Grant's completing his four articles and then writing an entire book. Weeks before this, Grant had written his wartime staff officer William R. Rowley that he intended to write and "probably will publish" something beyond his four articles, a work that would "finish all my connection with the war of the rebellion." He had also written a letter to his five-year-old granddaughter, Vivien Sartoris, who with her mother, Ellen (Nellie) Grant Sartoris, had come over from England to visit the past spring and departed at the end of July. Addressing her as "My Dear Little Pet Vivien," he said in part, "Your Grand-pa has been busy ever since you left writing his campaigns which he intends to publish in a book. It will probable [sic] be a year yet before it is ready. You must make your ma learn you to read so that you can read it when it is printed."

In light of these expressed intentions and his awareness of his military record, Grant was perhaps being a bit disingenuous when he now asked Smith, "Do you really think any one would be interested in a book by me?" Smith answered: "General, do you not think the public would read with avidity Napoleon's personal account of his battles?"

According to Johnson, at that point it was understood that Grant would write a book whose title would include the word "Memoirs," to be published by the Century on terms, as Johnson put it, "that should be satisfactory to the author." Smith certainly thought he had a deal: he wrote senior editor Gilder, "When the book is ready, he [Grant] is ready to come to us with it."

No contract was signed, however, and Grant continued working on his articles, substituting by mutual agreement the dramatic battle of Chattanooga for Lee's surrender at Appomattox. The possibility of a book that would be published by the Century remained unclear, but in terms of the articles Grant was writing, what Johnson had hoped would happen, did happen. Grant kept putting pen to paper day after day, and his experiences sprang ever more to life. This virile style, supple and powerful, had been observed, not in Grant's writing but in his conversation, by John Russell Young of the *New York Herald*, who accompanied the Grants on their trip around the world. Young came to see Grant as a man who could put everything together eloquently, colorfully: what he knew of history, what he was seeing in Athens, Constantinople, the Holy Land, Egypt—the monuments, the street scenes, the great leaders, the peasants, the beggars. He was, Young said, a fine conversational companion, "a remarkably good one."

His manner is clear and terse. He narrates a story as clearly as he would demonstrate a problem in geometry. His mind is accurate and perspicacious . . . The impression General Grant makes upon you is that he has immense resources in reserve. He has in eminent degree that 'two o'clock in the morning courage' that Napoleon said he alone possessed among his marshals and generals. You are also impressed with his good feeling and magnanimity in speaking of his comrades and rivals in the war. In some cases—especially in the cases of Sherman and Sheridan, [Major General James M.] McPherson and Lincoln—it becomes an enthusiasm quite beautiful to witness.

Young had the opportunity to spend many hours conversing with Grant. Grant was not known as a wit, but occasionally he came up with just the kind of droll anecdote that Lincoln used to great effect. At a reunion of his veterans, he told them this, in reference to his receiving an order from General Halleck to halt a major attack along

the Mississippi just after he had launched it: "The whole thing reminded me of a traveler who stopped at a restaurant and called for
a raw egg. As he swallowed it down he heard a chicken chirp, but
the wayfarer had only time to say, 'My friend, you spoke too late.'

Sitting on deck aboard the American battleship USS *Richmond*
as they steamed from the Chinese coast to the Japanese port of Nagasaki, Grant spoke to Young of Robert E. Lee's surrender at Appomattox Court House. Young wrote down what Grant had to say
about that greatly famous event, but, being a trained reporter,
moved on to ask Grant about his less-known role in saving Lee from
being tried as a traitor—something that could have resulted in Lee
being hanged for treason. That involved the actions taken by Lincoln's vice president Andrew Johnson soon after he became president upon Lincoln's assassination. This question from Johnson
brought forth Grant's concern for the nation, his belief in reconciliation that became manifest at Appomattox and never ceased.

> "Yes," said the General, "Mr. Johnson had made up his mind to
> arrest Lee and the leading Southern officers. It was in the begin-
> ning of his administration, when he was making speeches saying
> he had resolved to make all treason odious . . . I always said the
> parole of Lee protected him as long as he observed it."

Grant was referring to the oath that Lee and his men had taken,
"to be paroled and disqualified from taking up arms again." They
would not be marched off to prison camps. On the strength of their
promise to behave peaceably, they could leave the area of Appomattox Court House as disarmed individuals, paroled prisoners who
need not spend a day in captivity but were free to make their way
home as best they could.

In telling Young about his role in protecting Lee, Grant recalled what had been one of the greatest confrontations between

civilian and military authority in American history. When federal lawyers went ahead and indicted Lee for treason, Grant went to the White House and protested the action. As Grant told Young, President Johnson "wanted to know why any military commander had a right to protect an arch-traitor from the laws." Grant described his response.

> I was angry at this, and I spoke earnestly and plainly to the President. I said, as General, it was none of my business what he or Congress did with General Lee or his other commanders. He might do as he pleased about civil rights, confiscation of property, and so on. But a general commanding troops has certain responsibilities and duties and powers, which are supreme. He must deal with the enemy in front of him so as to destroy him. He must kill him, capture him, or parole him. His engagements are sacred so far as they lead to the destruction of the foe.
>
> I had made certain engagements with General Lee—the best and only terms. If I had told him and his army that their liberty would be invaded, that they would be open to arrest, trial, and execution for treason, Lee would never have surrendered, and we should have lost many lives in destroying him. Now my terms of surrender were according to military law, and so long as Lee was observing his parole I would never consent to his arrest.

Grant added to Young, "I remember feeling very strongly on the subject." He certainly had. Grant let it be known in Washington that he would resign from the army in protest if Lee were arrested. President Johnson and the federal prosecutors did not intend to argue with the victorious general in chief of the United States Army about the immunity conferred by a military parole. They quietly halted the treason proceedings, without dismissing them; Lee was never arrested. As Grant put it to Young as they sat on deck heading for Nagasaki fourteen years after the war's end, "The matter was allowed to die out."

~ II ~

General Adam Badeau, a temperamental man with an unusual history, would put forth a greatly different account of who spent the most time with Grant that August and September of 1884, and who had the greater influence on his work. This former member of Grant's wartime headquarters staff had entered the army from a background unlike the others of that group, four of whom were West Pointers. Badeau spent the years before the war in New York City as a theater critic and in 1859 published a collection of his reviews titled *The Vagabond*. He volunteered for the Union Army in 1862. On the day in 1863 that he was scheduled to report to Grant to serve as a military secretary, Badeau was severely wounded in the battle at Port Hudson, south of Vicksburg. Sent north to convalesce, he was nursed back to health in New York by two of his actor friends: Edwin Booth and Booth's younger brother, John Wilkes Booth, who would kill Abraham Lincoln two years later. (There is no evidence that Grant ever knew of this relationship.)

Returned to duty in 1864, Badeau played the role of an efficient military secretary on Grant's staff, rising to the rank of lieutenant colonel by the war's end. He remained on his staff while Grant commanded the postwar Regular Army from its headquarters in Washington.

Badeau always had a wide circle of acquaintances. While living in a Washington boardinghouse during the years after the war, he found himself sharing a table at every meal with the author Henry Adams, of the legendary Massachusetts political family. In his autobiography *The Education of Henry Adams*, he observed that Badeau was "exceedingly social, though not in appearance imposing. He was stout: his face was red, and his habits were regularly irregular, but he was very intelligent, a good newspaperman, and an excellent military historian." Adams's reference to Badeau's "irregular" habits included drinking to excess. "He talked much about Grant, and showed a certain feeling for analysis of character, as a true literary critic would naturally do. Loyal to Grant, and still more so to Mrs. Grant, who acted as his patron, he said nothing, even when far gone, that was offensive about either."

When Grant became president in March of 1869, Badeau, by now promoted to the brevet [honorary] rank of brigadier general, lived and worked for a time in the White House. He recalled that he had "some charge of Grant's unofficial letters for a while," and with Grant's permission used his wartime records for what eventually became Badeau's *Military History of Ulysses S. Grant*. Badeau worked slowly and argued with publishers along the way. The third and final volume of this work was not published until two years before the Grant & Ward failure.

In 1870, after Badeau had served in the White House for several months, Grant rewarded him for his six years of loyal work in war and peace by sending him to London as consul general. He held that post for eleven years, during which he also acted briefly as Grant's aide-de-camp when the Grants visited England, Scotland, and Ireland as part of their round-the-world trip. After that, Badeau became consul in Havana, but he had resigned earlier in 1884 in a dispute with the State Department over the department's unwillingness to investigate his allegations of "culpable frauds at the Consulate." Badeau was also involved in a suit against the United States government in the federal Court of Claims, based on his contention that his having retired from the army so that he could accept diplomatic rank should not affect his right to a military pension. (This paralleled Grant's situation of forfeiting his pension as a lieutenant general when he became president, but Grant was able to get Badeau a military pension of $1,500 a year.) His lawyers' fees continued to mount; he was also having differences with the State Department about what he called his "London accounts." He and Grant had corresponded frequently over the years and seen each other a number of times; when Badeau and Grant met again in New York in 1884, both men needed money.

According to Badeau, he was in on Grant's article describing Shiloh from the start. He said that when Grant went to Long Branch that summer of 1884, "[he] soon after sent for me and showed me a few pages he had written and called an article. The fragment was terse and clear, of course, like almost everything he wrote, but too laconic and compact, I knew, to suit the editorial purpose." As Badeau later wrote of it, he made the same suggestions to Grant that Johnson did, and Grant "seized the idea, and developed the sketch into a more protracted effort."

Whatever Badeau's contribution to the Shiloh article may have been, Johnson was not impressed by what he knew of it. He later said that when the page proofs of that article were sent to Grant, "a duplicate set was sent to General Badeau, who made a few single-word corrections of no importance, such as 'received' for 'got'—by no means an improvement on the General's Saxon style."

Although other factors would come into play as Grant's writing about the Civil War developed, a rivalry began between Johnson and Badeau. Because Badeau had a way of being controversial, frequently treating even Grant in an abrupt manner, his side of the story gained less credence, but he saved letters from Grant that showed Grant did indeed want his help, and received it. On July 3, at a time when Grant's first inadequate article on Shiloh was causing "dismay" at the *Century* office in Manhattan, Grant wrote Badeau, "I commenced on the Vicksburg campaign to-day." Looking just ahead, and aware that Badeau was planning a visit to his hometown of Tannersville in the Catskill Mountains ninety miles north of New York City, Grant referred to his proposed articles on the Battle of the Wilderness and Vicksburg as if he were reliving his leadership of those campaigns: "I do not think I will be able to get through the Wilderness before you go to the Mountains. But I will take Vicksburg and will be glad to see you here." Speaking of what he had begun to write about Vicksburg, Grant added, "In fact I do not want to submit my article until you have approved it." Eighteen days later he followed that up by writing Badeau that he would have the Vicksburg article "finished, ready for revision, to-morrow. If you feel like a change of mountain air to sea air for a while I will be glad to see you here. If you are not through with your article [one that Badeau was writing about Grant] you can finish it here." Grant wrote yet another letter five days after that, telling Badeau on August 26, "I will be glad to see you for at least a week."

Badeau came to Long Branch and began a form of working relationship with Grant that never became clear—a role something between an editorial adviser and a secretary. Grant was tackling his new task with the energy and absorption that had made his military planning so effective. In an upstairs room he had maps and reports and writing materials spread out on a white pine table that had been brought up from the kitchen. Julia sat in a wicker chair nearby, watching him work. Badeau later wrote this about his stay with the Grants.

> When I went to General Grant's house after this invitation he informed me that he wanted to write his "Memoirs" and particularly desired my assistance. Indeed, he said he should not think of attempting the work unless with my aid—and concurrence; for he had always promised that my history *[Military History of Ulysses S. Grant]* should take the place of all that he would have to say on the subject. He accordingly made me a proposition which he requested me to keep entirely secret between him and me, not divulging it even to his family; and I accepted his terms.

Badeau closed this passage with, "I stayed ten days at his house planning the entire work with him, revising once more what he had written about Vicksburg and Shiloh, and mapping out what was yet to be done with the articles on Chattanooga and the Wilderness for *The Century Magazine*."

This letter contained the first mention of a financial arrangement, identified by Badeau's use of the words "proposition" and "terms." In a memorandum that Grant wrote the following February and Badeau endorsed three weeks later, the conditions were spelled out: if Grant could find a publisher for this project, he would pay Badeau $5,000 from the first $20,000 the book earned, and $5,000 from the next $10,000.

As Badeau wrote of it, the implication was that Grant reached the decision to write his memoirs on his own, and Grant's correspondence supports that. By September Grant had clearly reinforced his decision to expand his four articles about key moments during his Civil War leadership into a book about his entire involvement with the war. (He later wrote to Julia's brother George W. Dent that writing the articles "filled up my time so pleasantly that I concluded to continue the work and write my life to the close of the rebellion.") Grant would add chapters about his life before the war and the background from which he sprang: he started his first chapter with the words, "My family is American, and has been for generations, in all its branches, direct and collateral." (The Grants had indeed been American "for generations." Matthew and Priscilla Grant had come to Massachusetts aboard the *Mary and John* in 1630, only eight years after the Mayflower landing, and subsequent generations settled in Connecticut, then in Pennsylvania, and then in Ohio, where Ulysses S. Grant was born at the town of Point Pleasant on the Ohio River on April 27, 1822.)

After Grant established his genealogical credentials at the beginning of his book, his work would grow to two volumes, and he decided to take his story to shortly beyond May 23 and May 24, 1865. On those two days, six weeks after Lee's surrender at Appomattox and five weeks after Lincoln's assassination, vast crowds gathered in Washington to bid an emotional farewell to 145,000 men of the wartime Union Army as they marched up Pennsylvania Avenue and into history in the final parade known as the Grand Review. Grant would add a chapter titled, "Conclusion"—two thousand words of summation of his view of the war, what it had accomplished, and what remained to make of the peace. There is no evidence that he ever intended to enlarge this—no reference, for example, to his eight years in the White House.

By deciding to give his work the full title, *Personal Memoirs of Ulysses S. Grant*, he did himself a great favor. He could write about the things he wished to put before the reader, and omit those he did not. At one stroke, he relieved himself of the obligation to include everything he might know about a battle or a person, while reserving the right to dwell on a smaller matter or fleeting perception. There is nothing Olympian about Grant's description of the behavior of his troops in November of 1861 at the Battle of Belmont, Missouri, which a number of Northern newspapers, starved for a Union success, hailed as a far greater victory than in fact occurred. Grant poured his troops ashore in an amphibious landing on the western bank of the Mississippi, attacking a Confederate camp and causing the enemy to flee. In his book he would tell what happened next to the men under his command.

> The officers and men engaged at Belmont were then under fire for the first time. Veterans could not have behaved better than they did up to the moment of reaching the rebel camp. . . . The moment the camp was reached our men laid down their arms and commenced rummaging the tents to pick up trophies. Some of the higher officers were little better than the privates. They galloped

about from one cluster of men to another and at every halt delivered a short eulogy upon the Union cause and the achievements of the command.

At that moment the Confederates swept back into view in a counterattack, and this situation developed:

The alarm "surrounded" was given . . . At first some of the officers seemed to think that to be surrounded was to be placed in a hopeless position, where there was nothing to do but surrender. But when I announced that we had cut our way in and could cut our way out just as well, it seemed a new revelation to officers and soldiers . . . The enemy was soon encountered, but this time his resistance was feeble.

Grant's men cut their way out and reembarked. The battle was a successful large-scale amphibious raid, but in Grant's account he looked beyond the statistics of killed, wounded, and missing. "The National [Union] troops acquired a confidence in themselves at Belmont that did not desert them through the war." Grant understood morale. He understood that morale could be built on as simple a statement as, "We had cut ourselves in and we could cut ourselves out." His comrade Sherman said that he did not understand Grant, and that he thought Grant sometimes did not understand himself. That may have been true, but from within Grant had come words that resonated in the American soul. As he began his great final year of campaigning against Robert E. Lee in Northern Virginia, the man who said, "We had cut ourselves in" gave America this: "I propose to fight it out along this line if it takes all summer."

6

To Eat a Peach,
and Soldier On

O<small>N</small> J<small>UNE</small> 2, about two weeks before the *Century*'s Johnson first
visited Grant at Long Branch, something happened that Julia
Grant described in these words:

> There was a plate of delicious peaches on the table, of which the
> General was very fond. Helping himself, he proceeded to eat the
> dainty morsel; then he started up as if in great pain and exclaimed:
> "Oh my, I think something has stung me from that peach." He
> walked up and down the room and out to the piazza, and rinsed
> his throat again and again. He was in great pain and said water
> hurt like fire.

For the moment, the family thought that something in the peach
had hurt him; perhaps a fragment of the pit was caught in his throat.
Julia said she "thought it was a sting from some insect in the peach."
The pain persisted, day after day; Julia later wrote, "I begged him
to see a doctor, but he said: 'No, it will be all right directly, and I
will not have a doctor.'"

Everyone knew that Ulysses S. Grant could be stubborn. A man who met him late in the war said, "He habitually wears an expression as if he had determined to drive his head through a brick wall, and was about to do it."

Grant wrapped a silk scarf around his neck, went on refusing to see a doctor, worked on his articles, and kept smoking cigars. "So it continued for weeks," Julia recalled, "until Dr. [Jacob Mendez] Da Costa was called in."

The "called in" occurred when Grant told his neighbor George Childs about pain and dryness in his throat. Childs replied that his friend Dr. Da Costa, an eminent surgeon from Philadelphia, was arriving for a week's visit, and that he would send Da Costa over to the Grants' cottage next door to examine him. Da Costa appeared, had Grant sit down on his porch in bright sunlight, and asked him to open his mouth. He saw something, a small growth that he could not identify but that troubled him; he wrote Grant a prescription, and told him to see his regular physician. Julia remembered, "As soon as Dr. Da Costa saw the General's throat, he recommended immediate attention." Grant ignored the advice: Julia said of that time at Long Branch, "All that summer was spent by my dear husband in hard work: writing, writing, writing for bread."

Grant was later to write his daughter Nellie that for some time he did not take his illness seriously, but it is possible that another reason he delayed further medical treatment was that he wanted to wait to be examined by his regular doctor, who was in Europe. That was Fordyce Barker, a friend and a famous physician who was said to be the first in America to use a hypodermic needle. Barker, a graduate of Bowdoin who had received advanced degrees, appointments, and honors from institutions on both sides of the Atlantic, had been spending months of every year in Europe for twenty-three years; in London he moved in literary circles in which he met Charles Dickens, who had published his novel *Great Ex-*

pectations in 1859. Although Grant occasionally experienced considerable pain, he continued to write in his house on the Jersey shore. He sought no "immediate attention" for whatever was happening in his throat.

Despite Grant's delay in seeing a doctor, he nonetheless had a lawyer in New York named William A. Purrington prepare a will, which was dated and witnessed on September 5, 1884. Grant appeared to have a double motivation in doing this. First came the desire of a prudent man who knew something was the matter with him to have an up-to-date will. The second motivation, which appeared within the first long paragraph, went back to the events of May.

I make this my last Will and Testament . . . with the intention of providing for . . . my family, who have been deprived of their fortunes by the fraudulent conduct of Ferdinand Ward, the partner in my late firm of Grant and Ward, to whom was entrusted by myself and my son Ulysses S. Grant Jr the business management of said firm at his own request and in reliance upon our belief in his integrity . . .

I make the foregoing recital of the abuse of our trust . . . for the reason that the said breach of trust has resulted not only in depriving me and my sons of . . . very nearly all our worldly possessions, but also in creating a vast aggregate of debts . . . contracted without my knowledge or approval, and in greater part, as it now appears, upon fraudulent, fictitious and illegal consideration.

Grant stated that it was his desire to honor any just debts, but he had been advised that there would be so "many claims . . . founded in fraud and collusion" that he could not deal with them "in this instrument." Thus he was turning over to his sons the responsibility of "taking such measures in concert with honest creditors as may lead to just and honorable settlements."

Next came what clearly weighed most on his mind: "I devise and bequeath all of my said entire estate, both real and personal to my dear wife Julia Dent Grant." Julia was to be sole executrix of his will.

~II~

As Grant worked on at Long Branch during this September of 1884, the anniversary came and went of a date that marked what many regarded as having been the great calamity of his eight years in the White House. On September 18, 1873, the financial crisis began that became known as the Panic of 1873. Six months into Grant's second term, Jay Cooke & Company, the nation's most important investment banking firm, which was speculating heavily in railroad securities, found itself unable to find buyers for an issue of several million dollars in Northern Pacific Railway bonds. Cooke & Company was forced to declare bankruptcy, which set off waves of selling on Wall Street. Two days later, the New York Stock Exchange closed for ten days.

The bill had come due for eight years of post–Civil War economic overexpansion. Fifty-six thousand miles of new railroad lines had been laid, mostly in the booming West. After September 18, all forms of production began to stop; as months passed, eighty-nine railroads went bankrupt, three hundred of the nation's seven hundred iron and steel mills closed, and half a million laborers lost their jobs. By 1876, unemployment stood at an alarming 14 percent. Dismal business conditions continued, beyond the end of Grant's second term in 1877: between 1873 and 1879, forty thousand businesses failed.

The Democrats in particular blamed all this on Grant, but there were also international economic forces in play that few American financiers understood. This crisis had in fact begun with the seemingly unrelated collapse of banks in Vienna, then the capital of the Austro-Hungarian Empire. The erosion of capital and confidence spread west across Europe to the markets of Berlin, the Paris Bourse, the London Exchange. The first transatlantic cable had been active for fifteen years; news of these financial failures reached New York by telegraph within minutes, adding to the domestic turmoil.

Despite the American newspaper clamor for scapegoats, Grant's popularity survived it all. Crowds in the North and West continued to think of him primarily as the general who saved the Union. As the years of his presidency passed, however, Grant made his own analysis of his performance as president.

When it came time to leave the White House, with his eighth and final Annual Message to Congress (now known as the State of the Union Address), he apologized to the nation's legislators, and through them to the American people, for his inadequacies as president. This remarkably candid statement, unique in presidential history, was an apology in the classic sense—not an expression of remorse or a plea to be forgiven, but an *apologia*, an explanation for his actions. He began with this:

> It was my fortune, or misfortune, to be called to the office of Chief Executive without any previous political training . . . Under such circumstances it is but reasonable to assume that errors in judgement must have occurred . . . But I leave comparisons to history, claiming only that I have acted in every instance, from a conscienscious [sic] desire to do what was right, constitutional within the law, and for the very best interest of the whole people. Failures have been errors of judgement, not of intent.

Grant reminded the senators and representatives of the circumstances under which he took office. "Less than four years before, the country had emerged from a conflict such as no other nation had survived. Nearly one half the states had revolted against the Government." He recalled the death of Lincoln and the political turmoil that followed: "Immediately on the cessation of hostilities the then Noble President, who had carried the country so far through its perils fell a Martyr to his patriotism, at the hands of an assassin . . . The intervening time, to my first inauguration, was filled up with wranglings between Congress and the new Executive [President Andrew Johnson] as to the best mode of 'reconstruction' . . ."

Despite his apology, during his presidential years he had often served the reunited nation better than it knew. By signing legislation on March 1, 1872, creating the Yellowstone National Park, Grant thereby created the country's national park system—something that many people have ascribed to Theodore Roosevelt. The American national parks were the world's first national parks.

Also in his presidential years, Grant took a view of the Indians different from that of his wartime subordinates Sherman and Sheridan, both of whom believed in Sherman's dictum that, "The only good Indian is a dead Indian." Grant wrote this: "It may be the Indians require as much protection from the whites as the whites do from the Indians. My own experience has been that little trouble would have been had from them but for the encroachments & influence of bad whites." Grant pursued this policy until the Battle of the Little Big Horn. After the massacre of Custer and his Seventh Cavalry, the public reaction was such that Grant decided to spend his limited political capital on other issues.

Grant's political values were never better expressed than in a comment he made concerning the consolidation of the great work of freeing the slaves begun by Lincoln. As for civil rights, Grant paid this tribute to the ratification of the Fifteenth Amendment, designed to protect the rights of blacks to vote, "A measure which makes at once four million people voters who were heretofore declared by the highest tribunal in the land to be not citizens of the United States, nor eligible to become so . . . is indeed a measure of grander importance than any other act of the kind from the foundation of our free Government to the present day."

Grant Puts On
His Armor

As summer ended, William Vanderbilt had made it clear that the Grants were free to move back to 3 East Sixty-sixth Street. By early October the Grants had finished moving there from Long Branch. Grant and Julia had separate bedrooms on the second floor. On the floor above them lived their oldest son, retired army colonel Frederick Grant, his wife Ida, and Frederick and Ida's children: Julia's namesake Julia Dent Grant, now eight, and three-year-old Ulysses S. Grant III, who would himself become a general and one day write a biography of his grandfather. The next to move in were the Grants' son Buck and his wife and little daughter Miriam, who was two months younger than her cousin Ulysses. Grant continued to urge Adam Badeau to come and stay with them, specifically describing both a room in which he could stay and another where he could work.

Facing his and Julia's ongoing financial straits, on October 4 Grant wrote the secretary of the Madison Avenue Congregational Church, "I herewith resign my place as Trustee . . . I have given notice—and now repeat it—that I give up my pew in the church because of my inability to pay the [pew] rent."

As if it were not enough to start writing a book while in pain, Grant felt it his duty to respond to the request of a three-man federal "commission to Central and South America" that he testify before them concerning proposed funding of "a consular and diplomatic appropriation act"—legislation for regulations and funding to improve commerce with that region. These men had been interviewing various figures in the world of import-export trade at the New York Customs House, but in deference to Grant they came to 3 East Sixty-sixth Street on the morning of Wednesday, October 9. None of the questions and answers resulted in producing meaningful legislation, but this meeting brought Grant back in touch with a man who had served him exceptionally well during the war and thereafter. This was the commission's chairman, retired Major General George H. Sharpe, who had run Grant's Bureau of Military Information, the sophisticated and highly effective intelligence-gathering unit that Grant had incorporated into his headquarters at City Point, Virginia, during the last year of the war. Creating this sixty-four man group had been Grant's idea, once again belying the image of Grant as a bulldog who knew nothing but how to throw wave after wave of troops at the enemy.

During his presidency, Grant had given Sharpe two Federal appointments, one of which put him dead center in an area of virulent political corruption. As United States Marshal for the Southern District of New York, Sharpe's task was to root out the criminal practices of Democrat "Boss" Tweed and his infamous Tammany Hall–based "Tweed Ring." Tweed's henchmen looted the municipal treasury to the extent of $200 million, in one instance charging New York City $8 million for construction of an unfinished courthouse that had been planned to cost $250,000. George Sharpe's life was often threatened by Tweed's political gangsters, but he brought in conviction after conviction, including those of two of Tweed's ringleaders accused of rigging elections. Grant rewarded Sharpe

with the federal government's plum patronage job: the lucrative position of Collector of [taxes for] the Port of the City of New York.
Tweed died in jail in 1878.

~ I I ~

Within a few days of the morning session with General Sharpe and
his colleagues, Adam Badeau moved in with the Grants at Sixty-
sixth Street. Grant had still not had the strongly recommended
medical consultation about his throat; Badeau described Grant's
condition in these terms: "At this time he seemed in tolerable
health. He was crippled and unable to move without crutches, but
he walked out alone, and he had driven me once or twice at Long
Branch behind his own horse. He gave up driving, however, after
his return to town. But he was cheerful; his children and grandchildren were a great solace to him; many friends came in to see
him and to testify their undiminished respect." As for his writing,
"He worked often five, and six, and seven hours a day." In terms of
his overall production to date, in a letter to his friend General Sherman he said that he was "now about one third through. My idea was
that it would be a volume of from four to five hundred pages. But
it now looks as if it will be two volumes of nearly that number of
pages each."

Badeau soon revised his estimate that Grant was "in tolerable
health," saying that "he complained constantly of pains in his
throat." On October 22, now with continuous throbbing pain in the
area of his mouth and throat, Grant finally went to see his regular
physician Dr. Fordyce Barker, who had recently returned from his
long stay in Europe. After a brief examination, that same day Barker
sent him to see Dr. John Hancock Douglas, one of the nation's leading throat specialists. Douglas, a tall man with a full white beard,
had seen much of Grant during the war. An important figure in the

United States Sanitary Commission, which provided medical services and support to the Union Army, he had watched Grant in action at Shiloh and in the Wilderness. He admired Grant's organizational ability, as well as his strategic vision and tactical skill. Douglas greeted Grant as a friend and asked what was the matter. Grant answered that, in addition to the injury that kept him on crutches and occasional severe headaches from which he had suffered for many years (something a later medical generation would call "migraine") he had a pain in his throat and difficulty swallowing.

The doctor had his patient sit down. Using a new device, a reflecting mirror, he made a detailed examination. He discovered that, while Grant might be feeling pain in his throat, the cause of the pain was actually at the base of the tongue. In the tissue on the right side he found a dark swollen inflammation, some of it crusty, and the gland beneath the tissue enlarged. On further examination, Douglas found some ulceration on the right tonsil. Finally, checking the roof of the mouth, he found an irritated area with three cancerous warts, each less than an eighth of an inch in length.

As Douglas pulled back the mirror and let Grant close his mouth, Grant looked at the expression on the doctor's face and asked, "Is it cancer?"

Douglas replied, "General, the disease is serious, epithelial in character [linked to tumors], and sometimes capable of being cured." Then he applied a solution of cocaine and water to the affected area, which gave Grant immediate relief from pain. After that Douglas swabbed away a buildup of mucous and other discharges from what was in effect an open internal wound. Finishing his first examination with this still-incomplete diagnosis, Douglas told Grant, whose house was two miles from the doctor's office, that he would have to come to him twice a day for treatment.

Leaving Douglas's office after receiving news that would prostrate most men, Grant boarded a streetcar and headed for the offices of the Century Company. Perhaps what he had heard from Dr. Douglas stimulated his desire to complete a book that could make enough money to provide for Julia after his death. He was ushered in to see Century president Roswell Smith, who later made this note of the visit: "General Grant has just been in, spent some time, and wants us to publish his book or books." Smith sketched out the terms of a publishing contract, offering a 10 percent royalty on each copy of his memoirs, with a projected sale of 25,000 copies. Grant seemed amenable to that; Smith added that a formal agreement would be drawn up, and that in the interim Grant ought to go on polishing the articles he had agreed to write for the *Century Magazine*.

Grant went home and said nothing to Julia or his son Fred about what he had learned from Dr. Douglas. The next day he began making the twice-daily trips to Douglas's office, using the horse-drawn streetcars rather than spending the money to take a cab. He also continued to smoke cigars.

Within a week, on about October 29, Julia and Fred decided to ask Dr. Douglas what was going on and went to his office. He told them that Grant had a "complaint with a cancerous tendency" and outlined for them the regimen that had to be observed.

Although Julia remained outwardly calm, she said that from Dr. Douglas's saying "cancerous tendency" she "learned the dreadful truth but still could not believe the malady was a fatal one." Still thinking of her husband's health in terms of the energetic man that he had so long been, she described her actions and feelings.

> I asked again and again if it were not curable and was answered that there had been instances when it had been cured. Then hope returned to me. My husband was healthy, temperate, strong. Why should he not be well and strong again? And down in my heart, I could not believe that God in his wisdom and mercy would take

this great, wise, good man from us, to whom he was so necessary and so beloved.

Now arriving at Dr. Douglas's office every day in a cab, Grant was accompanied by his black manservant, "Faithful Harrison" Terrell, who had been with the family for three years. Terrell had a son of exceptional ability, a fact demonstrated by a letter that Grant had written to an official in Boston on July 3 of 1883. In it he asked that, for the second year in a row, Robert Herberton Terrell be employed at the Boston Customs House during his summer vacation from Harvard. "As you are aware," Grant said, "Terrell is a colored man now in the Senior class at Harvard and has to earn his own living while prosecuting his studies. My special interest in him is from the fact that his father—a most estimable man—is my butler, beside I should feel an interest in any young man, white or colored, who had the courage and ability to graduate himself at Harvard without pecuniary aid other than what he could earn." Young Terrell graduated *cum laude* in the Harvard Class of 1884 and received the degrees of Bachelor of Laws and Master of Laws from Howard University. When he was appointed to the District of Columbia Municipal Court, he became the first African American judge to serve in Washington.

In one of these visits to Dr. Douglas's office in early November, Grant was examined by two more specialists, after which Douglas removed a small bit of tissue from the base of Grant's tongue and turned it over to yet another specialist, Dr. George Elliott, for a biopsy. To verify his finding, Elliott brought the specimen to Dr. George Shrady, a man who was a microbiologist as well as a surgeon, and a leader in the new field of plastic surgery, which included rebuilding the faces of cancer victims who had to have parts of their faces removed. Initially, Elliott did not tell Shrady the name of the patient. Then they had this exchange. Shrady told Elliott, "This specimen comes from the throat and base of the tongue and is affected with cancer."

Elliott replied, "Are you sure?"

"Perfectly sure. This patient has a lingual epithelioma—cancer of the tongue."

"This patient is General Grant."

"Then General Grant is doomed."

Over the next several weeks, other doctors conferred, and at some point told Grant that he must restrict himself to three cigars a day. The public knew nothing of the situation, nor did any prospective publisher. Eventually there were going to be all sorts of rumors and varying newspaper reports, but Dr. Shrady later wrote that the unanimous diagnosis was that the cancer had spread too far for surgery to save Grant. He summed it up with these words: "The wisdom of such a decision was manifested in sparing him unnecessary mutilation and allowing him to pass the remainder of his days in comparative comfort. Relatively, however, it meant suffering for him until the end."

~III~

As November went on, Grant continued to write. At 3 East Sixty-sixth Street, the second floor became a literary workshop. Grant worked many hours a day at a little desk in a small room with two windows facing south across Sixty-sixth Street. In a nearby room, Frederick Grant and Badeau shared the responsibility of arranging all the records and maps needed for the initial stages of outlining a book and checking facts from these sources. Then Badeau would take over to Grant a stack of notes that would be added to what lay immediately ahead in the writing and discuss with him how this fit into the changing outline of the book. After that, Grant would make his own selection of the materials, writing for hours a day with a concentration that seemed to wall off his pain. When he finished a section, he sent it back to Badeau and Frederick for rechecking and revision suggestions. At the end of the working day the three of them would discuss where and how to start the next morning. Occasionally Badeau would become argumentative about these decisions as to what should come next. Grant would simply stop talking to him.

Two other figures became indispensable parts of this inner circle. Julia's bedroom was at the back of the second floor, next to Grant's. She would spend much of each day there, knowing that he was fully aware of her presence; when he had just written a passage that particularly pleased him, he would pass the word in his weakening voice that she should come in and let him read it to her.

The November days kept passing: Harrison Terrell became a silent figure, sitting in a corner a few yards from where Grant worked. He sensed what Grant needed and would rise quietly, readjust the shawl that Grant kept constantly wrapped around his throat, and resume his seat. Twice a day, he brought Grant a glass of milk on a tray and patiently insisted that Grant drink all of it. He continued to accompany Grant on his visits to the doctors and was the one who kept track of when and in what quantity Grant's medicines were to be taken. Becoming more of a nurse than a valet, he added the postprocedure swabbing of Grant's throat with "Cocaine water" to the other duties he undertook. During November, Grant had to have a large molar extracted, and it was Terrell who took him to the dentist. As Badeau described this further complication in Grant's declining health, "Grant's fortitude was such that the operator [dentist] was doubtless deceived, and proposed the extraction of three others, and the shock to the General's system was one from which he did not recover for weeks."

Perhaps even more than Julia did, Harrison Terrell understood the pain that Grant increasingly felt, and how important it was to relieve it in every possible way. He saw that Grant, who now could only swallow such liquid meals as soups and oatmeal, often would leave the table so that the family would not see the blazing pain that even the act of swallowing caused. Out of Julia's sight, Terrell would spray Grant's throat with a mixture of cocaine and disinfectant, but even this kept the pain at bay for only a short time. As for this pain, when Grant's close friend the Philadelphia publisher George Childs later invited the Grants to visit him in Philadelphia for a week, Grant described his reasons for declining in these words.

> The doctor will not allow me to leave until the weather gets warmer . . . nothing gives me so much pain as swallowing water. If you can imagine what molten lead would be going down your throat, that is what I feel when swallowing.

Of the doctors, at this point the microbiologist and surgeon George Shrady spent the most time with Grant. He tried to keep his visits brief, because he sensed how much Grant wanted to press on with his daily writing. Occasionally, however, Grant urged him to stay and talk of the Civil War incidents about which he was writing. Shrady developed a profound admiration for his patient. He saw that the man who once gave orders to a million men knew how to take orders himself and valued his own concentration so much that he would endure thirst for hours, rather than take a drink of water that would cause him so much pain that he would lose his narrative drive.

Shrady sometimes relieved Grant's pain when others could not. One night, so wracked with his suffering that he was gasping with every breath, Grant called out for Shrady, who quickly appeared. Taking stock of the situation, Shrady saw that Grant was not only in pain, but fearful of the additional pain the hours ahead might bring. He promised Grant that he would feel better if he would change the way he was lying in bed. "Pretend you are a boy again," he quietly told Grant. "Curl up your legs, lie over on your side and bend your neck while I tuck the covers around your shoulders." When Grant trustingly did this, Shrady said to the former president of the United States, "Now go to sleep like a good boy."

Within a minute the man who had been gasping with pain was peacefully asleep. Shrady turned from Grant's bedside and saw that Julia had been silently standing in the darkened doorway. Fumbling for words, he told Julia that he did not mean any disrespect to Grant, but wanted only to give him some rest.

"There is not the slightest danger of that" Julia replied quietly. "He is the most simple-mannered and reasonable person in the world, and he likes to have persons whom he knows treat him without ceremony." Julia turned and went to her room.

The teamwork at 3 East Sixty-sixth Street was effective, but friction developed between Grant's son Frederick and Badeau. Frederick felt that Badeau treated him with condescension; worse, he felt that Badeau increasingly acted as if they were working on *his* book, rather than his father's. (When Frederick compared Badeau to the *Century*'s Johnson, he said it was Johnson who acted as his father's "literary tutor.") At the moment, there was no indication that Badeau would go on to allow the public to think that he, not Grant, was doing the writing that Grant was doing skillfully and carefully while suffering worsening pain, and that Grant would strike back forcefully.

8

Mark Twain Strides
onto the Stage

I N MID-NOVEMBER, a man appeared who eclipsed Johnson and Badeau. This was Mark Twain, one of the many prominent individuals who had occasionally dropped in to see Grant in his office at Grant & Ward. Twain was close to publishing his novel *Huckleberry Finn*, and he wanted to publish Grant's memoirs himself.

At this moment Grant and Mark Twain—the pen name taken by Samuel Clemens—were the two most famous men in America. But when they first met in 1869, Twain was a writer just beginning to be known, and Ulysses S. Grant was the man who had led the Union Army to victory and was in his first term as president. "I had just arrived in Washington from the Pacific Coast," Twain later wrote, "a stranger and wholly unknown to the public." Actually, Twain had already started building his reputation with such books as *Roughing It* and his stories of life in the mining fields of the West. He had also done some secretarial work for Senator William M. Stewart of Nevada, who asked Twain if he would like to accompany him to the White House and meet Grant. They entered Grant's office.

General Grant got slowly up from the table, put his pen down, and stood before me with the iron expression of a man who had not smiled for seven years, and was not intending to smile for another seven. He looked me steadily in the eye—mine lost confidence and fell. I had never confronted a great man before, and was in a miserable state of funk and inefficiency. The Senator said:

"Mr. President, may I have the privilege of introducing Mr. Clemens?"

The President gave my hand an unsympathetic wag and dropped it. He did not say a word, but just stood. In my trouble I could not think of anything to say . . . There was an awkward pause, a dreary pause, a horrible pause. Then I thought of something, and looked up into that unyielding face, and said timidly: "Mr. President, I–I am embarrassed. Are you?"

His face broke—just a little—a wee glimmer, the momentary flicker of a summer-lightning smile, seven years ahead of time—and I was out and gone as soon as it was.

Twain and Grant next met ten years later in Chicago, when Sherman's veterans held a reunion of the legendary Army of the Tennessee in Grant's honor upon his return from his postpresidential trip around the world. In the meantime, Twain had published *Innocents Abroad*, *The Adventures of Tom Sawyer*, and *The Gilded Age*, and become a nationally known author and lecturer. He had also developed his persona: the shaggy, wavy white mane, and the never-trimmed bushy eyebrows. On the first day of the reunion Twain found himself watching some eighty thousand Union veterans forming up in downtown Chicago, with a similarly large crowd gathering to see them parade past the former general in chief of the Union Army. People were on the sidewalks, at windows, on roofs. Twain was escorted to Chicago's leading hotel, the Palmer House, the balcony of which, draped in red, white, and blue, was to be the re-viewing stand. As he gazed over the enormous crowd, he heard a roar: Grant had just appeared behind him. Carter Harrison, the mayor of Chicago, brought Grant over to where Twain stood, and presented him to Grant.

> General Grant was looking exactly as he had looked upon that try-ing occasion ten years before—all iron and bronze self-possession. Before I could put together the proper remark, General Grant said, "Mr. Clemens, I am not embarrassed—are you?"—And that little seven-year smile twinkled across his face again.

Grant bowed to the crowd, which was still cheering. Wanting to give Grant more room, Twain said, "I'll step back, General, I don't want to interrupt your speech."

"But I'm not going to make any," Grant replied, perhaps with that same momentary sparkle in his eye. "Stay where you are—I'll get you to make one for me."

Neither man spoke because at that moment General William Tecumseh Sherman, then the army's commanding general, appeared on the platform and greeted them. With Grant and Sherman stand-ing side by side, the excited crowd had a view of the two Union gen-erals most responsible for winning the war: Grant, dark-haired, compact, and calm, and the ever-animated Sherman, tall, lanky, stooped, with a thatch of wiry red hair and a short bristly beard. Soon the parade began, led by yet another of the great Union gen-erals, the swarthy cavalry leader "Little Phil" Sheridan, whom Grant had described as "the embodiment of heroism, dash, and impulse." A newspaper account said: "When the head of the procession passed it was grand to see Sheridan, in his military cloak & plumed cha-peau, sitting as erect & rigid as a statue on his immense black horse . . . and the crowd roared again."

That evening, during a tribute to Grant held at Chicago's
Haverly's Theatre, Twain had another unobstructed view of him. In
a letter to a friend, he described how the evening began. Three thou-
sand of Grant's veterans waited for him to appear. On the stage where
Grant was also to take his place sat generals Sherman, Sheridan,
Logan, Pope, and Schofield, each scheduled to pay tributes to Grant.
Twain wrote of the meeting's opening moments.

Imagine what it was like to see a bullet shredded old battle flag
reverently unfolded to the gaze of thousands of middle aged soldiers, most of whom hadn't seen it since they saw it advancing
over victorious fields when they were in their prime. And imagine what it was like when Grant, their first commander, stepped
into view while they were still going mad over the flag, and then
right in the middle of it all, somebody struck up "When We Were
Marching Through Georgia."

Twain described Grant's rocklike manner:

Grant seated himself in an armchair in the middle of the row of
his generals, but the crowd remained on its feet, steadily applauding. [Thereafter Grant] was under a tremendous bombard-
ment of praise and gratulation, but . . . he never moved a muscle
of his body . . . Perhaps he never *would* have moved, but at last a
speaker made such a particularly ripping & blood-stirring remark
about him that the audience rose & roared & yelled & stamped
& clapped an entire minute . . . Gen. Sherman stepped up to him,
laid his hand affectionately on his shoulder, bent respectfully down
& whispered in his ear. Then Grant got up & bowed, & the storm
of applause swelled into a hurricane.

* * *

THE FINAL EVENT of the three days' tribute to Grant was the Grand Banquet, a long and liquid feast held at the Palmer House. Before that night passed, Twain engaged in an exceedingly risky toast to General Grant. If it had failed to be funny, and was seen as insulting, the audience of five hundred prominent men that included the principal speaker General Sherman, as well as generals Sheridan, Schofield, Pope, and scores of leaders in civic life, would never have forgiven him. Twain was to be the final speaker, with fourteen notable national figures before him each working up to a toast paying tribute to Grant. Correctly assuming that all the other celebrities would spend their time in earnest and perhaps repetitive praise of the guest of honor, Twain had chosen as his topic, "The Babies—as they comfort us in our sorrows, let us not forget them in our festivities."

When Twain's turn finally came, it was past two in the morning. He began by approaching his real target obliquely: "We have not all had the good fortune to be ladies. We have not all been generals, or poets, or statesmen; but when the toast works down to the babies, we stand on common ground." He then expanded on this first of his points: brave as all these veterans had been, every one of them had surrendered to the charms and demands of tyrannical male infants. "You could face the death-storm at Donelson and Vicksburg and give back blow for blow; but when he clawed your whiskers, and pulled your hair, and twisted your nose, you had to take it."

Twain moved to the fact that some infants were destined to become more important than others. How fortunate it would be, "if we could know which ones they are." As an example, Twain reverted to Civil War heroes, telling his distinguished wine-soaked audience, "In one of these cradles the unconscious [Admiral "Damn the torpedoes!"] Farragut of the future is at this moment teething." He moved on to this: "And in still one more cradle, somewhere under the flag, the future illustrious commander in chief of the American armies is so little burdened with his approaching grandeurs and responsibilities as to be giving his whole strategic mind at this moment to trying to find out some way to get his big toe into his mouth."

This elicited nervous laughter: everyone understood that the hypothetical infant under discussion was the eminently dignified Ulysses S. Grant. Twain plunged on, saying that this ambitious and determined baby had a goal: trying to swallow his big toe was "an achievement [to] which, meaning no disrespect, the illustrious guest of this evening turned *his* entire attention . . . some fifty-six years ago."

With his eyes wide open, Twain had walked himself out on a tightrope above his audience; he recalled a "shuddering silence" as he evoked this image of Grant as a baby struggling to swallow his big toe. He paused, and turned to Ulysses S. Grant. "And if the child is but a prophecy of the man, there are mighty few who will doubt that he *succeeded.*"

The collective holding of breath was broken by the rarely heard sound of Ulysses S. Grant laughing. With that, everyone roared. Twain recalled the moment: "Gen. Grant sat through fourteen speeches like a graven image, but I fetched him up. I broke him up, utterly! He told me that he laughed till the tears came & every bone in his body ached. (And do you know, the biggest part of the success . . . lay in the fact that the audience *saw* that for once in his life he had been knocked out of his iron serenity.)"

Something else about Twain might have knocked Grant out of his iron serenity, had he known of it. When the Civil War began, Mark Twain, still with the name of Samuel Clemens, had joined the Missouri State Guard—a Confederate militia. His particular unit, the Ralls County Rangers, elected Clemens, a twenty-five-year-old Mississippi riverboat pilot with not a day of military experience, as one of their lieutenants.

The Rangers never pulled themselves together. Aware that a Union Army regiment had entered Missouri and was basing itself some twenty-five miles to the north of them in Clemens's home town of Hannibal, they never moved in that direction and spent their time asking local farm housewives to cook meals for them, after which they slept in the barns of these Confederate sympathizers who they were supposed to be protecting. If a more serious Confederate officer tried to give them an order, they laughed at him. When they finally received news that the Union regiment at Hannibal was slowly coming their way, a number of the Rangers deserted. Among them was Lieutenant Samuel Clemens, who did not stop heading away from the war until he reached Carson City, Nevada, two thousand miles from where he had been sworn into the service of the Confederate States of America.

What Ulysses S. Grant, the former commander of the Union Army, might have thought of this now-famous man had he known he was a deserter, no one can say. What is known is that the Union regiment moving toward the Rangers was the Twenty-first Illinois, and that its then-commander was Colonel Ulysses S. Grant.

* * *

TWAIN HAD SEEN Grant a number of times in the five years that had passed since that weekend in Chicago. Now, in mid-November of 1884, Twain reappeared in a new way.

> I had been lecturing at [Manhattan's] Chickering Hall and was walking homeward. It was a rainy night and but few people were about. In the midst of a black gulf between lamps, two dim figures stepped out of a doorway. I heard one of them say, "Do you know General Grant has determined to write his memoirs and publish them? He has said so today, in so many words."

In fact, Twain had been hearing for some time that Grant might be inclined to write his memoirs, and that the Century Company wanted to publish them. Twain had more than a passing interest in the matter. Three years before this he had gone to visit Grant in his 2 Wall Street office, accompanied by his friend, the esteemed author, editor, and literary critic William Dean Howells, who hoped that Grant would use his influence to extend the term of his father's post as American consul in Toronto. Before making his suggestion that Grant should write his memoirs—an idea that got no response— Twain asked Grant "if he wouldn't write a word on a card which Howells could carry to Washington and hand to the President [Chester A. Arthur.]"

Twain never forgot what came next.

> But, as usual, General Grant was his usual self—that is to say, ready and also determined to do more for you than you could possibly have the effrontery to ask him to do. Apparently he never meets anybody half way: he comes nine-tenths of the way himself voluntarily. "No" he said,—he would do better than that and cheerfully: he was going to Washington in a couple of days to dine with the President and he would speak to him himself and make it a personal matter. . . .
>
> Within a week came a letter from the Secretary of State, Mr. Freylinghuysen, to say that in no case would old Mr. Howells be disturbed. [And he wasn't. He resigned, a couple of years later.]

Having obliged Howells and having pointed out to Twain "that he had no necessity for any addition to his income"—certainly true three years before the Grant & Ward debacle—Grant hospitably ordered in a lunch of baked beans and coffee; Howells, already famous but deeply impressed by meeting Grant, remembered the experience in these terms. The "baked beans and coffee were of about the railroad-refreshment quality; but eating them with Grant was like sitting down to baked beans and coffee with Julius Caesar, or Alexander, or some other great Plutarchan captain."

Despite the lack of interest that Grant had shown three years before in writing anything about himself, Twain, now forty-nine, was a man who forgot little, and kept himself and those around him in constant motion. A person of enormous ambition and energy, he was a remarkable self-promoter: in addition to his copious writing, during a twelve-month span in 1871 and 1872 he gave seventy-seven lectures to well-paying audiences in American cities and towns, and three lectures in England. Despite his profits from all this, his handsome house in Hartford, Connecticut, was costing him more than he could afford, and a few years later he began losing thousands of dollars in developing a new method of engraving called Kaolatype. That past May, near the time the Grant & Ward fraud had become public, Twain set up his niece's husband, Charles L. Webster, in a publishing company to be known by the Webster name. The company's principal activity was to publish Twain's books. At that point Twain had not been thinking of Grant as an author, but in recent weeks he had alerted young Webster to be ready to compete for Grant's book if the opportunity arose. Still, during some recent social calls that Twain had made at Sixty-sixth Street, neither he nor Grant had raised the subject of Grant's working on a book.

Overhearing this conversation in the rainy night, Twain caught up to the two "dim figures" ahead of him and found that one was Richard Gilder, the Century Company's senior editor, who had recently bought three chapters of *Huckleberry Finn* for serialization in the *Century Magazine*. Gilder invited Twain to dine with him and his friend at Gilder's house on Fifteenth Street. As they ate, Gilder spoke freely of what he now considered to be a fait accompli: he told Twain that Grant would be signing a contract with him for his memoirs at any time.

Early the next morning, Twain made his way to Grant's house. At 3 East Sixty-sixth Street he found Grant and his son Fred in the library. As Twain wrote of that moment, "The general said in substance this: 'Sit down and keep quiet until I sign a contract'—and added that it was for a book which he was going to write."

Twain sat, thinking that he was witnessing the end of any chance to publish whatever Grant was writing, but then realized that Frederick Grant was giving it a final reading. The younger Grant finished, nodded his approval, and put the contract down on a table; his father rose, moved to the table, and picked up a pen.

Twain spoke up. "Don't sign it. Let Colonel Fred read it to me first."

Grant agreed to this; Twain began listening to the terms. Soon Fred came to a stipulation that Grant would get 10 percent of the sales price of each copy sold. Twain stopped him. His voice rising, he told Grant, "Strike out the ten per cent and put twenty per cent in its place. Better still, put seventy-five per cent of the net returns in its place."

Grant shook his head, and replied that the Century Company would never go along with that. Twain explained that while the Century people knew how to sell magazines, they did not understand that the way to sell a book like Grant's was by advertising it for sale by subscription, with the readers committing themselves in advance to buying their copies, rather than just printing books and placing them on the shelves of bookstores. He added that the Century editors were simply unaware of the possibilities that a book by Grant presented, and that there was "not a reputable publisher in America who would not be very glad to pay" 20 percent or even 75 percent for a book by "such a colossus as General Grant." Reading on through the contract, Twain snorted at the idea that, from Grant's 10 percent, the Century Company wanted to deduct what he called expenses for "the book's share of clerk hire, house rent, sweeping out the offices, or some such nonsense as that." He also felt that Grant was being paid far too little for his articles scheduled to appear in the *Century Magazine*. In an account of this meeting, Twain wrote, "I didn't know whether to cry or laugh."

Grant fell back on his military code of loyalty, telling Twain that he had been dealing with one or another of the Century staff for months. By backing out, he "did not want to be thought of as dishonest or as a thief, a 'robber of a publisher.'" As he said that, Grant was still holding the pen in his hand, ready to sign the contract. He challenged Twain to be specific and to name a publisher who would in fact give him everything that Twain said he could get.

"I named the American Publishing Company of Hartford. He asked if I could prove my position. I said I could furnish the proof by telegraph in six hours."

This impressed Fred Grant, who knew that particular firm had profitably published several of Twain's enormously successful books. Grant stood there, still ready to sign the contract. Fred tried to break the impasse, telling his father that nothing could be lost by considering the matter for another twenty-four hours.

Grant agreed to do that. The next morning, Thursday, November 20, Twain arrived early again, finding Grant in a good mood but still not persuaded by his arguments. When Grant resumed talking about his dealings with the Century people, Twain decided to throw in the reserves. Dropping all that he had said the previous day about the American Publishing Company or book publishers in general, he told Grant, "Sell *me* the memoirs, General . . . I have a checkbook in my pocket; take my check for fifty thousand dollars now, and let's draw the contract." He went on to say that he could make an initial $100,000 on the book in six months.

Somewhat bemused, Grant told Twain that he regarded him as a friend, and did not want him to lose money on a risky venture. Twain repeated his offer. Grant paused, and said that he would consult with his friend, the Philadelphia newspaper publisher George Childs, whose lawyer had already studied a version of the Century contract.

Mark Twain had seen a lot of card games during his years as a riverboat pilot on the Mississippi. He sensed that, after starting the previous morning with the odds completely against him, he might conceivably win the pot for which he was playing, but not if he tried to raise the present stakes. Twain promptly agreed that this was just what Grant should do: consult his friend George Childs. He said good day to Grant and his son, and left the house. Twain always had many irons in the fire; he headed out of Manhattan on one of his lecture tours, appearing that evening of November 20 up the Hudson River in Newburgh, New York, the first of nineteen places where he would appear before the end of the year. He left the negotiations, if there were to be any, to his young partner Webster and Frederick Grant. "I wanted the General's book," he wrote later, "and I wanted it very much, but I had very little expectation of getting it."

Three days later, on November 23, Grant wrote to Childs. Only part of his letter has survived intact, but in that portion he said, "On re-examining the Contract prepared by the Century people I see that it is all in favor of the publisher, with nothing left for the Author. I am offered very much more favorable terms by the Charles L. Webster & Co." Characteristically getting right to the point, Grant continued, "Mark Twain is the Company. The house is located at 658 Broadway. I inclose [sic] you their card. If you are coming to the city any time soon I will be very glad to see you and talk this . . ." [Here the fragment ends.]

On the same day that he received Grant's letter, Childs evidently consulted with his lawyer, who had prepared a lengthy memorandum based on the earlier "papers in reference to the proposed Contract." As days passed, it came down to this: Grant could have 70 percent of the net profits, or a 20 percent gross royalty on the sales. Grant feared Twain would bankrupt himself in either arrangement, and Twain was convinced that Grant would make more money by taking 20 percent of the gross sales. George Childs and his lawyer reviewed everything, preferred the 20 percent arrangement, and forwarded to Grant and Charles L. Webster their recommended revisions.

As he studied the evolving document over several weeks, Grant was surprised to see how far Twain was willing to go to protect the Grant family's interests rather than his own. Some of the generous terms had not even been discussed. Grant was to receive an immediate advance of $10,000, not a customary practice at the time, for living expenses for himself and his family while he continued writing the book. Twain was also willing to go along with a recommendation by Childs's lawyer that the contract should be written between Julia and whoever proved to be the publisher, to forestall Grant's creditors from seizing any profits.

At that moment, only a handful of people knew that Grant had cancer, and Twain was not among them. He nonetheless saw that Grant, overweight, on crutches, and clearly experiencing discomfort, was in ill health. By assigning the legal rights to Julia, she would receive the profits if Grant should die when enough of the book was completed to enable it to be published.

Studying this, Grant's pride came to the fore. He said that he would not take the $10,000 advance, but would accept a sum of $1,000. Twain immediately grasped that Grant realized that both the $10,000 and the $1,000 were bonuses that need not have been given. He later said of the situation: "It was a shameful thing that a man who had saved his country and its government from destruction should still be in a position where so small a sum—$1000—could be looked upon as a godsend."

Kindhearted though some of the terms he had included were, Twain nonetheless felt that he had made a great coup, in terms of money and prestige. Taking a few moments from his lecture tour, he wrote Charles Webster this:

> If these chickens should really hatch . . . General Grant's royalties will amount to $420,000, and will make the largest single check ever paid an author in the world's history. Up to the present time the largest one ever paid was to Macaulay on his History of England, 20,000 [pounds]. If I pay the General in silver coin at $12 per pound it will weigh seventeen tons.

There were the Grant and Twain of fame, and the Grant and Twain seen at 3 East Sixty-sixth Street by Julia Grant's eight-year-old granddaughter and namesake, Julia, who was living there. "I still enjoyed my privileges," she said of her relationship with her grandfather. "If I was in the sitting-room my little chair was drawn close to my grandfather's and he would stroke my hair or cheek or hold my hand a little while. I remember how beautiful his hands were—large, classic, with long, capable fingers and perfect nails, to which Nature had left nothing for the manicure to do." Julia added, "The hands looked strong, and so did the wonderful face with its quiet, firm expression of mouth and deep eyes, calm in spite of his constant pain." She also learned that "my father spent twenty-three out of twenty-four hours" in one of the two front rooms, "sleeping on a sofa in the office, always dressed and ready to spring to his father's side if the latter woke at night and wanted to write . . . [always] there, gentle and smiling, to help look up a date, or to verify a date, hand a pillow, or do anything else he could." Speaking of her mother, Ida Grant, she said, "my mother said it was unhealthy for my father to be awake and working thus day after day, keeping himself alive with black coffee, but she could do nothing with him."

Little Julia had a unique reaction to Mark Twain.

One visitor frightened me dreadfully—Mark Twain, with his . . . protruding eyebrows, which almost hid the deep-set eyes shining beneath them . . . he had a vague way of strolling into a room and moving about without seeming to aim for any special spot. Somehow, though I did not dare say it, I got the idea he was a crazy man, and I would draw close to one or another of the grown-ups when he was around. I think I would never have had the courage to be in the same room with Mark Twain alone.

9

Horses, and a
Last Cigar

A s November ended, Grant felt somewhat better, and made a trip that gave him considerable pleasure. Alden Goldsmith, a prominent horse breeder, invited him to visit his Walnut Grove Farm in Goshen, New York, a town west of the Hudson River some sixty miles north of Manhattan, and one of the centers of American horse racing. Many of the greatest trotting races of that era were held at its track.

While Grant and Goldsmith were looking over some of the finest horses in the nation, C. E. Meade, a well-known New York newspaper correspondent and a relative of Union General George Gordon Meade, joined them. Meade, then forty-five, had been born and brought up in Goshen, but he had not been back for many years. He later wrote, "I learned that Gen. Grant was visiting at the Goldsmith stock farm, some five or six miles below the town." Meade's reportorial instinct impelled him to go there, and he found Goldsmith and Grant "viewing some fine colts in the yard of one of the great stables."

Surrounded by the beautiful autumn countryside, magnificent horses, and in the company of a relative of one of his principal

generals, Grant engaged in many pleasant reminiscences. These
included memories of the good side of his cadet life at West Point,
located only a few miles away, where he had demonstrated his
unique skill with horses.

Grant on a horse cut a different figure from Grant on the
ground. Walking along, he struck one observer as an "ordinary,
scrubby-looking man, with a slightly seedy look . . . He gets over
the ground queerly. He does not march, nor quite walk, but pitches
along as if the next step would bring him on his nose." Once Grant
swung into a saddle, a transformation occurred. Frederick Grant
had this to say of his father's equestrian gifts:

> My father was the best horseman in the army, he rode splendidly
> and always on magnificent and fiery horses . . . He preferred to
> ride the most unmanageable mount, the largest and the most
> powerful one. Oftentimes I saw him ride a beast that none had
> approached.

Grant's control of a horse made a lasting impression on those
who saw it. A spectator remembered the moment when Grant and
a horse named York set a record-breaking jump at a West Point
graduation exercise: "[York] bounded into the air and cleared the
bar, carrying his rider as if man and beast had been welded together.
The spectators were breathless."

The training that turned out results like this was not for show,
but to produce a warrior who could use a horse skillfully in com-
bat. At the Battle of Monterrey during the Mexican War, as Grant's
regiment advanced through city streets in house-to-house fighting,
his colonel realized that his men were running out of ammunition.
Someone had to ride back through two miles of streets swept from
one side by enemy fire, carrying the order to bring up more ammunition immediately. Believing that whoever tried to carry this

message would probably be killed, the colonel assembled twelve officers and asked for a volunteer. Grant alone stepped forward. He swung up on a grey mare named Nellie and put his arm around the horse's neck and a foot over the hind part of her saddle. Then, hanging down the side of the horse away from the enemy, he "crossed at such a flying rate," he said in the *Personal Memoirs* he was now writing, "that generally I was past and under cover of the next block of houses before the enemy fired. I got out safely without a scratch." Mary Robinson, a slave who belonged to Grant's father-in-law, Frederick Dent, in pre–Civil War Missouri, said of this brave feat that Grant "appeared to look upon Nellie's conduct as more courageous than his own."

By the time that Grant and Julia took their postpresidential trip, he weighed 181 pounds, thirty-five pounds more than he had at the end of the Civil War. It was arranged that while they were in Milan he would review the Italian army's elite Bersaglieri cavalry regiment. A knowledgeable American on the scene learned that some of the prankish young officers had schemed to have Grant mounted on an enormous ill-tempered horse "that had never been ridden. I was in mortal fear that our general would be speedily thrown and crushed to death by the cruel hoofs."

While the aristocratic Italian cavalrymen were winking at each other in anticipation of what was to come, Grant's eyes lit up admiringly as he studied this "blooded bay horse of immense proportions." Grant mounted the horse awkwardly, but "as soon as he was seated his horsemanship so impressed the crowd that it broke into spontaneous applause."

* * *

As Grant's visit to Goldsmith's farm ended, C. E. Meade experienced a poignant moment.

. . . the General took out his cigar case, passing it to Mr. Gold-smith and myself, then silently picking one out and holding it be-tween his fingers, he looked at it sadly for a moment.

"Gentlemen," he said, and I thought there was a slight quaver in his voice, "this is the last cigar I shall ever smoke. The doctors tell me that I will never live to finish the work on which my whole energy is centered these days . . . if I do not cease indulging in these fragrant weeds. It is hard to give up an old and cherished friend, that has been your comforter and solace through many weary nights and days. But my unfinished work must be com-pleted, for the sake of those that are near and dear to me." . . . and then the General slowly lighted the solacing torch and for a few moments gazed over the browning fields and the rich coloring of the autumn foliage among which myriads of migrating blackbirds made merry as they clung to the limbs, and the golden sunshine filled the world about us with a wealth of autumn glories. Still amidst the beauty of the surroundings a sadness filled my heart that hushed my lips to silence as I contemplated the stricken hero before me slowly puffing his last cigar.

To that moment, the only people who knew that Grant was suf-fering from terminal cancer were his doctors, his family, his servant Harrison Terrell, and possibly his live-in editorial assistant, Adam Badeau. Mark Twain knew only that Grant had "something the mat-ter with his throat." Now a leading reporter from New York had a sensational scoop: Ulysses S. Grant, the great victorious general who had gone on to serve two terms as president, had told him that he was under a sentence of death from smoking tobacco. C. E. Meade put not a word of this into print.

In the public mind, Grant had always been a smoker of cigars, but that was not entirely the case. As early as 1850, when Grant was a twenty-eight-year-old captain, a brother officer commented on his smoking a pipe, and the former Dent family slave Mary Robinson said that during the time he farmed some of the Dent land during the prewar years "he smoked a pipe, which his wife threw away whenever she could find it. She did not object to cigars, but she detested the pipe." In addition, Mary Robinson recalled that "he chewed tobacco excessively." It was only after Grant became nationally known for his "Unconditional Surrender" demand when he captured Fort Donelson in Tennessee on February 16, 1862, that he began smoking so many cigars. He explained the circumstances to his aide Horace Porter, a twenty-six-year-old West Pointer who joined his staff sixteen months after Grant sensationally took Donelson.

> I had been a very light smoker previous to the attack on Donelson, and after that battle I acquired a fondness for cigars by reason of a purely accidental circumstance. Admiral [Samuel] Foote, commanding the fleet of gunboats which were cooperating with the army, had been wounded, and at his request I had gone aboard his flag-ship to confer with him. The admiral offered me a cigar, which I smoked on my way back to headquarters.
>
> On the road I was met by a staff-officer, who announced that the enemy were making a vigorous attack. I galloped forward at once, and while riding among the troops giving directions for repulsing the assault I carried the cigar in my hand. It had gone out, but it seems I continued to hold the stump between my fingers during the battle.
>
> In the accounts published in the papers I was represented as smoking a cigar in the middle of the conflict; and many persons, thinking, no doubt, that tobacco was my chief solace, sent me boxes from everywhere in the North. As many as ten thousand were soon received. I gave away all I could get rid of, but having such a quantity on hand, I naturally smoked more than I would

have done under ordinary circumstances, and I have continued the habit ever since.

~ II ~

When he returned to Manhattan, Grant continued to work in his uniquely dedicated manner. (Modern though the phrase sounds, throughout the Civil War Grant would exhort his commanders to "keep the ball rolling.") Many people, both during the war and later, described Grant's combination of mental and physical discipline, but none did so better than Horace Porter, who came to see him in New York in early December of 1884.

Porter, then a captain, had first met Grant at Chattanooga, which was to remain Grant's least appreciated victory. After the nearly disastrous Union defeat at Chickamauga in September of 1863, the Confederate general Braxton Bragg advanced eleven miles north to place seventy thousand men on the towering mist-covered ridges that surrounded the little city of Chattanooga on three sides—Missionary Ridge on the east, Lookout Mountain to the south, and Raccoon Mountain on the west. In that rain-soaked bowl in the hills, forty-five thousand Union troops looked up apprehensively, expecting at any hour to be struck by an attack that could destroy them all. The stakes were high: Chattanooga was a vital communications hub, the principal southern rail center, the crossing point of an X that connected lines running southwest-northeast and northwest-southeast. If Chattanooga, only recently taken by Union troops, were recaptured by the Confederate Army, it would be a great strategic loss for the Union and a rejuvenation for Southern morale after the defeats at Gettysburg and Vicksburg earlier in the year.

Porter, whose valor in rallying fleeing troops at Chickamauga set in motion paperwork that years later would bring him the Congressional Medal of Honor, was billeted in the small one-story frame house that served as the headquarters of Union General George Thomas. On October 23, Grant arrived out of the night, newly ordered to command all the forces between the Mississippi River and the Appalachian Mountains. He was in pain. Close to a month before, Grant had been injured when he had fallen from a horse during a brief trip to New Orleans. He was now ending what he described in a letter to Julia as the last part of a rushed six hundred-mile roundabout trip from Vicksburg to Chattanooga: a two-day "horse-back ride of fifty miles through the rain over the worst roads I ever saw." At times, Grant had to be lifted off his horse and carried across washed-out places where horses might slip and fall. On the second day, his horse slipped coming down a mountain trail while he was in the saddle, further damaging his leg; to enter Thomas's headquarters he had to be carried out of the darkness at nine at night.

Soon after Grant arrived, Porter entered the main room of the little headquarters, and saw an exhausted mud-spattered general slumped in a chair in front of the fireplace, holding a lighted cigar in his hand. Grant declined the offer of food and a chance to change into warm clothes. A large map was set up, and various senior officers pointed out the Union defensive positions. Porter described the tense scene. "General Grant sat for some time as immovable as a rock and as silent as the sphinx, but he listened attentively to all that was said. After a while he straightened himself up in his chair, his features assumed an air of animation, he began firing whole volleys of questions at the officers present."

The atmosphere in the room changed. This man had not come to plan a retreat. He had not even come to improve a defense. He was asking the kind of questions a commander asks when he intends to go on the offensive. The next day, although Grant's "lameness was very perceptible," he made an inspection of the Union lines.

Returning to Thomas's headquarters that evening, he sent word that Porter was to report to him. "As I entered," Porter recalled, "he gave a slight nod of the head by way of recognition, and, pointing to a chair, said rather bluntly, but politely, 'Sit down.'" After asking some questions "in regard to the character of and location of certain heavy guns which I had recently assisted in putting into position in the advanced portion of our lines," Grant began writing some reports.

"I arose to go, but resumed my seat as he said, 'Sit still.'" Porter watched as Grant went to work on a long report. "His thoughts flowed as freely from his mind as the ink from his pen . . . he sat with his head bent low over the table . . . Upon this occasion he tossed the sheets of paper across the table as he finished them, leaving them in the wildest disorder. When he had completed the dispatch, he gathered up the scattered sheets, read them over rapidly, and arranged them in their proper order. Turning to me after a time, he said, 'Perhaps you might like to read what I am sending.'"

Porter thanked him, and read both the overall plan for the coming battle, and "Directions . . . for the taking of vigorous steps in every direction throughout his new and extensive command."

What Porter did not know was that, after first seeing him twenty-four hours before, Grant had decided to add him to his staff. He would stay with Grant for the next, and final, eighteen months of the war. Porter accompanied Grant east when Lincoln brought him to Washington in March of 1864 to take command of the entire Union Army, and to face Robert E. Lee in Northern Virginia. Porter went every step of the way with Grant to Appomattox Court House, and in his book *Campaigning with Grant* wrote the most complete eyewitness account of the historic surrender meeting between Grant and Lee.

During most of Grant's first term in the White House, Porter served as one of his personal secretaries, while remaining in the army and rising to the rank of general. Porter resigned from the army in 1872 and left the White House. Striking out on a business career in his midthirties, Porter eventually became president of the Pullman Car Company, originally named the Pullman Palace Car Company because of the comparatively palatial amenities of the new sleeping cars.

Now when Porter came to see Grant at 3 East Sixty-sixth Street twenty-one years after they met on the eve of the Battle of Chattanooga, Grant confided that he was dying of cancer. Among the things they talked about were the second night of the Battle of the Wilderness, some six months after Porter joined Grant's staff, and the first battle in which Grant fought Lee. During that second day of unequaled violence, Grant had smoked twenty cigars. In his *Campaigning with Grant*, Porter described what happened that night.

> The general, after having given his final orders providing for any emergency which might arise, entered his tent, and threw himself down upon his camp-bed. Ten minutes thereafter an alarming report was received from the right. I looked in his tent, and found him sleeping as soundly and as peacefully as an infant. I waked him, and communicated the report. His military instincts convinced him that it was a gross exaggeration, and as he had already made every provision for meeting any renewed attempts against the right, he turned over in his bed and immediately went to sleep again.
>
> Twenty-one years thereafter, as I sat by his death-bed, when his sufferings had become agonizing, and he was wracked by the tortures of insomnia, I recalled to him that night in the Wilderness. He said: "Ah, yes; it seems strange that I, who always slept so well in the field, should now pass whole nights in the quiet of this peaceful house without being able to close my eyes."

* * *

UNTIL THIS POINT in his illness, Grant had suffered physical pain, but now in December he also began to have nightmares. One night a frightened cry brought his son Frederick to stand listening outside his bedroom door. "The cannon did it!" he shouted.

He began talking of his dreams to Dr. Douglas, who had seen him in action at Shiloh and in the Wilderness, but the stressful dreams he spoke of were not explicitly of battle. Grant told Douglas this:

> It seemed to me as though I had been traveling in a foreign coun-try. I had only a single satchel and I was only partially clad. I found to my surprise that I was without any money and separated from my friends. While I was traveling I came to a fence. There was a stepping stile but it led up to only one side. I climbed over, how-ever, and then found I had left the satchel on the other side. Then I thought I would go back home and borrow the money from Mrs. Grant. I asked her for it, but she said she had only seventeen dol-lars and that was not enough; at which I awoke.

10

A Bittersweet Christmas

Adam Badeau, still working closely with Grant and Frederick, later described the swings of mood that he witnessed while living in the Grant household during this time before Christmas.

> In December his pains became still more excruciating; he could not swallow without torture, and his sufferings at table were intense . . . I shall always recall his figure as he sat at the head of the table, his head bowed over his plate, his mouth set grimly, his features clinched in the endeavor to conceal the expression of pain, especially from Mrs. Grant, who sat at the other end. He . . . was often obliged to leave before the meal was over, pacing the hall or the adjoining library in his agony.

At times, Badeau thought that Grant had given up. "[He] often sat for hours propped in his chair, with his hands clasped, looking at the blank wall before him . . . It was like a man gazing into his open grave. He was in no way dismayed, but the sight was to me the most appalling I have ever witnessed—the conqueror looking at his inevitable conqueror; the stern soldier to whom so many armies had surrendered, watching the approach of that enemy before whom even he must yield."

Grant rallied. According to Badeau, Grant said to him, "I am not going to commit suicide," and went back to working hard. "He liked to have his pages read aloud to the family in the evenings, so that he might hear how they sounded and hear their comments." And there were the three grandchildren who were living in the house.

> Daily about one o'clock he was interrupted by his grandchildren who stopped as they passed to their lunch . . . They came, indeed, like a burst of light into the sick man's study, three of them, dancing, gamboling, laughing—as pretty a brood of merry, graceful grandchildren as ever a conqueror claimed for descendants, or looked upon to perpetuate his name . . .
>
> I shall never forget the frolic with the little ones on Christmas Day. They all came to dinner, and the two youngest sat on each side of him. He was comparatively free from pain . . . [The children] monopolized the conversation, and when their mamas endeavored to check them, the General interposed and declared that this was their day. So they prattled across their grandpapa, and made preposterous attempts at jokes . . . and no one [laughed] more heartily than the great warrior, their progenitor. It was a delicious morsel of sweet in the midst of so much bitter care, a gleam of satisfaction in the gloom of that sad winter, with its fears, and certainties, and sorrows.

Badeau had conflicting emotions about his own situation. On the one hand, despite the financial arrangement that he had agreed to with Grant concerning his work on Grant's *Memoirs*, he always remembered that prior to that Grant "had always promised that my history *[Military History of Ulysses S. Grant]* should take the place of all that he should have to say on the subject." On the other hand, he had a great admiration for Grant, and the quietly ardent side of Grant's nature. He was to write:

> No one, indeed, can understand the character of General Grant who does not know the strength of his regard for his children. It was like the passion of a wild beast for its cubs, or the love of a mother for a sucking child, instinctive, unreasoning, overween-ing; yet, what everyone can appreciate; natural, and in this grim veteran touching in the extreme.
>
> He not only thought his sons able, wise, and pure; he had a trust in them that was absolute and childlike . . . He rose from his death-bed to work for them, and when he thought he was dying his utterances were about his "boys." [And] this feeling, lavished on his own children, reached over to theirs. No parent ever enveloped his entire progeny in a more comprehensive or closed regard.

That same side of Grant had been witnessed twenty years before by Horace Porter. In the autumn of 1864, when Grant had his family living with him at his headquarters at City Point, Virginia, one morning Porter stepped into Grant's tent and saw this:

> I found him in his shirt-sleeves engaged in a rough-and-tumble wrestling match with his two older boys [Fred, then fourteen, and Buck, twelve]. The lads had just tripped him up, and he was on his knees grappling with the youngsters, and joining in their merry laughter, as if he were a boy again himself. I had several dispatches in my hand, and when he saw that I had come on business, he disentangled himself with some difficulty from the young com-batants, rose to his feet, brushed the dust off his knees with one hand, and said in a sort of apologetic manner: "Ah, you know my weaknesses—my children and my horses."

~ II ~

During the same days around Christmas that Badeau described, General William Tecumseh Sherman came calling on Grant at his house in Manhattan. When Grant was elected president in 1868 he appointed Sherman to succeed him as commanding general of the United States Army. Ten months before this trip to New York from St. Louis, Sherman retired from the army after forty-seven years of service, including his time as a cadet at West Point. When Philip Sheridan replaced Sherman, that completed the sequence of post-war commanders that Grant always hoped the army would have.

Sherman, who said of his and Grant's immensely important friendship and military relationship, "We were as brothers, I the older man in years, he the higher in rank," was an entirely differ-ent man from Grant. In contrast to Grant's muscular medium build, greying dark hair, and quiet manner, Sherman was tall and rangy, with wiry red hair and bristly beard, constantly gesturing as he spoke. Nonetheless, Grant relaxed in his company as he did with no other officer.

Grant's granddaughter Julia described her impressions of Sherman:

> He talked a lot, was tall and vital, with a distinguished face, his head well poised, and he had a charming, confiding manner."

And Sherman knew his old commander well, as Julia remem-bered in this exchange between her grandmother and Sherman.

> Seeing grandmama's worry over my grandfather's silence, which she attributed to pain, I remember that one day when her hus-band having left the room she mentioned this, General Sherman, walking up and down, said to her: "But the general was always silent, Mrs. Grant. Even at the worst times of strain, during the

war, I used to go to see him at his headquarters, and he would sit perfectly still, like he did here today. I just walked up and down and swore then; and I'm sure it did your husband lots of good, ma'am, and relieved his mind to have me do it for him." Grandmama laughed and was consoled.

On this visit to New York in December, Sherman wanted to learn the truth about the rumors of his friend's condition. When Julia and Frederick told him that Grant had cancer, Sherman, who always thought of Grant as indestructible, found that hard to believe. Although Grant was younger, Sherman, who lost his father at the age of nine, had always looked to him as something of a father figure. He expressed his faith in Grant when he wrote this to him in March of 1865, summing up the two years they had campaigned together before Lincoln brought Grant east to become general in chief: "I knew wherever I was that you thought of me, and if I got in a tight place you would come if alive."

Sherman remained doubtful that Grant was dying, and they clearly enjoyed their hours together. Among other memories they had in common was that of the graduation balls they attended at Annapolis and West Point in June of 1869, soon after Grant become president and Sherman became the army's general in chief. Protocol dictated that the president should lead off the opening quadrille in the "set of honor." It became apparent that Grant had learned nothing about dancing since he avoided the dance floor during the "hops" when he was a cadet at West Point. A witness reported to the *New York Times* that Grant "had a scared look on his face that moved your heart."

He turned away too soon from his partner, and turned to the next lady, holding his hands up appealingly, like an innocent kitten with its burnt paws, and lost himself constantly almost beyond recovery. For every step he took he seemed he would prefer facing another [Fort] Donelson.

As for Sherman, he was seen as "exhibiting an immense amount of motive vim, but wanting sadly in judgment." The outcome at both graduation balls was the same. "At Annapolis, we are told, GRANT, instead of 'leading off' in his set, was very submissively led off, evidently knowing no more of the figures, and doing them no better, than a 'frozen-toed turkey.' SHERMAN, on the other hand, was . . . awkward, and quite as bold as awkward, taking steps like his soldiers marching to the sea." Both men "deserted the Terpsichorean field," but the *Times* put the matter in perspective: "Not every one that shone at Waterloo cut a fine figure at the Brussels ball the night before."

On Christmas Eve, Sherman wrote his wife, Ellen, in St. Louis, "Grant says my visits have done him more good than all the doctors." Still dubious about how serious Grant's condition was, he nonetheless saw that the Grants needed money. On December 29, he wrote Sheridan about Grant: "I made him two long visits and found him much better than Fred had described—but his business condition is worse than I supposed . . . I found Grant, Fred and Badeau at work on his book which he says has made such progress that he expects to have it ready for the Press in . . . May." Evidently uncertain about that schedule and how much the book might in fact make, Sherman began to organize a group of prominent Americans to raise some money for the Grants. He relied primarily on Cyrus W. Field, the financier who promoted the first transatlantic telegraph cable. Sherman also brought into this group Grant's friend the Philadelphia publisher George W. Childs, the prominent Philadelphia banker Anthony J. Drexel, and Hamilton Fish, the patrician New Yorker who had been Grant's secretary of state. Stories alluding to this effort ran in the *New York Times* on December 29 and New Year's Eve. On January 6 of the new year 1885 Grant wrote to Field, saying, "I appreciate both the motive and the friendship on your part, but on mature reflection I regard it as due myself and my family to decline this generosity."

At this point, Grant received from the Century Company their check for $1,000 for his article on the Battle of Shiloh. Immediately, the man who had just asked the millionaire Cyrus W. Field to stop raising money for him sent $1,000 to Charles Wood of Lansingburgh, New York, the first person in the nation to step forward and send him $500 when news of the Grant & Ward failure appeared the previous May. In doing so, Grant said, "I wish to state to you . . . how great was the relief afforded by your timely loan. At the time I had not a hundred dollars in my pocket." Saying that he hoped to mail him another check, repaying the rest of the $1,500 total that Wood had sent him, Grant added, "It affords me greater pleasure from the fact that I have earned this from my own work." Wood donated the money to charity.

* * *

WORD SPREAD around the country that Grant was ill of an unidentified disease and in need of money. The *New York Herald* reported that Sherman had received "a remittance of $100, the gift of an ex-Confederate soldier, to be used in behalf of General Grant, in remembrance of his magnanimity toward the South." At the same time, some largely inaccurate newspaper stories appeared concerning the arrangement that William H. Vanderbilt had made with Julia for her to turn Grant's swords, medals, and gifts from foreign heads of state over to the federal government after Grant's death. All these objects were to remain in her custody until that time. The stories suggested that Vanderbilt was in some way trying to recover the personal loan of $150,000 he had made to Grant on the fateful weekend in May of

1884 that the Grant & Ward collapse began. In fact, Vanderbilt, destined to live less than a year, was still trying to protect Grant and Julia from creditors of Grant & Ward who might be able to attach these possessions, which had both great monetary and historical value. On January 11, Julia wrote Vanderbilt, calling Vanderbilt's actions "generous and princely," but reiterating that she and her husband still intended to pay off their debt to Vanderbilt when they could.

Julia's letter to Vanderbilt never became public, but the widespread talk of the Grants' difficulties brought a most unusual man into the picture—P. T. Barnum, the greatest showman of the nineteenth century. Among Barnum's many shrewd judgments as to what people were prepared to pay money to see, he had sent the midget Tom Thumb on a stupendously successful international tour, and four years before this had started the three-ring Barnum & Bailey Circus, featuring the giant elephant, Jumbo, as the star of the "Greatest Show on Earth." Barnum wrote Grant a letter. He began by saying, "The whole world honors and respects you. All are anxious that you should live happy and free from care. While they admire your manliness in declining the larger sum recently tendered by your friends they still desire to see you achieve financial independence in an honorable manner."

Barnum had the solution. Grant's valuable mementoes, "bestowed upon you by monarchs, princes, and peoples throughout the globe," were for the time being in a legal limbo. Barnum would pay handsomely for the privilege of putting them on tour to large cities in America and Europe. "I will give you $100,000 cash, besides a portion of the profits, assuming all risks myself, if I may be permitted to exhibit them to a grateful and appreciative public."

This overture got Barnum through the door of 3 East Sixty-sixth Street. In a story the *New York Tribune* printed on January 13, he told a reporter, "I conversed with him [Grant] to-day at his house on the subject. He says the trophies are beyond his control."

That ended Barnum's efforts, but during the remaining weeks of January, more and more mail piled up at Sixty-sixth Street. One letter that Grant particularly liked came from a Captain H. S. Dixon of Fresno, California. Dixon commanded a new type of veterans' organization, the Fresno Camp of Blue and Gray Veterans, whose membership included men who had fought for the South, as well as those who fought for the North.

This letter contained copies of that group's resolutions that urged Congress to place Grant officially on the list of retired army officers. Because former presidents did not then receive pensions, if Grant could receive the military pension, it would ensure him and Julia a pension of more than $20,000 a year, but bureaucratic regulations held that by becoming president he had waived his right to a general's pension. To get past that would require a special act of Congress; such a bill, Senate Bill 2530, was now under consideration, but some of the Confederate veterans serving in Congress opposed it.

In replying to Captain Dixon, Grant asked him to thank his Blue and Gray Veterans for their efforts on his behalf, but emphasized his pleasure in seeing that this came "from an association composed of veterans of both armies . . . I hope that the fraternity practiced by the veterans of Fresno may be patterned after by all the citizens of our country before many years roll over."

The calls for Grant to receive a pension increased. At the end of the month, former Confederate Brigadier General Raleigh E. Colston put the matter clearly in a letter to Grant.

It is the nearly unanimous sentiment of the Confed. Veterans, especially those of the Army of N. Va. [Lee's Army of Northern Virginia] that it is only bare equity to restore you to a position as good as that which you gave up at your country's call, and that because you served as President, it should not deprive you of the rights & privileges enjoyed by your brother officers to the end of their lives.

It would have been but justice, had you been placed on the retired list immediately after the termination of your presidential term.

Colston accompanied this with a copy of a letter he had written to the editor of the *Washington Post*, saying, "Let the survivors of the Confederate army urge their representatives in Congress to hasten the passage of the Senate bill as a matter of strict equity, and a relief which Gen. Grant can accept with *just pride*. I doubt not he will be gratified to know that those whom he treated generously in the day of their sorrow remember him gratefully in his hour of tribulation."

* * *

ON FEBRUARY I, 1885, Grant wrote to his friend George Childs that his health was "now improving." That was not so, but Grant wanted to believe it. As if what he added to this proved it, he said, "I am now quite well in every way except soreness of the tongue about the root, and the same thing of the tonsil just over it. It is very difficult for me to swallow enough to maintain my strength, and nothing gives me so much pain as swallowing water." Grant's beloved only daughter, Nellie, who lived in England with her faithless husband, Algernon Sartoris, and their children, received mixed reports on her father's condition and decided to write straight to him. Replying to her on February 16, he once again mixed optimism with what could only be considered bad news. "The sore throat which you recollect I had all the time we were at Long Branch last summer has proven to be a very serious matter. I paid no attention to it until it had run four months. It has troubled me so much to swallow that I have fallen off nearly thirty pounds."

What came next was the Grant who wrote Lincoln, "I propose to fight it out along these lines if it takes all summer." He first put emphasis on what hope could be found in his medical condition and then moved to his work on his book. "It has only been within the last ten days that the doctor has been willing to say that the ulcers in my throat are beginning to yeald [sic] to treetment [sic.]"

Then he put on paper his version of Napoleon's "Two o'clock in the morning courage."

It would be very hard to be confined to the house so long a time if it was not that I have become interested in the work which I have undertaken. It will take several months yet to complete the history of my campaigns. The indications now are that the book will be in two volumes of about four hundred and fifty pages each. I give a condensed biography of my life up to the breaking out of the rebellion. If you ever take the time to read it you will find out what sort of a boy and man I was before you knew me. I do not know whether my book will be interesting to other people or not, but all the publishers want to get it, and I have had larger offers than have ever been made for a book before. Fred helps me greatly in my work. He does all the copying, and looks up references for me.

We have all been as happy as could be expected considering our great losses and my personal suffering. Philosophers profess to believe that what is, is for the best. I hope that it may be so with our family.

All join in sending love and kisses to you and all the children.

Your affectionate Papa

Nellie booked her passage to cross the Atlantic. Grant continued to look for good news of any kind. He learned that Fred had been able to rent the big summer house at Long Branch, and he enjoyed seeing the stack of ten copies of the issue of the *Century Magazine* that arrived, containing his article on Shiloh. As for his *Memoirs*, day after day he was serving up to his future readers a masterful overview of his campaigns and battles, and doing it with an approach and style entirely his own. He repeatedly conveyed his feeling for the uncompromising nature of war, in all its aspects. "I always admired the South, as bad as I thought their cause," Grant wrote, "for the boldness with which they silenced all opposition and all croaking, by press or individuals, within their control." War should be avoided if at all possible. "But, once entered into, it is too much for human nature to tolerate an enemy within their ranks to give aid and comfort to the opposing section or nation."

Grant gave his readers a classic example of an historical "What If?" In a section of a chapter in Volume One titled, "The Coming Crisis," he looked back on the seven years between his resignation from the army in 1854 and the outbreak of the Civil War. Speaking of the issue of secession, he said, "The fact is that the Constitution did not apply to any such contingency as the one existing from 1861 to 1865. Its framers never dreamed of such a contingency occurring. If they had foreseen it, the probabilities are they would have sanctioned the right of a State or States to withdraw rather than that there should be a war between brothers."

Here was Grant, who with Lincoln did more to preserve the Union than anyone else, positing the idea that the Constitution could have been amended to avoid war over the issue of secession. "The framers were wise in their generation and wanted to do their very best possible to secure their own liberty and independence, and that of their descendants to the latest days."

His summation on this issue: "It is preposterous to suppose that the people of one generation can lay down the best and only rules of government for all who are to come after them, and under unforeseen contingencies." Elsewhere, in Volume Two, Grant made it clear that slavery was the issue that led to the war, and added that, while originally he did not agree with the concept that "a state cannot exist half slave and half free," after the war he came to believe "that the saying is quite true."

In addition to his daily work on the *Memoirs*, Grant now finally came to grips with his choice of a publisher. In a memorandum, he wrote in part, "I have made up my mind that I prefer Webster & Co to publish my book . . . I believe the above company can sell a greater number than the Century. They have no other business which this will come in competition with . . . Webster offers better terms." Since Mark Twain had created Webster and Company largely to publish his own books, this added a dimension to what was already a close relationship. Twain returned to New York from a lecture tour on February 21 and went immediately to Grant's house. He was shocked to see how thin and pale Grant had become, but believed that Grant still possessed the strength and determination to finish this last thing he had set out to do. As Twain was leaving, Frederick Grant went downstairs with him, seeing him to the door; there he told him in confidence that the doctors thought that Grant might not live longer than a few more weeks.

This shook Twain. Nonetheless, six days later he signed the contract with Grant for his *Personal Memoirs*. The arrangement was the one on which Grant, his friend Childs, Childs's lawyer, and Twain, had all finally agreed: Grant would get a 20 percent gross royalty on sales, and the *Memoirs* would be published on the subscription basis Twain had recommended.

Knowing that Grant might not live to finish the work, Twain looked at it this way. Speaking of the first volume, he wrote his nephew Charles Webster, "As I understand it, it lacks 2 or 3 chapters. Well, if the lack is at the *end* of the volume, we will end the volume *without* them; if they are to be supplied by another hand, they may begin the 2d vol., not mar the 1st, which must be *all* General Grant, if possible." Twain understood what was at stake, not only for Grant and himself, but for the nation: What can this historic man impart to us all before he succumbs to death and his experience and wisdom will be lost to all of us?

Twain threw himself into the practical side of the venture, immediately canceling a planned lecture tour of England and Australia. At the same time that the completed book contract arrived at 3 East Sixty-sixth Street, Twain hired a stenographer to speed up Grant's writing. This was Noble E. Dawson, who had acted as Grant's secretary during one of his postpresidential trips to Mexico. He had been working as a stenographer for the Senate Interstate Commerce Committee, but when it became known that Grant wanted his services, he was immediately released to go to New York. Dawson and Grant quickly began working well together; Dawson would arrive at Grant's house early in the morning, and work all day, setting down in shorthand what Grant said, dictating to Dawson now instead of writing. Then Dawson would read the dictated text back to Grant, making corrections as Grant directed. Dawson said this of their sessions:

> General Grant dictated very freely and easily. He made very few changes and never hemmed and hawed. Mr. Mark Twain was shown the manuscript of the first volume during one of my dictation sessions with the General. Mr. Twain was astonished when he looked at it and said that there was not one literary man in one hundred who furnished as clean a copy as Grant. The General's sentences rarely had to be revised in any way.

Twain was in the process of having a stronger reaction than that. He had started his effort to publish Grant's *Memoirs* because he thought they would be a financial success. Now he saw that they had a remarkable literary quality. He later compared them with Caesar's *Commentaries*, saying this:

> . . . the same high merits distinguished both books—clarity of statement, directness, simplicity, manifest truthfulness, fairness and justice toward friend and foe alike and avoidance of flowery

speech. . . . General Grant's book is a great, unique, and unapproachable literary masterpiece. There is no higher literature than these modern, simple *Memoirs*. Their style is flawless . . . no man can improve upon it.

With all his growing respect for a man he already greatly admired, Twain nonetheless stayed right on the commercial path. At the office of Webster and Company, he designed a new letterhead, which had beneath the firm's name, "Mark Twain's Books and the forthcoming personal Memoirs of General Grant." Twain ordered that these last five words, "personal Memoirs of General Grant," should be printed in "just a shade larger type, and in RED INK."

~ I I I ~

On March 1, the *New York Times* came out with a story headlined: GRANT IS DYING.

This was not caused by any new development, but with this, the public learned what Grant's doctors, family, and friends had known or feared for months. The other New York papers—the *Tribune*, *World, Sun, Post, Journal, Daily News, Brooklyn Eagle*—swiftly appeared with their own stories, which were variations on the *Times*'s subheads: DYING SLOWLY FROM CANCER; GRAVELY ILL; SINKING INTO THE GRAVE; GEN. GRANT'S FRIENDS GIVE UP HOPE. Within twenty-four hours all the metropolitan papers had their reporters standing across the street from 3 East Sixty-sixth Street, assigned to a twenty-four-hour watch. Reporters from all the major East Coast cities soon joined them; within a week journalists came in from St. Louis, Chicago, San Francisco, and Los Angeles. A group of reporters rented the basement of a nearby house on Madison Avenue and used it to string telegraph wires to link up with downtown newspaper offices and out-of-town news services. One reporter charmed a chambermaid in a neighboring house into letting him look through a window to see what was going on inside 3 East Sixty-sixth Street.

The doctors decided to issue two medical bulletins a day, usually through Dr. Douglas, although they seldom offered anything new. For a time, three "bulletin boys" were allowed to be in the main hall of Grant's house; working for the Associated Press, the United Press, and Western Union, their job was to grab copies of the medical bulletins and get them to their news services as quickly as they could run.

The March weather was cold, rainy, and gloomy, but Sixty-sixth Street became crowded with those who came to stare at Grant's house. At one point, three thousand unanswered letters and telegrams from well-wishers, along with stacks of packages, were piled in the library. When Grant would appear, crossing the sidewalk to get into a friend's carriage for a ride through the neighborhood and into Central Park, the crowd would part to let him through, sometimes remaining respectfully quiet, with men taking off their hats, and sometimes applauding. At the end of the first week of what was becoming a circus, New York's police chief Adam Gunner called on Julia and said that he was assigning additional policemen to patrol the street and keep order.

Some in the crowds proved to be eccentrics. A man named John Hansfelt tried to force his way through the front door. When a policeman stopped him, Hansfelt declared that he had written Julia that her husband would live if only he stopped drinking coffee. "The Lord moved me to write," he said, "but He did not move her to respond."

"Well," the police officer responded in the witty tradition of his department, "now *I'm* moving *you*."

A different story emerged when a reporter from the *New York Tribune* approached a middle-aged countryman with a missing arm who was limping along with a cane. Asked why he had come to Sixty-sixth Street, the man replied:

> He's my old commander and I love him. When the Battle of the Wilderness was over and the Rebs had taken to their heels, I was a-lying in a shady spot I had a-crawled to, when the General rode by. My arm and my leg was a-hanging by a thread and as he passed me I shouted, "Hooray!" and the General's face lit up with a smile of joy and sadness. That was my last battle and I never saw him again.

As for Grant, he went on writing as well as dictating, usually wearing a shirt that had become one or two sizes too big for him, and a scarf and a knit wool skating cap. During most of his daytime and night hours, he would curl up in a combination of two large overstuffed black leather armchairs, bending forward during the day to write on a board that would be set across the space above his thighs. At night he would lean back against one or more cloth pillows, remaining sufficiently erect to avoid his throat filling with mucus and pus. Aware that people often stood outside his house during the day, Grant would occasionally get up from his work, make his way to the window, gaze expressionlessly for a few seconds at the crowd that gathered below even in the rain, and return to his mass of documents and maps.

Apart from his work, Grant read several newspapers a day, and thus learned virtually everything being written about him. On one occasion, when Twain came to the house, Grant greeted him with this. "You would think the newspapers could get my weight right. While I was out riding, the thought occurred to me that I would like to be weighed. When I got to a store, I got out and slipped on the scales . . . [which] balanced at 146. Well, I read six newspapers this morning. No two of them have the same figures and no one of them is right."

Trying to expand the frame of reference of their stories, newspapers went well beyond Manhattan. A reporter for the *Boston Globe* called on former Confederate president Jefferson Davis at Beauvoir, the plantation in Mississippi where Davis and his wife, Varina, were living, and asked him to comment on Grant's career. Davis replied, "General Grant is dying. Instead of seeking to disturb the quiet of his closing hours, I would, if it were in my power, contribute to his peace of mind and the comfort of his body." Learning of this and other conciliatory remarks by former enemies, Grant responded, "I am very glad to hear this. I would much rather have their good will than their ill-will. I would rather have the good will of any man than his ill-will."

Some of Grant's strongest supporters began to speak of him in the past tense. In a telegram, Sheridan said, "He was a far greater man than people thought him to be. He was always able, no matter how situated, to do more than was expected of him."

Occasionally the press got hold of a story that Grant was better. Several weeks after the *Times* headline that stated GRANT IS DYING, the *New York World* came out with the headline, NOT CANCER AFTER ALL. The accompanying story suggested that Grant's doctors were incompetent. That brought a retort from Grant, who had faith in his doctors. He authorized Dr. Douglas to release a statement to the press. "This paper, the *World*," Grant said, "is a reformer in medicines. It is an advertising medium for quack medicines prepared by ignorant people. If I were left to their treatment, I would die within a few days, suffering the extremist [sic] agony in the meantime."

Things Come Together

Amidst all this attention in Manhattan, in Washington the effort to get Grant his deserved military pension seemed to be stalled. Sherman was in Washington, lobbying to get this for Grant, but there were still pockets of congressional resistance. Nonetheless, Grant had a friend from the party that had so often opposed him. Representative Samuel J. Randall, the Democratic Speaker of the House, was ready to do some extraordinary maneuvering on his behalf. Senate Bill 2530 was a "companion bill," identical to one in the House. If both House and Senate approved it, Grant would get his deserved pension, but time was running out. A constitutionally mandated brief congressional recess had to occur before a new president was inaugurated; at noon on March 4, the presidency of Chester Arthur would end, and Grover Cleveland would be sworn in. When Grant learned that the House had adjourned the night before the inauguration without taking action on his behalf, he said to his friend Childs, who was visiting the Grants in New York, "You know during the last day of a session everything is in turmoil. Such a thing cannot possibly be passed."

Grant had underestimated the parliamentary skill and imagination of his Democratic supporter Randall. The Speaker reconvened the House on Inauguration Day, March 4, and instructed the clerk to date the day's paperwork, still to be done before noon, as having been done the previous day. The House passed the Grant bill a few minutes before noon, but the Senators were no longer in the Senate chamber and were beginning to gather in the Capitol's rotunda for the coming inauguration ceremonies. Randall rushed out of the House chamber and urged the senators to reassemble in the Senate chamber and pass their identical version of the same bill. As they came in to do so, the hands of the clock passed noon, but Randall had a clerk climb a ladder and turn the clock back twenty minutes, during which the Senate passed the bill that gave Grant his pension.

At one that afternoon, Grant was sitting in the room in which he worked, chatting with Mark Twain, his son Fred, George Childs, and Adam Badeau. Julia was in the next room. Noon had come and gone; all of them assumed that, for whatever combination of reasons, the bill had failed to become law. A telegram was brought upstairs to Childs. He handed it to Grant, who looked at it and said, "I am grateful the thing has passed." Julia rushed in from the library, beaming as she exclaimed, "Hurrah! Our old commander is back!" Twain wrote of the moment: "Every face there betrayed strong excitement and emotion, except one—General Grant's. He read the telegram, but not a shade or suggestion of a change exhibited itself in his iron countenance." That may have been the way Twain remembered it later, but that night he sent a telegram to his wife saying that when Grant read the message about his pension, "The effect upon him was like raising the dead."

As for Twain, now that he had the contract to publish Grant he began frequently rushing from his house in Hartford to New York, where he divided his time between 3 East Sixty-sixth Street and the Webster publishing house down on Fourteenth Street. This was Twain, as venture capitalist. Working with his nephew, Charles Webster, he began signing every kind of contract—to buy huge amounts of paper, to reserve time on printing presses throughout the New York area, and to arrange with book binderies in several cities to do the work of placing the two volumes in cloth covers when they were printed. He even rented a building in Manhattan and created a bindery of his own, buying the machinery and bringing up from Philadelphia special workers to run the machines. Twain calculated that once the presses started to feed the combined binderies, a copy of Grant's book would come off the line every second.

As for how to sell the manufactured book, Twain demonstrated what he had told Grant the past November: the best way to publish a work like this was to sell it by subscription, with the readers committing themselves in advance to buying their copies, rather than the publisher just printing the books and placing them on the shelves of bookstores. There were many agencies all over the country that specialized in having their traveling salesmen go out in a form of door-to-door selling and canvas prospective buyers of books. Twain's nephew Webster held a large meeting in Manhattan of men who ran or were sales managers for this type of agency. In New York they learned that they would be offering the two volumes in three different qualities of bindings at three prices. Collectively, these men pledged to sell 250,000 sets of Grant's book and returned to their various cities carrying a prospectus that announced that Volume One would be published on December 1 of this year of 1885, and the second volume four months later. This commitment to a sales campaign enabled Twain to write Webster that "It *insures* a sudden sale of 250,000 copies of the first volume." Twain wanted to watch every detail and to be "close at hand all the time while General Grant's book is passing through the press . . . I want no mistakes to happen, nothing overlooked, nothing neglected." Grant, too, wanted to give his book exactly the same attention to detail, and while Twain was monitoring the sales campaign, Grant had already decided to begin his second volume with the Battle of Chattanooga, and go on from there to the end of the war.

In addition to the managerial problems of producing Grant's book, the question arose of who had the publishing rights to the various parts of Grant's writing on the Civil War. Twain saw that Grant was basing significant sections of his book on the four articles for which the *Century Magazine* had a contract. If the *Century* had the exclusive rights to the wording of those articles, Grant, who needed to keep moving ahead, might have to revise those texts in order to be able to use them in his book. Twain also understood that the *Century* management had not been pleased with Grant when, after months of dickering with them, he chose Twain to be his publisher.

Accompanied by his nephew Charles Webster and a lawyer named Clarence A. Seward who acted as Grant's legal adviser, Twain strode into the Century Company's offices to meet with its president Roswell Smith. Going on the offensive, Twain put it to Smith that Grant was the rightful owner of everything he had written on the Civil War.

Smith let Twain's jaws snap on thin air. He agreed; all rights would revert to Grant, but not until the *Century Magazine* had published all four of the articles for which they had paid Grant. (Grant had yet to finish revising his article on the Vicksburg campaign.) Somewhat defiantly, Smith pulled out the receipt for that transaction.

On the spot, Twain became the agreeable man he could be. He realized that this piece of paper covered those four articles and nothing more. Any further use of that material would require an additional contract. Grant need not change a word of what he was using from those articles in his *Personal Memoirs*. Twain then confronted Smith on the subject of what he felt was the Century's inadequate payment to Grant for his four articles. This was pure friendship on Twain's part; he had no share in anything but the profits from Grant's book. Since the magazine started publishing Grant, its subscriptions had steadily risen, and would increase by 40 percent in the next sixteen months. Although the magazine was publishing other significant work—excerpts from William Dean Howells's masterpiece *Silas Lapham*, Henry James's *The Bostonians*, and Twain's own *Adventures of Huckleberry Finn*—no one doubted that Grant was the magazine's big attraction for 1885. Once again, Smith was amenable. In a conversation with Grant some months earlier, he had come up from $500 to $2,000 per article, and now agreed to raise that to $4,000 apiece.

Thinking of everything, Twain also moved to insulate Grant's book from the possibility of a pirated publication—something that had happened to Twain himself. At that time there was no international copyright protection. Unscrupulous Canadian publishers would steal page proofs of new works by popular authors from American printers, copy them word for word, and have them out and for sale before the American editions were manufactured. Since the American copyright laws granted copyright only to printed matter, if one or more Canadian publishers could get ahead of the printed edition of Grant's book, Twain would have no recourse. To forestall this, Twain had Webster keep the page proofs in the company safe as they came in from the printers, and Webster and Company guaranteed a $6,000 bonus to the printers and binders who could account for every proof sheet. To top off these security measures, Twain bought an insurance policy to reimburse Webster and Company should any of these proofs be stolen or lost.

~II~

While Twain worked on the publishing side of Grant's efforts, during the first half of March Grant produced a remarkable spurt of work. He finished his Vicksburg article, and expanded that material for what he was writing to conclude his first volume before opening his second volume with the Battle of Chattanooga. On some days, working from morning to night, he wrote ten thousand words—an effort that moved Twain to say, "It kills me these days to write half of that."

On March 20, Twain appeared with a gifted young sculptor named Karl Gerhardt, who had returned from studies at the École des Beaux-Arts in Paris that Twain had been subsidizing. A few days before this, Twain had shown his protégé Gerhardt a photo of Grant, and from that the artist had swiftly produced a small clay bust that Twain found to be a nearly perfect likeness. When Gerhardt now showed this little statue to the Grants, Julia and Fred found it exciting, and Julia insisted on bringing both the artist and his bust in to where Grant sat working. Grant greeted him pleasantly; seeing that Julia wanted young Gerhardt to continue working on it then and there, he put aside his work while Julia had him turn his head at different angles, saying, "stop moving," and "move your head just this way, Ulyss," followed by "just a bit more." This cooperation pleased Julia, and Grant suggested that a small table be set up on which Gerhardt could place his bust to continue his work on it while Grant resumed his writing. After a final affectionate but impatient request from Julia— "Ulyss! Ulyss! Can't you put your feet on the floor?"—everyone became quiet, Twain reading a book he had picked up, Grant writing, and Harrison Terrell watching from the back of the room. After awhile, Grant fell asleep as Gerhardt continued moving his hands on the clay.

When Grant awoke an hour later, the entire family gathered to admire the sculptor's work. Harrison Terrell declared, "That's the General. Yes sir, that's the General. Mind! I tell you that's the General."

Gerhardt had so improved the bust that, reproduced in terra cotta in thousands of copies, it became known as "the most nearly correct likeness of the general."

* * *

IN LATE MARCH, everything seemed to be moving forward on schedule. Besides his writing, Grant enjoyed some lively, pleasant hours. His daughter, Nellie, had arrived from England. On afternoons when the early spring weather was good, he and Nellie would go for a ride in Central Park in Senator Chaffee's carriage. Sometimes they were accompanied by the senator and by Grant's friend Matias Romero, Mexico's minister to the United States, who often came to see him in New York. (Romero was to say that Grant's joy at having Nellie with him again kept him from sleeping at night.) At other times the tall, white-bearded Dr. John Hancock Douglas joined them on these outings.

Two new figures joined the group at the Grants' house. In addition to Harrison Terrell, a male nurse named Henry McSweeny was hired to assist in caring for Grant. A woman who knew him said, "Henry McSweeny was a tall fine looking well poised young man who was without question very fond of General Grant." To distinguish him from Harrison Terrell, the *New York Times* referred to him as Grant's "white nurse."

As the weather turned warmer, Grant received frequent visits from the other new figure, Reverend John Philip Newman, pastor of the Central Methodist Episcopal Church of New York City—the congregation of which Grant had been a trustee until he resigned because he could no longer pay the rent for his pew. The Grants had met Newman in Washington during Grant's presidency, when he was pastor of the Metropolitan Church where Grant had occasionally attended services. Newman did not shy away from publicity; as he went in and out of 3 East Sixty-sixth Street, he would stop and answer reporters' questions. Prayers, Newman told them, hundreds of thousands of prayers, were keeping Grant alive. Senator Chaffee finally said to the same reporters, "There's been a good deal of nonsense in the papers about Doctor Newman's visits. General Grant does not believe that Doctor Newman's prayers will save him. He allows the doctor to pray simply because he does not want to hurt his feelings." Grant was later reported to have said that he did not care how much praying went on at Sixty-sixth Street as long as it made Julia feel better. Despite Julia's reliance on Newman's spiritual counsel, Mark Twain saw him as something of a religious mountebank, saying of one of Newman's claims of praying with Grant, "This piece of reporting comports with Newman, gush, rot, impossible."

In addition to the stimulus of having many of his family and friends around him, on the evening of Thursday, March 26, Grant gave testimony against Ferdinand Ward's partner James Fish. Grant had requested the right to give this deposition, and his doctors had agreed that he could do that. Lawyers for both the federal government and Fish's defense lawyers conducted the forty-five minute examination at 3 East Sixty-sixth Street. Fish was not present; already behind bars for months for theft in the Grant & Ward swindle, he now faced additional prosecution for violating national bank (embezzlement) laws. Among those in the room were reporters from the *New York Times* and *Tribune*, as well as Frederick Grant and his brother Buck. (It sometimes seemed as if the *Times* had nearly twenty-four-hour knowledge of what occurred at the Grants' house.)

On this occasion Grant gave his testimony with the same clarity he usually employed in writing his book, and with the same sense of indignation that he had felt ever since he learned of the way in which Ward and Fish stole his family's money. He displayed no forgiveness: here sat the Grant for whom the battle was never over, the man who marked Sheridan for higher command after that general chased the fleeing Confederates at Chattanooga down the reverse slopes of mountains and through the night until two in the morning.

The defense lawyers had a supremely difficult task. On the one hand, their job was to demonstrate that Grant had in some way, perhaps in letters he signed, been party to deceiving the investors in Grant & Ward. On the other, they had to word their questions in a way that avoided any suggestion of that. They tried, and came up with a portrait of a financial babe in the woods. In one part of his testimony, Grant said this about his way of filing papers.

> I have never been in the habit of preserving private letters, and if I was to try I suppose I should make a poor record. My business in life has always been such that somebody else has always taken care of letters that had to be saved, and the only way I have now of preserving a letter that I wish to preserve until I do something with it is to put it in my side coat pocket or put it in the drawer where I write, and then when I look for a letter it is about the last one I find.

In reply to a question on redirect by the defendant's counsel concerning whether he had, previous to the failure of Grant & Ward, "any mistrust on your part in respect to Mr. Ferdinand Ward?" Grant replied: "I am sorry to say that I did not. I had no mistrust of Mr. Ward the night before the failure, not the slightest . . . It took me a day or two to believe it was possible that Ward had committed the act he had."

The most important thing for the government's lawyers to establish was that Grant had not, as some had alleged, been involved in getting Grant & Ward favorable treatment in receiving government contracts. On this Grant was rock solid.

There is nothing wrong in being engaged in Government contracts more than in anything else, unless made wrong by the acts
of the individual, but I had been President of the United States,
and I did not think it was suitable for me to have my name connected with Government contracts . . . I did not think it was any
place for me.

After taking Grant's deposition, the *New York Times* reported, the
lawyers for the prosecution and the defense " . . . had a pleasant talk
with the General, expressing deep regret at his affliction and ven-
turing to hope that the further progress of his disease might finally
be stopped. 'You're certainly looking remarkably well,' remarked
Lawyer Smith [Edwin B. Smith of the defense] in the course of the
conversation. 'I don't know about that,' responded the patient, with
a slight shake of the head: 'I am conscious that I am a very sick man.'"

Just how "very sick" Grant was became clear a few hours later,
when he began coughing uncontrollably. The doctors immediately
gave him a solution of cocaine and morphine; Grant found the morphine a particularly powerful sedative, and tried to avoid it because
he felt it clouded his mind. He awoke the next day and went back
to work, but had another choking fit that evening, and the next three
evenings. When he was stricken on March 30 for the sixth night in
a row, Grant's friend Romero told reporters this: "The truth is the
disease has gotten away from the doctors. It is possible that he may
die tonight and at the very best he cannot live ten days. As he is too
weak, he cannot expectorate the blood and will choke to death."

The crisis reached such proportions that the doctors considered
removing Grant's tongue, or cutting into his windpipe in the pro-
cedure known as a tracheotomy. In deciding not to do that, Dr.
Shrady stated, "It is doubtful if the General's heart could stand another choking attack. We have decided he could not survive a tracheotomy for very long."

General Grant at Cold Harbor: Grant lost 7,000 or more men dead or wounded in one hour at Cold Harbor. Nonetheless, he remained aggressive and determined. Lincoln said of him, "Once Grant gets possession of a place, he holds on to it as if he had inherited it." *Library of Congress*

Nellie Grant: Of Grant's four children—three sons and a daughter, Nellie—she was clearly his favorite. In 1874, when at the age of eighteen she married the Englishman Algernon Sartoris in the White House in what was called "The Wedding of the Century," Grant wept throughout the ceremony. After the bride and groom left to sail for England the next day, Grant was found lying on Nellie's bed, sobbing. Eleven years later, when Nellie, living in England, learned that her father had cancer, she returned to be with him during the final months of his life. In the days right after she came back, Grant was so happy to see her that he could not sleep, not because of pain, but from joy. Nellie's husband turned out to be a philandering alcoholic. Four years after Grant's death in 1885, she was divorced and returned to the United States for good, bringing her four children with her. Julia, now rich from royalties from the *Memoirs*, welcomed her daughter and grandchildren, but happiness eluded Nellie for the rest of her life. *Library of Congress*

Julia, Grant's wife: Because of a cross-eyed condition known as strabisimus, she always tried to have herself photographed in profile. The Civil War historian Bruce Catton said of their marriage, "They shared one of the great, romantic, beautiful loves of all American history." *Library of Congress*

Grant, Julia, and their youngest son Jesse: Grant was in his first term as president when this photograph was taken in the summer of 1872 at their seaside retreat in Long Branch, New Jersey. *Library of Congress*

General Philip Sheridan: Swarthy and barrel-chested, "Little Phil" Sheridan had emerged from the Civil War as the greatest Union cavalry leader. As Grant had planned it, in 1883 he succeeded Sherman as the Army's general in chief, and was its commander at the time of Grant's death. Sheridan first came to Grant's attention at the Battle of Chattanooga, when he kept his troops chasing the retreating Confederates through the darkness until two in the morning. Grant described him as "the embodiment of heroism, dash, and impulse."
National Archives

General Horace Porter: Another officer who first came to Grant's attention at Chattanooga was Captain Horace Porter, twenty-six-year-old West Pointer whose recent leadership and valor at Chickamauga resulted in his receiving the Medal of Honor. After observing him for a day, Grant added him to his staff. Porter continued in that capacity to the end of the war, emerging as a brigadier general and going on to serve Grant in the White House as a personal secretary. Porter wrote a book, *Campaigning with Grant* which, combined with the passages in Grant's *Memoirs*, presents by far the best account of the surrender at Appomattox Court House.
Library of Congress

General William Tecumseh Sherman: "We were as brothers," General Sherman said of Grant, "I the older in years, he the higher in rank." Of his faith in Grant's ability and personal loyalty, he said in speaking to Grant of their immensely successful military partnership, "I knew wherever I was that you thought of me, and if I got in a tight place you would come if alive." When Grant was dying of cancer, Sherman wrote his wife, "Grant says my visits have done him more good than all the doctors." *Library of Congress*

General Robert E. Lee: Of meeting with Lee to discuss surrender terms at Appomattox Court House, Grant said, "Whatever his feelings, they were entirely concealed from my observation; but my own feelings, which had been quite jubilant upon receipt of his letter [asking for the surrender meeting] were sad and depressed. I felt like anything rather than rejoicing at the downfall of a foe who had fought so long and valiantly, and had suffered so much for a cause, though that cause was, I believe, one of the worst for which a people ever fought, and one for which there was the least excuse." *Library of Congress*

General William Scott Hancock: Accompanied by twenty other generals on horseback, General Hancock, who threw back Pickett's Charge at Gettysburg, led Grant's funeral procession up Broadway. This picture from *Harpers* shows the way in which the United States Army was experimenting with dress uniforms in 1885. Some of these officers are wearing fore 'n' aft hats like those worn by admirals, and others are in German-influenced helmets topped by spikes or plumes.

Grants on a World Tour: After his second term as president, in 1877 Grant and his wife Julia embarked on a two-year tour around the world. Here they are in front of ancient walls in Egypt, with Grant seated in the front row wearing a white sun helmet; Julia, to his right, has on a wide-brimmed straw bonnet. *Library of Congress*

Grant's Parlor on Sixty-sixth Street: In this ornately-decorated parlor of the Grants' house at 3 East Sixty-Sixth Street in Manhattan, Mark Twain began talking to Grant about becoming the publisher of his *Memoirs*. Twain always thought big. To his nephew Charles Webster, who was to publish Grant's book, he wrote, "If these chickens should really hatch . . . General Grant's royalties will amount to $420,000, and will make the largest single check ever paid an author in the world's history . . . If I pay the General in silver coin at $12 per pound it will weigh seventeen tons." In fact, the advance orders on Grant's book guaranteed that it would make half a million dollars before it was printed.(*from* Artistic Houses, Being a Series of Interior Views of a Number of the Most Beautiful and Celebrated Homes in the United States, *published by D. Appleton & Co., 1883*

William H. Vanderbilt: When the Grants moved to Manhattan, they were befriended by William Henry Vanderbilt, son of the great entrepreneur Cornelius Vanderbilt, from whom he had inherited nearly $100 million dollars—a sum he was greatly increasing through his own business ventures. Grant was at no time wealthy by the standards of New York's millionaires, but they saw in him the same sort of vision and determination that had brought them success in other fields. Vanderbilt said of Grant, "He is one of us." Grant was duped into asking Vanderbilt for a short-term loan of $150,000 to save the firm of Grant & Ward—a sum that he thought would be repaid within two days by Ferdinand Ward, known as "The Young Napoleon of Wall Street." When Ward turned out to be guilty of criminal misappropriation of funds, Vanderbilt went out of his way to stop the Grants from trying to repay him. At the time he died, three months after Grant did, Vanderbilt was the richest man in the world, with a fortune of 193 million dollars. *Library of Congress*

P. T. Barnum: When Grant's swords, medals, and lavish gifts from foreign heads of state fell into a legal limbo in the aftermath of the Grant & Ward financial disaster, Grant heard from P. T. Barnum, the greatest showman of the nineteenth century. Barnum had sent the midget Tom Thumb on a stupendously successful international tour, and had started the three-ring Barnum and Bailey's Circus, featuring the giant elephant Jumbo as the star of the "Greatest Show on Earth." Barnum said that he would put these national treasures on tour to large cities in the United States and Europe. "I will give you $100,000 in cash, besides a portion of the profits, assuming all risks myself, if I may be permitted to exhibit them to a grateful and appreciative public." When Grant explained that the trophies were "beyond his control," they parted in friendly fashion. *Library of Congress*

Mark Twain: Twain, thirty-two in 1867 when this photo was taken, had deserted from the Confederate Army at the beginning of the Civil War. Seventeen years after this, when Grant lost all his money in a Wall Street swindle, Twain saved him financially by publishing his *Personal Memoirs. Library of Congress*

Robert Underwood Johnson: In the summer of 1884, Robert Underwood Johnson was one of America's best young magazine editors when he approached Grant about doing one or more articles about the Civil War for the *Century Magazine*. Arriving at the Grants' summer cottage on the New Jersey shore, he was thrilled to be in the presence of the greatest living survivor of that convulsive event. In his fine autobiography *Remembered Yesterdays* Johnson explained how he found Grant humiliated and bitter about the way he and his family had been defrauded on Wall Street. "He gave me the impression of a wounded lion. He had been hurt to the quick in his proud name and his honor, and the man who, we had been told, was stolid and reserved showed himself to be a person of the most sensitive nature and the most human expression of feeling." Under Johnson's tutelage, Grant quickly developed four excellent articles that led on to his writing his *Memoirs. New York Public Library*

Adam Badeau: A man who had once been a theatre critic in New York City, Adam Badeau was unlike any other figure on Grant's wartime staff. During the war, he was badly wounded at Port Hudson, south of Vicksburg and returned to New York to convalesce. There he was nursed back to health by his actor friends Edwin Booth and Booth's younger brother, John Wilkes Booth, who assassinated Lincoln. (There is no evidence that Grant ever knew of this relationship.) In a partly secretive arrangement, Badeau helped Grant in organizing the materials for his *Memoirs*, and then disgraced himself by allowing people to think he had written them himself. *Library of Congress*

Dr. John Hancock Douglas: Dr. Douglas was the physician who spent the most time with Grant during the final year of his life. One of the nation's leading throat specialists, during the Civil War Douglas had been an important figure in the United States Sanitary Commission, which provided medical services and support to the Union Army. In that capacity he had watched Grant in action at Shiloh and in the Wilderness, and they had become friends. Douglas made the initial diagnosis of cancer, and was present at the moment Grant died. *National Archives*

Reverend John Philip Newman: The Revered Newman had been pastor of a church in Washington that the Grants had occasionally attended when he was president. Later, after moving to a church in Manhattan, he became a frequent visitor to Grant and Julia during his illness. The prayers of hundreds of thousands of Americans, he told the reporters who were constantly on watch outside 3 East Sixty-sixth Street, were what was keeping Grant alive. Senator Jerome Chaffee of Colorado, whose daughter was married to Grant's second son Ulysses S. Grant, Jr., said to the same reporters, "General Grant does not believe that Doctor Newman's prayers will save him. He allows the doctor to pray simply because he does not want to hurt his feelings." Mark Twain saw Newman as something of a religious mountebank, saying of one of Newman's claims of praying with Grant, "This piece of reporting comports with Newman, gush, rot, impossible." *Library of Congress*

Grant's Cottage: The twelve-room house at Mt. McGregor, in upstate New York, high in the hills nine miles north of Saratoga Springs, that became known as "The Grant Cottage" was where Ulysses S. Grant spent the last five weeks of his life. Located on the grounds of a large new four-story resort hotel called the Balmoral, it belonged to the philanthropist Joseph W. Drexel, who offered it to the Grants and had it refurbished before they arrived. Grant's physician John Hancock Douglas said of this haven, "That is just the place I have been looking for. There is little heat there, it is on the heights, it is free from vapors, and above all, it is among the pines, and the pure air is especially grateful [beneficial] to patients suffering as General Grant is suffering." This historic structure is preserved and maintained as it was in 1885 by the Friends of the U. S. Grant Cottage.

Grant at Mt. McGregor: Grant spent the last five weeks of his life at Mt. McGregor, in upstate New York. Suffering from cancer of the throat, he worked many hours of each day, racing death as he finished writing his *Personal Memoirs*. He finished his massive and brilliant book on July 20, 1885, and died three days later. *Library of Congress*

The Room at Mt. McGregor where Grant Died: The flash in the center of this photo, taken in 1890, is characteristic of the amateur photography of the day. Nothing in the room has been changed since the moment of Grant's death on the morning of July 23, 1885. When he expired, his son Frederick waited long enough to make sure that he had breathed his last, and then stopped the hands of the clock on the mantel at 8:08. They remain in that position to this day.

New York Times **Headline:** In the era when newspaper headlines and sub-heads were mechanically restricted to one column, this is how the *New York Times* told its readers of Grant's death. For months the *Times* had been preparing parts of a fifty-seven page account of Grant's life, which appeared soon thereafter.

Grant's Funeral: Thousands of carriages carried officials and other mourners up Broadway in the five-mile-long funeral procession to Grant's temporary tomb. In all, more than a million persons—the largest crowd ever to gather on the North American continent— turned out to say good-bye to Ulysses S. Grant. *Library of Congress*

Grant's Temporary Tomb: Grant's body lies in a coffin before being placed in a temporary tomb high above the Hudson River in Manhattan. When a bugler played "Taps" at the close of this interment ceremony, General William Tecumseh Sherman wept as he saluted his friend in farewell. *Library of Congress*

Both the doctors and the press came to the conclusion that Grant would die at some point on Tuesday, March 31. Preparations for national mourning began: telegraph companies held their wires open to flash the news of his death across the country. Twain wrote in one of his notebooks, "Many a person between the two oceans lay hours awake listening for the booming of the firebells that should speak to the nation simultaneously and tell its calamity. The bells' strokes are to be 30 seconds apart and there are to be sixty-two, the General's age. They will be striking in every town in the United States at the same moment."

At some time after midnight on April 1, Grant fell asleep under the influence of a heavy dose of morphine. Julia sat beside him, weeping. At 5 a.m., the dozens of reporters keeping vigil across the street saw lights come on throughout the house. Harrison Tyrrell appeared on the front steps; hailing a cab, he soon returned with Dr. Shrady. Dr. Douglas came out of the night and rushed into the house. Harrison Terrell reappeared; taking another cab, he went downtown to the St. Cloud Hotel, bringing back Grant's son Buck and the Reverend John Philip Newman.

A crowd began to gather in the misty first light. Inside, Julia told the Reverend Doctor Newman that she was not sure her husband had ever been baptized; could that be done now? Newman recalled that "I said, 'I will baptize him if he is conscious. I cannot baptize an unconscious man.' As I began to pray, the General opened his eyes and looked steadily at me . . . I said, 'General, I am going to baptize you,' and he replied, 'Thank you, Doctor. I intend to take that step myself' . . . As the physicians believed he could not live five minutes longer, I prayed that God would receive his departing soul . . ."

At this point, memories of those next five minutes diverge. In Newman's account, he baptized Grant, and Julia and the clergyman knelt side by side as he "offered the Lord's prayer." Doctor

Douglas remembered that he had filled a syringe with brandy after Grant gasped, "If you doctors know how long a man can live under water, you can judge how long it will take me to choke when the time comes." Doctors Douglas and Shrady watched as Grant's pulse kept weakening; saying that the time had come to inject the brandy if it was to be of any use, Shrady inserted the syringe in Grant's right arm. "As the pulse did not respond satisfactorily," he wrote in his diary, "a second injection was resorted to, and at once the heart regained its action." Shrady added, "Throughout this time the General was conscious, spoke clearly and was the least perturbed of those present."

This second injection saved Grant's life. Moments after the additional brandy went into his arm, he vomited a thick fistful of slimy diseased tissue. He could breathe again. Grant soon fell asleep.

The next day he lay curled up in his combination of two massive armchairs, his breathing still labored, but by afternoon he slept soundly once more. The following day, Thursday, April 2, Grant began moving shakily around the house on the arm of his son Fred. On the day after that, Good Friday, he mixed getting back to work with a ride in Chaffee's carriage, and then did something analogous to his action in making a will the past September. He signed a letter addressed to "The President of the United States," whoever that person might be in 1898. Grant said:

> May I ask you to favor the appointment of Ulysses S. Grant, the son of my son Frederick Grant as a cadet, at West Point, upon his application.
>
> In doing so, you will gratify the wishes, of U. S. Grant

(Looking thirteen years ahead, on March 30, 1898, President William McKinley endorsed this letter with the words, "I direct the appointment to be made." That would begin the military career of

Grant's grandson Ulysses S. Grant III, three years old in 1885, who graduated from West Point in 1903. He served in both World Wars, retiring as a major general, and in 1969 published a biography of his grandfather, titled *Ulysses S. Grant: Warrior and Statesman*.)

* * *

ON EASTER SUNDAY, April 5, thirty-three members of the Excelsior Chapter of the Columbia Council, a Masonic organization, marched up to the front door of 3 East Sixty-sixth Street to serenade Grant. (There is no evidence that Grant was ever a Mason.) He came out to the front stoop, bundled up in his dark overcoat and white silk scarf, tipped his top hat to them, and remained there for a time as they sang. (Grant was not known for his musical taste, and was in fact tone-deaf. He once said, "I know two tunes. One is 'Yankee Doodle,' and the other isn't.")

Grant went back into his house, reappeared briefly at his library window, curled up in his two chairs, and fell asleep. When he awoke, Dr. Shrady was preparing the afternoon medical bulletin. Shrady suggested that, since most of the churches in America had prayed for him on this Easter Sunday, Grant should dictate to him a message of thanks to the public. Grant quickly had Shrady take this down:

> I am very much touched and grateful for the sympathy and interest manifested in me by my friends—and by those who have not hitherto been regarded as my friends. I desire the goodwill of all, whether hitherto friends or not.

Just then, Julia came into the library and Grant read her the bulletin that he and Shrady had composed. Julia told both men, who seemed pleased with themselves, that there was no hint of spirituality in this Easter Sunday message. At least, she told them, they could substitute "prayerful" for "sympathy."

This baffled both Shrady and Grant, neither of them known as ardent churchgoers. (When a delegation of ministers called on Grant at the White House in 1872, he told them that there were three political parties in America—Republicans, Democrats, and Methodists.)

Nonetheless, they quickly agreed to make the soothing change. When this word "prayerful" went out on the wires, it sounded so unmedical that several editors thought that perhaps Grant had died. Frank Mack of the Associated Press leapt into a carriage and rushed uptown to 3 East Sixty-sixth Street to see if Grant was still alive.

Everyone found Grant's recovery, even if temporary, to be remarkably impressive. In the early hours of Wednesday the nation's telegraph lines had been held open to flash the news of his death from coast to coast. On Friday he could go for a ride in a carriage, and on Sunday he could stand for a time in front of his house, listening to a group serenade him. The Reverend Newman told reporters that Grant's life had been saved through the prayers of countless thousands of Americans. Dr. Shrady told the same reporters that the brandy had revived his failing heart and enabled him to clear his blocked throat.

Twenty Years After the Nation's Great Redemptive Moment

O N April 9, four days after Easter Sunday, much of the nation marked the fact that twenty years had passed since April 9, 1865, the date when Robert E. Lee surrendered his Army of Northern Virginia to Grant at Appomattox Court House. Messages arrived for Grant from veterans' organizations in Philadelphia, Springfield, Massachusetts, and Rock Island, Illinois. In Indiana, the State senate and house passed a resolution that spoke of Grant as certain to die at any hour: "[We] join with the American people of every shade of opinion in the voice of sympathetic regret that his life is to be lost to his country."

The most eloquent and sincere combination of appreciation for Grant and sympathy for his current suffering came from the city of Cleveland. As carried in the *New York Times*, the statement sent from there read:

The soldiers and sailors of Northern Ohio, assembled in Cleveland to celebrate the twentieth anniversary of the surrender of

Gen. Lee, with hearts surcharged with the tenderest affection for their old commander, which the lapse of 20 years has only served to strengthen and intensify, send to you their most sincere sympathy in this hour of your great physical suffering. With admiration and love for you as a soldier and as the first citizen of the Republic, which only broadens and deepens as time passes, we tender a soldiers' greeting and God bless you.

Most of page five of the *New York Times* was devoted to an unusually detailed account of how he had spent the previous day. It began with, "From 5 o'clock to 7:30, when the General rose, he dozed in his chair, scarcely awake. Then, of his own accord, he raised himself to his feet while the white nurse, Henry, changed his pillows. A little later, when the family began to appear on the sick room floor, they found the General sipping his mixture of warm milk and egg and looking really refreshed after his rest."

Among the messages received on this April 9 anniversary, one for Julia carried memories of the trip around the world on which they had embarked only six years before. A telegram came for Julia from Queen Victoria's lady-in-waiting, the Dowager Marchioness of Ely, saying, "The Queen who feels deeply for you in your anxiety commands me to inquire after General Grant." On behalf of his mother, Frederick Grant replied, "Mrs. Grant thanks the Queen for her sympathy and directs me to say that General Grant is no better." At this stage of Grant's illness, the right side of his neck had on it a swelling the size of an egg.

As the day went on, flowers arrived. "Just before noon the room was brightened by a great collection of flowers from the conservatory of George W. Childs, at Wooton, near Philadelphia." Buck Grant's father-in-law Senator Chaffee came and spent nearly an hour. Colonel Ira Ayer, who had served under Grant in the Wilderness, came to see him, as did General Thomas Rosser, the dashing

Confederate cavalry leader. Twenty years and four days before this, Rosser and Robert E. Lee's nephew Fitzhugh Lee had fought against the Union cavalry general and future Indian fighter George Armstrong Custer at Amelia Court House in the closing days of the war. Making a brief visit to Grant, Rosser drove up to 3 East Sixty-sixth Street in a carriage and entered the house carrying a basket of flowers.

It was indeed a time of memories. Grant asked Dr. Shrady if he could have "one or two puffs" on a cigar. Shrady agreed; Grant settled down in one of his armchairs, and smoked with a contented expression. No one he spoke to on this anniversary of Lee's surrender ever mentioned what he said to them. The classic measured images of the surrender—Lee's dignity, Grant's generosity of spirit and action—had engraved themselves on the American mind, yet they were static images. But for the men who brought the war to a close, those last days were ones of cyclonic action. Twenty years before, the man who now leaned back smoking in the high-ceilinged room at Sixty-sixth Street had driven himself and his men for weeks to reach that supreme hour. Day after day, constantly riding from place to place, studying maps and reading reports and issuing orders, Grant had orchestrated and executed his Appomattox campaign. More than Shiloh, more than Chattanooga, more than the Wilderness or his Overland Campaign to the James River, the final push to the Appomattox Court House had been his masterpiece of war, equaled only by his Vicksburg campaign.

During those climactic days Grant had brought everything to bear: his knowledge of Virginia's geography, his knowledge of his own generals, his knowledge of Lee and his generals. From the time on March 29 when he telegraphed Sheridan from his field headquarters at Gravely Creek, "I now feel like ending the matter," until the moment on April 9 when he received a note from Lee requesting a meeting "with reference to the surrender of this army," Grant sent 112 messages moving his forces around the Confederacy's collapsing theater of war in Northern Virginia.

After his March to the Sea from Atlanta to Savannah, Sherman had turned north to disembowel the states of South Carolina and North Carolina. Pursuing the remaining large Confederate forces under Lee's West Point classmate Joseph E. Johnston, Sherman saw that the end was soon to come. By April 8, Grant's troops had occupied Petersburg and Richmond; at Sayler's Creek they had fought what was in all probability the last major battle of the war. The remnants of Lee's gallant army were disintegrating in a final retreat to the west. With Sherman's usual admiring and generous spirit, he wrote Grant, "I am delighted and amazed at the result of your move to the South of Petersburg, and Lee has lost in one day the Reputation of three years, and you have established a Reputation for perseverance and pluck that would make Wellington jump out of his Coffin."

On April 7, two days before the surrender, Grant sent Julia, who was at City Point, a telegram entirely different from his orders directing the movements of scores of thousands of troops. He had rented a house for her in Burlington, New Jersey, and she had been living there when she was not at his headquarters at City Point. From Burkeville, Virginia, thirty miles east of Appomattox Court House, he wired her, "I think you had better return home [Burlington] as it may be 10 or 12 days before I return."

Julia, who felt that great events were moving even faster than her husband realized, later wrote on the reverse side of this telegram: "I did not obey. I waited and returned with the victorious Genl's."

* * *

IT FELL TO Horace Porter, and to Grant himself in his *Memoirs*, to portray the most revealing moments of the day of surrender. The night before, Grant had tossed and turned sleeplessly on a sofa in a large white farmhouse in Curdsville, Virginia, located a few hundred yards from the field headquarters of General George Gordon Meade, Grant's day-to-day commander of the Union's Army of the Potomac. Grant was having one of his blinding migraine headaches. He later wrote that he spent hours that night "in bathing my feet in hot water and mustard, and putting mustard plasters on my wrists, and the back part of my neck, hoping to be cured by morning."

Nothing worked. Exhausted, near noon the next day Grant was riding his horse, Cincinnati, on the road that ran from Curdsville towards Appomattox Court House when Lieutenant Charles E. Pease of Meade's staff caught up to him. He handed Grant a letter from Lee. Grant read the soon-to-be-famous words, "with reference to the surrender of this army." Pease also handed Grant a note from Meade that told him that, pursuant to Lee's request, Meade had read this request to discuss surrender terms, and in consequence had ordered a short truce. Grant said of that moment, "When the officer reached me I was still suffering with the sick headache: but the instant I saw the contents of the note I was cured." He dismounted, penned a letter to Lee asking him to send word as to where they should meet, and "hastened on." As Grant was soon to meet Lee, his words on the subject of what he was wearing take on significance. "When I had left camp that morning I had not expected so soon the result that was taking place, and consequently was in rough garb. I was without a sword, as I usually was when on horseback in the field, and wore a soldier's [enlisted man's] blouse for a coat, with the shoulder straps of my rank to indicate to the army who I was."

At one o'clock Grant and his staff rode up the single street of the little village of Appomattox Court House, with its half-dozen houses. As they went up this slight slope, they could see beyond it a broad valley, filled with Confederate columns and wagon trains.

Beyond the enemy units Grant saw major forces of his own cavalry and infantry. Holding the high ground to the south and west, they were blocking any possibility of a further retreat by Lee. The hopelessness of Lee's situation was there to see.

Grant approached a group of his generals who were standing in the street. Sheridan was among them, an exultant expression on his flushed face. In response to Grant's "How are you, Sheridan?" Sheridan replied in a near-shout, "First-rate, thank you; how are you?"

"Is Lee over there?" Grant said, pointing up the street.

"Yes, he is in that brick house, waiting to surrender to you."

"Well, then," Grant said, "we'll go over."

Porter noted this of the house they approached. "[It] had a comfortable wooden porch with seven steps leading up to it . . . The building stood a little distance back from the street, with a yard in front, and to the left on entering was a gate for carriages, and a roadway running to a stable in rear."

Porter went on to describe one of the most significant handshakes in American history.

> General Grant mounted the steps and entered the house. As he stepped into the hall, Colonel Babcock [Brevet Brigadier General Orville E. Babcock of Grant's staff] who had seen his approach from the window, opened the door of the room on the left, in which he had been sitting with General Lee and Colonel Marshall awaiting General Grant's arrival. The general passed in, and as Lee arose and stepped forward, Grant extended his hand, saying "General Lee," and the two shook hands cordially.

At this point in his account, Porter recalled that generals Sheridan, Edward O. C. Ord, and a number of other officers remained out in the yard. They felt that Grant might want to be alone with Lee during the first part of their meeting, but "In a few minutes

Colonel Babcock came to the front door, and, making a motion with his hat toward the sitting room, said: 'The general says come in.'"

> We entered, and found General Grant seated in an old office arm-chair in the center of the room, and Lee sitting in a plain arm chair with a cane seat beside a square, marble-topped table near the front window. We walked in softly, and ranged ourselves quietly about the sides of the room, very much as people enter a sick-chamber when they expect to find the patient dangerously ill.

Here was a moment of the highest drama, made all the more affecting by the silence inside the house and out.

> The contrast between the two commanders was singularly striking . . . as they sat, six or eight feet apart, facing each other. General Grant, then nearly forty-three years of age, was five feet eight inches in height, with shoulders slightly stooped. His hair and full beard were nut-brown, without a trace of gray in them . . . The boots and portions of his clothes were spattered with mud. He had worn a pair of thread gloves of a dark-yellow color, which he had taken off on entering the room. His felt "sugar-loaf," stiff-brimmed hat was resting in his lap. He had no sword or sash, and a pair of shoulder-straps was all there was about him to designate his rank . . .

Grant's officers were fascinated to be in the presence of the legendary Robert E. Lee. Like almost everyone who saw Lee, Porter imagined him to be at least six feet tall, whereas Lee was only two and a half inches taller than Grant.

> Lee, on the other hand, was six feet and one inch in height, and erect for one of his age, for he was Grant's senior by sixteen years.

His hair and full beard were a silver-gray, and thick, except that the hair had become a little thin in front. He wore a new uniform of Confederate gray, buttoned to the throat, and a handsome sword and sash.

At last, Grant began the discussion of the surrender terms. Again, the magnitude of the occasion contrasted with the prosaic nature of the arrangements that must be made. Here sat two professional soldiers, bringing to an end the largest war the world had then seen. Their words and tone were mutually respectful and businesslike, but, facing Lee as he spoke, Grant had more than the laying down of arms on his mind. In his *Memoirs*, he described his thoughts.

What General Lee's feelings were I do not know. As he was a man of much dignity, with an impassible [sic] face, it was impossible to say whether he felt inwardly glad that the end had finally come, or felt sad over the result, and was too manly to show it.

Whatever his feelings, they were entirely concealed from my observation; but my own feelings, which had been quite jubilant on the receipt of his letter, were sad and depressed. I felt like anything rather than rejoicing at the downfall of a foe who had fought so long and valiantly, and had suffered so much for a cause, though that cause was, I believe, one of the worst for which a people ever fought, and one for which there was the least excuse. I do not question, however, the sincerity of the great mass of those who were opposed to us.

In an effort to make things as easy as possible for Lee, Grant led them into a conversation "about old army times," and their service in the Mexican War. After a few minutes, "General Lee called my attention to the object of our meeting," and, after a few more digressions, Lee made the eminently reasonable suggestion, as Grant put it, "that the terms I proposed to give his army ought to be written out."

> When I put my pen to the paper I did not know the first word that I should make use of in writing the terms. I only knew what was in my mind, and I wished to express it clearly. As I wrote on, the thought occurred to me that the [Confederate] officers had their own private horses and effects, which were important to them, but of no value to us; also that it would be an unnecessary humiliation to call upon them to deliver their side arms [pistols and swords].

Here, Lee explained to Grant that in the Confederate army, in addition to the officers, the cavalrymen and artillerymen owned their own horses. Grant swiftly grasped the point.

> I took it that most of the men in the [Confederate] ranks were small farmers. The whole country had been so raided by the two armies that it was doubtful whether they would be able to put in a crop to carry themselves and their families through the next winter without the aid of the horses they were then riding . . . I would, therefore, instruct the officer I left behind to receive the paroles of his [Lee's] troops to let every man of the Confederate army who claimed to own a horse or mule take the animal to his home.

During the working out of these terms of surrender, Porter noted that Lee twice showed signs of gratitude. The first was when he saw that Grant was allowing the defeated officers to take home their horses, swords, and pistols. As Porter recorded it, "[Lee] said with some degree of warmth in his manner, 'This will have a very happy effect on my army.'" The second was when he understood that Grant was allowing *all* of his men who owned horses or mules to take them home and put in a crop that might well preserve the lives of many Southern children in the winter to come. "Lee now looked greatly relieved, and though anything but a demonstrative man, he gave every evidence of his appreciation of this concession, and said: 'This will have the best possible effect upon the men. It will be very gratifying, and will do much towards conciliating our people.'"

Grant spoke of a last exchange that took place after he had presented all of the Union generals in the room to General Lee:

> General Lee, after all was completed and before taking his leave, remarked that his army was in very bad condition for want of food . . . that his men had been living on parched corn exclusively, and that he would have to ask me for rations . . . I told him "certainly," and asked for how many men he wanted rations. His answer was "about twenty-five thousand;" and I authorized him to send his own commissary and quartermaster to Appomattox Station, two or three miles away, where he could have . . . all the provisions wanted.

Leaving the room in which he had signed his acceptance of the terms of surrender, Lee paused to compose himself in the hallway just before stepping through the open door onto the porch. A Union general named George Forsyth caught a glimpse of Lee at a moment when he thought no one could see him. Forsyth saw that Lee was turning red, "a deep crimson flush, that rising from his neck overspread his face and even tinged his broad forehead . . . Booted and spurred, still vigorous and erect, he stood bareheaded, looking out of the open doorway, sad-faced and weary."

Lee put on his hat and stepped out. Several Union officers who were resting on the porch, having no idea that the meeting had ended, jumped to their feet and saluted. Lee returned the salute "mechanically but courteously." At the top of the steps he pulled on his gauntlets, and gazed to the northeast, where the remnants of his Army of Northern Virginia remained in defensive positions a mile away, many with no idea that he had just surrendered them all.

Some Union officers in the yard below had come to attention, but Lee still stood at the top of the steps, staring toward his army, noticing nothing around him. Now he looked to his right and left, wondering where his horse was. "Orderly!" he called in a choked voice, "orderly!" Sergeant G. W. Tucker, the one other Confederate beside Lee and Colonel Marshall who had come to this meeting, appeared instantly, leading Lee's horse, Traveller.

Lee went down the steps, Marshall behind him, and paused on the lowest step while Tucker replaced Traveller's bridle. Again he looked sadly in the direction of his army, and "thrice smote the palm of his left hand slowly with his right fist in an absent sort of way." Then, as Tucker buckled the throat latch of Traveller's bridle, Lee finally looked at this grey horse he loved. He lifted Traveller's black forelock from under the brow band, parted and smoothed it, and patted Traveller's forehead.

Sergeant Tucker stepped back. Lee "swung himself slowly and wearily, but nevertheless firmly, into the saddle . . . as he did so there broke unguardedly from his lips a long, low, deep sigh, almost a groan in its intensity, while the flush on his neck seemed, if possible, to take on a still deeper hue."

As Lee turned Traveller's head away from the house, Grant came down the steps and started across the yard toward his horse, Cincinnati. Grant, too, was in an abstracted state. When he realized that this was Lee leaving, he stopped and took off his hat. So did every other Union soldier in the yard.

Lee raised his hat silently, and turned through the gate into the road.

Grant stood watching him ride away. The Union officers wanted to mount their horses and get back to their commands, but as long as Grant stood there they had to remain standing as they were. One of Grant's staff said to him, "This will live in history."

Grant did not reply, and watched Lee until he was out of sight.

It remained for Porter to record a final touch, both accurate and in perfect keeping with the Grant of Appomattox.

General Grant and his staff then started for the headquarters camp, which, in the mean time, had been pitched near by. The news of the surrender had reached the Union lines, and the firing of salutes began at several points; but the general sent an order to have them stopped, using these words: "The war is over; the rebels are our countrymen again; and the best sign of rejoicing after the victory will be to abstain from all demonstrations in the field."

13

Reactions to a
Sick Hero

As these days twenty years after Appomattox unfolded, the *New York Times* continued its close coverage of events at 3 East Sixty-sixth Street. On Sunday, April 12, an unnamed man who had been in Grant's bedroom during the day—the language sounds like that used by Adam Badeau—said this to a *Times* reporter. "When the General awoke at the breakfast hour he seemed dazed and looked about him wonderingly. It was the effect of the drugs. Two to three times the General has given evidence on awaking to a wandering mind and, on several occasions, unintelligible sentences have escaped his lips at such times." The man added:

> Sometimes I go into his room and I talk to him and he never even hears me. He looks at someone who speaks to him in an unconscious state, and closes his eyes without uttering a word. For hours he will sit in his chair without uttering a word. He talks to himself constantly. His talk is generally about the war. Almost every battle he directed is referred to while he has been in a semidelirious state. He calls his staff around him just as if it were twenty years ago.

By contrast, five days later, on Friday, April 17, readers saw this first-page headline and subheads in the *Times* about what took place at the Grants' house the day before.

ASTONISHING HIS FAMILY GEN. GRANT JOINING THEM AT THE LUNCH TABLE. TAKING HIS OLD PLACE AND EATING WITH RELISH—CONTINUED IMPROVEMENT BOTH LOCALLY AND GENERALLY.

While the Grant family were at lunch yesterday the dining room door opened and in walked the General. To the astonished greetings of the family, he made no direct response, but, turning to the waiter, he said: "Inform Dr. Douglas that we are waiting lunch for him."

A moment later the doctor joined the family. The General was seated in his old place at the head of the table. The meal passed in merry fashion. . . . Mrs. Sartoris was radiant with bright chat and infectious laughter, while the General, with assumed gravity, helped himself to some macaroni and a slice of cold mutton, which he cut in fine pieces, poured gravy over it, and ate it as naturally as though he had never got out of the way of eating solid food. After lunch he went upstairs . . .

Five days after that, the *Times* offered its readers this, mentioning among others Mrs. Jesse Grant, wife of the Grants' youngest son, Jesse.

GEN. GRANT'S IMPROVEMENT

TAKING A SHORT WALK AND SHOWING SIGNS OF BETTER HEALTH

The smiling and expectant faces of Mrs. Sartoris and Mrs. Jesse Grant drew the attention of passers along Sixty-sixth-street yesterday afternoon to the east window of the General's sleeping room. They were looking down on the stoop.

Presently the General came out. A red and gold scarf encircled his neck, showing above the collar of a heavy beaver overcoat. On reaching the sidewalk the General turned toward Madison-avenue. Col. Grant was at his side, and Harrison walked behind. The General limped, and had use for a light cane. At the corner of Madison-avenue father and son turned back. The walk lasted five minutes. It was slow, but not specially labored. Several salutations [greetings] were exchanged by the General, and to one or two who expressed pleasure at seeing him he replied thankfully. The walk did not seem to fatigue him, but Col. Grant passed an arm lightly under the General's in going up the stoop. The ladies stood at the upper window until the General was again indoors.

This was the General's second outdoor venture yesterday. The first time was at noon, when he went driving, his son Ulysses and wife and Mrs. Jesse Grant attending him, Harrison taking the box with the driver, as on Monday.

This minute attention to detail, the *Times*'s confidence that by now everyone knew that "Harrison" was Grant's faithful attendant Harrison Terrell, signified the public awareness of Grant's condition and daily life. His ability to take a walk that lasted five minutes and "did not seem to fatigue him" was seen as a hopeful sign. As for how much Grant was in the minds of his veterans during this month that marked the twentieth anniversary of Appomattox, the month during which he would soon have his sixty-third birthday, this tribute was paid him at a veterans' banquet at which "Gilt trimmings on military uniforms glittered in the gaslight of the Hotel Brunswick last night." The *Times* report of this dinner, which took place on the evening of the same day of Grant's five-minute walk, identified the elaborate dinner this way: "The Veteran Association of the Seventy-First Regiment, with invited guests from active companies and veteran associations of other regiments in the city, were dining for the seventeenth time, in annual anniversary of the Seventy-first regiment's departure for the war."

A tribute to Grant, and a reference to the perception that his health was improving, came about during the toasts.

> Col. C. F. Homer, in an after-dinner speech, said that not only every soldier and every veteran, but every true American citizen would rejoice in the news of Gen. Grant's victory over an enemy that threatened to carry him to the grave. Col. Homer offered a resolution, which was adopted with a unanimous roar of yeas, offering congratulations to Gen. Grant's family on his improvement, and expressing the hope that it would continue until it restored him to the Nation he had done so much to preserve.

Within 3 East Sixty-sixth Street, little Julia Grant was a witness to her grandfather's illness and the family's reaction to it. Speaking of herself and her younger brother, Ulysses, she later wrote, "Toward the end of spring we were scarcely ever allowed in the sick room . . . But I heard them talk of how the book was still progressing, how each day at the hours of least suffering some pages were added to it, and one person would say, "The book is killing him," and another would reply: "No, the book is keeping him alive; without it he would already be dead."

* * *

IT REMAINED for Grant to dispel some of the optimism being felt about his health. Shortly before the Appomattox anniversary he had said to his doctors, "My chances, I think, of pulling through this are one in a hundred." Now he consented to give one of his rare interviews, this one to a reporter from the *Philadelphia Times*. "Speaking of his disease," the journalist wrote, "he did not believe the relief was permanent, and when the suffering was so intense . . . he only wished for the one great relief to all human pain."

When the reporter commented on the outpouring of compassion and admiration from all over the country, Grant had this to say.

> The public only know of but a fraction of the expressions of sympathy which I have received. These come from friends without reference to politics or to the feeling which might be supposed to have grown out of the late war. I receive a hundred letters in a mail and several mails a day—in fact, many more letters than Fred can answer. They also come from State legislatures and organized bodies besides individuals.

Grant was indeed right in saying that "the public know of only a fraction of the expressions of sympathy which I have received." In the South, where Robert E. Lee died five years after the Civil War, the majority of white Southerners revered the memory of Lee as a beloved figure, the handsome and graceful aristocrat who fought so ably and boldly as the hero of "The Lost Cause." In the North, Grant's emotional hold on the public had developed in a different way. Twenty years after Appomattox, not only did his veterans pay constant tribute to him, but a new generation, not born at the time of the surrender, was growing up with an inbuilt feeling toward a man who, like Lincoln, had preserved the Union. During this April, which brought memories of the Appomattox surrender, consciousness of Grant's battle with his health, and increasing mention of his approaching birthday, his veterans showered good wishes upon him, but many young people felt a need to touch this quiet man in their own way. Maria Matalina Casagrande, a student at the Fifth Ward Industrial School of the Children's Aid Society of New York, wrote this to Grant.

Of course you do not know me, but Miss Satterie, who is our teacher, and we all love her dearly, but I do most of all because I am the oldest in the school, and I understand things better than the little ones do. So Miss Satterie, tells us everything about you, and dear General, we all pray that our dear Father in Heaven, will spare you to us until you are a hundred years old.

We know how you are every day, because all of our boys in school are either news-boys or boot-blacks, and the news-boys of course read it in the paper. And all of us girls know how you are. I buy a paper every night just to see how you are. Last night, I was so glad to read you had gone for a drive. Then we all of us, the big ones I mean, study History and we know what you did for us, before we were born. I am an Italian girl, almost all of us are down here in our school, but there are other children too. Some German, some Irish, and some colored children, but we all love you, and pray for you, with all our hearts and souls.

Another letter came from a more affluent group. "We little ones of the 'Childrens Hour' of the Sixty-First [Street] Methodist Church New York have heard that you are sick. We are very sorry and pray to God to make you well again. We know that you was once our President and have heard our fathers tell about how wise and brave you were in the great war[.] We shall remember you when the big people now living are dead. We hope your example will lead us to lead nobler lives than we would have done if we had never heard of you. Please accept our hearty love, good wishes and prayers."

Early on a Saturday morning, 350 children from this church paraded past 3 East Sixty-sixth Street. The next day's *Times* said this: "Gen. Grant was aware of their coming and although he had not risen for the day, hastily threw on a dressing gown as the children went by with flags and banners merrily waving. Later in the day the

General visited them in the Park, where they spent the day. They sang several songs for him and cheered him enthusiastically when he bade them good-bye."

Some of these communications revealed quite a bit about the lives of the young people who wrote them. In a letter that she sent to Grant a week after the twentieth anniversary of the Appomattox surrender, Winnie C. Dobell of St. John's, Michigan, told him this:

I am a little girl and have never been to school but do my lessons at home with mama. My reader is Harpers Young People and this morning I read such a nice story about you. I went down to the news-room to buy a copy to send to you but they were all gone so mama said I might write and tell you and if you could not read it your self perhaps some of the kind people who are with you would read it to you.

My papa was a soldier and loves you very much but he is a lawyer now and does not fight any more though mama says he often fights his old battles over again. He is commander of the [Grand Army of the Republic—Union veterans organization] post and last week Thursday the 9th they had a Camp-fire and every body made speeches about General Lee's surrender to General Grant . . .

I shall send you a Birthday card and it will be a truely [sic] present from me. I shall buy it with the money that I have earned. Mama says it is not a real present if you ask papa for the money to buy it with[.] I shall put my name on it so you will know it is from me for I suppose you will get a great many. Good bye dear General Grant. I love you very much and wish I could do something to make you well.

Another young female admirer, Maggie Irving of Louisville, Kentucky, sent him this. "I am a little Louisville girl that likes you so much. My father was one of your old soldiers and he never tires of telling us of the 'bravest soldier in the country.' Old General Grant, please, please get well. I hop [sic] you will live to be even older than that old rebel jeff davis. He don't even deserve to have his name spellt in capitale [sic]. General Grant, I don't write to you for your autograph or anything of the sort. I only write to let you know how we all love you. I hope you won't suffer a bit. General Grant pleas [sic] accept the best wishes and love of this little Louisville girl."

~II~

April 27 was Grant's sixty-third birthday. The *Times* account of his day said, "The perfume of flowers filled his house from early morning. Many callers left them with their cards, while messengers and expressmen, similarly laden, kept the bell ringing often until well into the afternoon." Andrew Carnegie sent him a large basket of sixty-three red roses surrounded by "Spring flowers," which Julia set aside to decorate the dinner table for the festive meal she was planning for the evening. A "beautiful bouquet" arrived from Grant's former secretary of state Hamilton Fish and his wife. Among scores of other tributes from prominent individuals and organizations, a letter came from Governor John A. Martin of Kansas, with a message accompanying an executive order honoring Grant on his birthday. It said in part, "The population of Kansas embraces a larger proportionate number of [Union veteran] soldiers than that of any other State. It is believed that every regiment of the Union army, and very nearly every Company, is represented in this population." Mayor R. L. Cofran of Topeka, Kansas, added this: "Twenty thousand citizens of Topeka, who have assembled in mass meeting in honor of your birthday, send greetings and breathe a fervent prayer for your speedy recovery."

A dramatic counterpoint to the tributes from Kansas was the resolution adopted by the Confederate Survivors' Association, meeting in Augusta, Georgia.

Remembering him now as the generous victor who, at the ever memorable meeting at Appomattox, to our immortal Lee and to the glorious 8,000 veterans, the surviving heroes of the Army of Northern Virginia, conceded liberal and magnanimous terms of surrender, do we, standing by the graves of our Confederate dead . . . respectfully tender to General Grant assurances of our sincere and profound sympathy in this the season of his direful extremity.

A larger crowd than usual gathered outside the house. During this mild spring day, Grant went for two rides in Central Park in the carriage of Buck's father-in-law, Senator Jerome Chaffee, accompanied by Julia, their daughter, Nellie, and their son Buck.

At 6:30 that evening, dinner was announced. Beside members of the immediate family, the guests included Mark Twain, General William Tecumseh Sherman, Reverend Newman and his wife, and Adam Badeau. The *Times* described the evening as it developed.

The family and guests had entered the dining room when the General came down stairs. He was joyfully greeted and seemed very happy. In the centre of the table 63 tapers were aflame amid banks of flowers. The mantelpiece and windows were also bright and redolent with flowers.

Dinner occupied about two hours, the General sitting through it and relishing as much as any one the pleasantries of the event. After dinner there were family devotions. Then all went into the parlor.

What came next in the *Times* story demonstrated again the depth of the newspaper's sources regarding events in the Grant household. Other accounts, some later cited in biographies of Grant, had him standing at a window as New York's Seventh Regiment, dressed in their grey uniforms with plumed black shakos, marched past the house in a salute to him. Here was the *Times* version.

Word had reached the house that part of the Seventh Regiment would march past, and the General said he would review them. With this purpose the parlor curtains were pushed aside and the house was lighted. People gathered in the street and looked in on a brilliant scene, the rich furnishings of the parlor being set off with bright faces [vases?] and flowers bunched in all colors and varieties, decorating the room wherever there was a place to put them. But the troops did not come and at 10 o'clock, thoroughly wearied by the unwonted excitement of the day, the General went to his room.

Exhausted though he was, before he went to sleep that night Grant penned what the *Times* termed "a comprehensive response" to all the communications he received that day.

To the various army posts, societies, cities, public schools, States, corporations, and individuals, North and South, who have been so kind as to send me congratulations on my sixty-third birthday, I wish to offer my grateful acknowledgments. The dispatches have been so numerous and so touching in tone that it would have been impossible to answer them if I had been in perfect health.

U. S. GRANT

~ III ~

Now Adam Badeau made a mistake that did nothing but harm, most of it to himself. Initially, the problem arose not from Badeau, but from the *New York World*. Based on gossip and speculation, none of it evidently coming from Badeau, on April 29 the *World* told its readers this.

The work upon his [Grant's] new book about which so much has been said is the work of General Adam Badeau. General Grant has furnished all of the material and all of the ideas in the memoirs but Badeau has done the work of composition. The most the General has done upon the book has been to prepare the rough notes and memoranda for its various chapters.

When Mark Twain saw this, his first instinct was to sue the *World* for libel. In support of that, Grant swiftly sent a letter to his and Twain's publisher, Webster and Company. He stated tersely, "Composition is entirely my own," and two lines later repeated, "The composition is entirely my own." He concluded with, "You may take such measures as you see fit to correct this report which places me in the attitude of claiming authorship of a book which I did not write and is also injurious to you who are publishing and advertising such a book as my work."

This was of course the moment for Adam Badeau, who was listening to Grant dictate his own words to stenographer Dawson every day, to step forward and deny that he was writing Grant's book for him. That is not what he did. A few hours after the *World* story appeared and Grant sent off his letter, Badeau came to where Grant was working. Silently, he handed Grant an envelope, bowed, and left. In the envelope was a letter to Grant. A thousand words long, it was divided into two topics. The first was his restatement of the financial agreement he and Grant had reached, concerning the compensation that he was to receive for his work on the book—terms that Grant had signed, and would never disavow.

Then Badeau began a recital of how his relationship with Grant and the *Memoirs* had harmed him. He had received little money thus far and had sacrificed his time to no personal advantage. To this point, although he had been treated as a member of the family— an experience so many Americans would have been happy to have—nothing he set forth early in the letter would touch a nerve with Grant.

Then he began to cross a line. "I must efface myself, and I can have no reputation or consideration for my connection with the book." Now Badeau started chipping away at Grant's work. He might not have been writing Grant's book, he said, but he had been connecting the "disjointed fragments" written by Grant. "Yours is not and will not be the work of a literary man, but the simple story of a great general. Proper for you, but not such as would add to my credit." In short, he was a better writer than Grant. Then came the deal: apart from and in addition to whatever else they had arranged, he wanted $1,000 a month "to complete the work from your dictation in the first person with all the supervision you are able to give but in any event to complete it." There was a suggestion of blackmail in what he wrote next. He would take 10 percent of the profits, and continue "to declare as I have always done that you wrote it absolutely." The result for Grant would be that he, Badeau, the better writer, would take Grant's book and improve it into "a monument such as no man ever put up to his own fame."

Badeau failed to realize that he was now addressing a man who was not only a general, but a man who had discovered that he loved to write, was proud of what he was doing for himself, his wife, and the nation, and intended to die doing it. Three days later he received Grant's answer. In a tone that combined finality with the patient sorrow that an uncle might feel for an erring nephew who had repeatedly become controversial during his own career, Grant began:

> I have concluded that you and I must part all association so far as the preparation of any work goes which is to bear my signature . . . I did not contemplate your writing anything for the book, but to help me arrange it . . . My name goes to the book and I want it so in the fullest sense.

. . . I understand you better than you understand yourself. You are petulant, your anger is easily aroused and you are overbearing even to me at times, and always with those for whom you have done, or are doing, literary work. Think of the publishers you have quarreled with. As an office holder you either quarreled or found great fault with those immediately over you . . . in matters affecting yourself you are beyond contact at times, and when you have tendered advice you sometimes become so enraged if it is not followed that you think yourself much injured. You have no idea of this yourself, but it has frequently happened with me. I have abstained from bringing it to your notice at the time, by ceasing to talk, or by half acquiescing and then doing as I thought right afterwards.

As for Badeau's idea of receiving $1,000 a month, "this would make you a partner with my family as long as the book found a sale. This is preposterous. Not for a moment has it been entertained." Although Grant closed his letter with the thought that, apart from the ending of their working relationship, "You can always be the welcome visitor at my house that you have been before," Julia was less forgiving. In her own memoirs, written years later, she spoke of being betrayed by one to whom Grant had been kind. She described Badeau as "an old staff officer who was at the time sharing his hospitality [and proved] his base ingratitude." Badeau moved out of 3 East Sixty-sixth Street; he and Grant never saw each other again.

Although Twain decided not to pursue his lawsuit against the *World*, much damage had been done. After waiting for a few days, Twain concluded that he "had not seen the World's lie in any newspaper," but for those who learned of the story, it cast a shadow that was never fully dispelled, over the subject of the true authorship of Grant's *Memoirs*. Ironically, many people thought that Mark Twain, who so admired Grant's ability and originality, was the real author. The greatest victim, however, was Badeau himself. He was seen as having wronged Grant at a time when the nation was watching Grant's brave race with time and cancer, trying to finish his book. Badeau had made himself a marked man: although he went on to write his *Grant in Peace*, which began at Appomattox and went to the end of Grant's life, with passages that expressed admiration for Grant, he managed to break into print in 1888. After Grant's death he threatened to sue Julia for $10,000—the amount originally stipulated in the 1884 agreement he and Grant had made. He was legally right, but was seen as troubling the national hero's widow. Julia wanted him to state specifically that he had not written her husband's book.

On October 31 of 1888 the *New York Times* carried a piece titled, "Gen. Badeau's Suit Ended." On his part he agreed that the composition of the *Memoirs* "was entirely that of Gen. Grant, and to limit his claim to that of suggestion, revision, and verification." Julia, who by this time had received at least $420,000 in royalties from the book and would eventually make more than $600,000, paid Badeau his $10,000.

Unmarked Anniversaries

A year had passed since the early days of May 1884, when the Grants lost their investment in Grant & Ward. Since then, Grant had come down with cancer and made enormous progress with his *Personal Memoirs*. There is not a single letter he wrote at this time a year later that refers to the Grant & Ward fiasco, nor is there a record of anyone writing to him about it, and there was no mention of it in the newspapers. He did, however, write letters to gatherings of his old veterans. The Society of the Army of the Potomac—whose meeting in Brooklyn he had attended the year before, appearing before them to immense applause—was meeting this year in Baltimore and had again elected him as its president. In accepting the honor, he wrote, "I wish my health promised the probability of my being at the next [annual] meeting," and closed with, "Wishing all members many happy re-unions." He also received this communication, from the nation's largest veterans' organization.

Resolved, by the Nineteenth National Encampment of the Grand Army of the Republic, assembled in the city of Portland, Maine, representing 300,000 soldiers and sailors in the United States, that

in this, the first hour of our assembly, we tender to the distinguished comrade, soldier and statesman, General *Ulysses S. Grant*,
our profound sympathy in his continued illness, and extend a soldier's greeting to our beloved Commander and Comrade, who has
for months endured unspeakable agony with that characteristic
fortitude that has challenged the admiration of the world.

Grant had his son Frederick telegraph his response. To the veterans he said in part, "General Grant wishes to take this occasion
to also thank them for their splendid services which have resulted
in giving freedom to a race, peace to a continent, and a haven to the
oppressed of the world." These few words demonstrated his continuing clarity of thought and precision of language; in his description of the nation as "a haven for the oppressed," he was referring
to those in the waves of immigrants who were escaping tyrannical
European regimes and pogroms. He also sent this message to the
gathering of GAR veterans in Maine, written in his own hand.

Tell the boys that they probably will never look into my face again,
nor hear my voic[e], but they are en[g]raved on my heart and I
love them as my children. What the good Lord has spared me
[f]or is more than I can tell, bu[t] it is perhaps to finish up my
book, which I shall leave to the Boys in Blue, and in which they
cannot only see me but follow me in the ac[tion]s in which they
helped me.

* * *

AMONG THE less-known milestones in Grant's life, thirty-nine
years before this May of 1885, he had come under fire for the first
time, in the Mexican War. Of all that happened to him before the
Civil War, the two incidents that most foretold his future ability oc-

curred in Latin America, one at the end of the Mexican War and one in Panama four years after that.

On September 13, 1847, the day before General Winfield Scott's victorious entry into Mexico City, Grant distinguished himself in the attacks made along the aqueduct road leading toward the complex of buildings and defenses on the city's outskirts known as the Garita [city gate] San Cosme. During the sixteen months of war that he had experienced since first being fired on in May of 1846, Grant had participated in most of the major battles. Serving at times as the regimental quartermaster of the Fourth Infantry Regiment, a position calling for attention to supplies and transportation at the rear of the fighting, Grant did all that and still repeatedly fought at the front. On this climactic afternoon Grant moved forward on his own, actually working his way around an enemy breastworks until he was behind the Mexicans who were firing at the Americans. Returning to the American lines, he asked for volunteers and got twelve men. Grant led them, and an American company he came upon that was just entering the battle, back around to the side of the enemy position, attacked the Mexicans on their unprotected flank, and forced a retreat. When the numerically superior enemy reoccupied the breastworks later in the day, Grant's Fourth Infantry led the counterattack that finally won it back: another lieutenant reported that he and Grant were "the first two persons to gain it."

As if that were not enough for this last afternoon of the Mexican War, Grant, scouting on his own again, made a discovery that he wrote about in his *Memoirs*. He said that he "found a church off to the south of the road, which looked to me as if the belfry would command the ground back of the Garita San Cosme." Trusting his instincts, he rounded up an officer in command of a mountain battery and its crew and directed them as they wrestled the small cannon up the steps of the bell tower. When they opened fire on the Mexican soldiers who were behind walls where they thought they could not be seen, "The shots from our little gun dropped in upon the enemy and created great confusion."

The commander of this wing of the American attack, Brigadier General William Worth, was studying the enemy position through a spyglass. These sudden unexpected explosions surprised him as much as it did the Mexicans. He sent his aide Lieutenant John C. Pemberton, the future Confederate general who would surrender Vicksburg to Grant sixteen years later, to bring Grant to him.

Telling the gunners of the mountain howitzer to keep up the fire, Grant reluctantly left the bell tower and reported to General Worth, who congratulated him, "saying that every shot was effective." Worth ordered Grant to take a captain with another mountain howitzer and its crew back with him, and get it up in the tower to double the fire.

"I could not tell the General," Grant wrote in his *Memoirs*, "that there was not room enough in the steeple for another gun, because he probably would have looked upon such a statement as a contradiction from a second lieutenant. I took the captain with me, but did not use his gun."

Grant faced another great test in the spring of 1852. After nearly four years of happily married postwar life, during which the young Grants lived at army posts in upstate New York and Michigan, his Fourth Infantry Regiment was ordered to California. At that time his and Julia's son Frederick was two, and she was due to have another baby in July. The route the Fourth Infantry was to take involved boarding a ship in New York to make the voyage to Panama; at that time, long before the construction of the Panama Canal, this had to be followed by an overland trip across the often disease-ridden isthmus to the Pacific, with the final leg on another ship to San Francisco. Despite their deep desire to stay together, the Grants decided that the risks to Julia and their son and unborn child were too great, and that he must make this voyage by himself.

On his regiment's harsh journey to California, Grant's hard-won knowledge of logistics, developed as a supply officer during the Mexican war, made him an unsung hero. His position as regimental quartermaster gave him the responsibility of drawing up and executing the plans for moving seven hundred soldiers, plus a hundred of their wives and children, across the Isthmus of Panama at a time when a cholera epidemic ravaged the area.

The disease killed a hundred of them. The toll would have been higher had it not been for Grant's energy and his willingness to take the initiative. The army had authorized Grant an allowance of sixteen dollars per mule to rent the beasts of burden to carry women, children, equipment, and what had been assumed would be a few sick persons. Finding no mules for rent at that price during a growing crisis, Grant threw away the bureaucracy's rules, hired mules at double the price, and, burying along the way the hundred who died—men, women, and seventeen children—got the survivors to Panama City. There the sick were separated and sent to a vessel, anchored well out in the harbor, that Grant leased as a hospital ship. For two weeks, as more died all around him, Grant remained aboard, arranging for food, medicine, and care. A witness to his efforts said that Grant emerged as "a man of iron, so far as endurance went, seldom sleeping . . . His work was always done, his supplies ample and on hand . . . He was like a ministering angel to us all."

15

The "Man of Iron" Keeps Going

O N MAY 10, Dr. Fordyce Barker came to see Grant at his house. Although Barker was not a specialist in conditions such as Grant's, he had been very much involved in his case, as well as in keeping up with his work in other branches of medicine. As one account put it, Barker had been "so much broken down by overwork that he considered it necessary to leave for Europe and came in to say good-bye."

This brought Grant and Barker to a special point in their relationship. From the time the Grants had moved to Manhattan, Barker had been Grant's physician, and the men became friends. Barker had been in Europe at the time in the summer of 1884 when Grant first began to feel pain in his mouth, and Grant had waited until Barker's return in October before coming to grips with his affliction. Now, "with marked evidence of suppressed emotion," Grant expressed his regard for Barker and thanked him for his part in his treatment. Grant added, "I suppose you never expect to see me again."

To this, Barker replied, "I hope I may."

Grant responded to that by saying sadly, "You do not say 'expect,' but 'hope.'"

Three days after this, Grant again took a turn for the worse. On May 16, his family and the doctors felt that he was much more depressed than he had been for some time. Dr. Douglas, aware that a "malarious condition" existed in Central Park, suggested that instead of a carriage ride in the park, Grant take a ride on a streetcar along part of Madison Avenue. "Upon his return from this trip," a contemporary account said, "his manner gave his family much uneasiness. His physicians decided that his depression of mind was due to the state of the weather. Mind and body, they maintained, needed a change of scene and air." Serious thought began to be given to what could be done to get Grant out of the summer heat that could descend on the city at any time. The house on the Jersey shore at Long Branch had first been rented; then on April 19 the *New York Tribune* reported that the family had decided to sell it. Something else had to be found.

The tumor on the right side of Grant's throat, once the size of an egg, grew to be twice as big; his voice grew weaker, "and at times became a mere whisper." Nonetheless, every day he pushed on with his work. Although he still had much to do to complete the book, on May 23 it occurred to Grant that he had never written a dedication for the *Memoirs*. He did so now, penning the words: "These volumes are dedicated to the American soldier and sailor." When Fred saw this later, he suggested to his father that perhaps he should specify that he meant the soldiers and sailors who had fought for the North. To that, Grant replied: "It is a great deal better that it should be dedicated as it is . . . As it is the dedication is to those we fought against as well as those we fought with. It may serve a purpose in restoring harmony."

Along with continuing his work on his *Memoirs*, Grant began to wind up matters of various kinds. He wrote to the Librarian of Congress, asking him if he was "authorized to receive" the property that the Grants had insisted that their friend William H. Vanderbilt should take as payment of their $150,000 debt to him, incurred during their bankruptcy the year before. Grant identified this as including "the medal voted to me by Congress, and other trophies of the war and of my trip around the world." That collection of greatly valuable objects still remained at 3 East Sixty-sixth Street, and Grant closed his letter with this: "I will soon be leaving the city and will be very glad to have it out of the house during the absence of myself and my family."

The medals and trophies were soon housed in the War Department in Washington, "to await the further action of Congress," but in his letter Grant had spoken of soon "leaving the city" for the summer. This letter was written on Friday, May 22, the day before Grant dedicated his *Personal Memoirs*. Such a move to get Grant out of Manhattan's approaching summer heat had been under discussion for some time, but now the family and the doctors had found an ideal place. Saratoga Springs, New York, 180 miles north of Manhattan, was known for the mineral waters of its fashionable spas, and as the site of the Saratoga Race Course, a track where thoroughbred horses had been racing since 1863. Nine miles northeast of there, at the top of a massive forested hill known as Mt. McGregor, twelve hundred feet above sea level, was a large new four-story resort hotel known as the Balmoral. Accommodating five hundred guests, it would soon open for the season. Among its facilities, it had a massive generator that would light the hotel with electricity; the Balmoral would be only the second hotel in America to be illuminated this way. On the grounds of this luxurious inn, which was reached by a small railroad line running up from Saratoga Springs, stood a spacious two-story private cottage recently acquired by the philanthropist Joseph W. Drexel, a member of the prominent Philadelphia banking family who now lived in New York.

Drexel already owned a fully furnished summer home in Saratoga, but had bought this still-empty cottage with a view to escape the occasionally tiresome social life and the greater heat to be found in Saratoga. Drexel knew and admired Grant; when he learned that Grant's family and doctors wanted a cool and healthy place for him, he offered his cottage to them. The Grants accepted, and Drexel and his wife set about renovating and furnishing it.

Grant's doctor John Hancock Douglas, who went to Saratoga every summer and knew Mt. McGregor, later recalled his reaction on learning this. "That is just the place I have been looking for. There is little heat there, it is on the heights, it is free from vapors, and above all, it is among the pines, and the pure air is especially grateful to patients suffering as General Grant is suffering." He concluded, "So it happened that just what we wanted we had."

Back in Manhattan, Grant continued to wind up his affairs, acting like a man who planned to be away a lot longer than the summer months. On May 29, under the heading *Memorandum*, he wrote, "Disposition I want made of the proceeds of my book, if sales amount to more than $100,000[.]" He then allotted various prospective sums to Julia and other members of his family. Perhaps still stung by the Badeau dispute, he set forth this, regarding his son Frederick: "Col. F. D. Grant is to have $10,000 for his *services as my Secretary*, and *his labors* in *helping me prepare my book!*"

Soon after this, he handed Harrison Terrell a letter of recommendation.

> I give this letter to you now, not knowing what the near future may bring to a person in my condition of health. This is an acknowledgment of your faithful services to me during my sickness up to this time, and which I expect will continue to the end. This is also to state further that for about four years you have lived with me, coming first at [as] butler, in which capacity you served until

my illness became so serious as to require the constant attention of a nurse, and that in both capacities I have had abundant reason to be satisfied with your attention, integrity and efficiency. I hope that you may never want for a place.

Yours,

U. S. Grant

~ II ~

On Saturday, May 30, Decoration Day, there was a parade down Fifth Avenue. Men wearing the dark blue uniforms and wide-brimmed hats of the Grand Army of the Republic (GAR) veterans' organization turned out for the day set aside to honor the memory of those who had died in battle.

The parade came down Fifth Avenue, bands playing and crowds cheering. As unit after unit came to Sixty-sixth Street, they turned left off their usual route on Fifth Avenue and began passing in review before Grant's house at 3 East Sixty-sixth. On this day a year before, Grant and Philip Sheridan had ridden in a carriage past cheering crowds in Brooklyn, but since then cancer had struck. Grant was having a bad day and was lying in bed, suffering. Horace Porter was in the room and described what happened when Grant realized what was going on.

> Now he heard the sound of martial music . . . Then came the heavy, measured steps of moving columns, a step which can be ac-quired only by years of service in the field. He recognized it all now. It was the tread of his old veterans.
>
> With his little remaining strength he arose and dragged him-self to the window. As he gazed upon those battle-flags dipping to him in salute, those precious standards bullet-riddled, battle-stained . . . his eyes once more kindled with the flames that had

lighted them at Shiloh, on the heights of Chattanooga, amid the glories of Appomattox . . .

Bareheaded, Grant was clearly visible at his second-story window as he gazed down at his "Boys in Blue." They took off their hats to him as they passed.

> . . . as those war-scarred veterans with uncovered heads and up-turned faces for the last time looked upon the pallid features of their old chief, cheeks which had been bronzed by Southern suns and begrimed with [gun]powder, were bathed in tears of manly grief.
>
> Soon they saw rising the hand which had so often pointed out to them the path of victory. He raised it slowly and painfully to his head in recognition of their salutations.

Porter said of the sudden silence, in the street and in the room where Grant still stood at the window, "The column had passed, the hand fell heavily by his side. It was his last military salute." A reporter from the *New York Tribune* wrote this of these same minutes after the column had passed out of sight:

> . . . the old warrior stood at his post in the window, like a statue, looking toward the Park. Someone came up from behind and touched him, and he moved slowly away . . . The sight of the old soldiers, many of whom had been with him in the Wilderness, touched him deeply, and he sat thinking in his chair for a long time after the sound of the music had died away in the distance.

Another Loan from Vanderbilt

A<small>T DAWN ON</small> T<small>UESDAY</small>, June 16, Manhattan's Grand Central Station became the scene of unusual activity. Workers were preparing the special train that would leave in two hours, taking Grant and his entourage to Saratoga Springs. The train consisted of a locomotive, a private car belonging to the sleeping car company owned by William H. Vanderbilt's son-in-law Dr. William Seward Webb, and Vanderbilt's private car, which the *World* described to its readers as being "fitted up most luxuriously and every detail which can add to his [Grant's] ease and comfort during the journey has been attended to." Among those modifications, three lounge seats had been removed, and a bed installed on which Grant could rest. Grant's two large overstuffed black leather armchairs were loaded onto Webb's car.

At about seven in the morning, Grant came out the door of 3 East Sixty-sixth Street, wearing a black coat, a black beaver-skin top hat with a five-inch crown, bedroom slippers, and a white silk scarf. His appearance shocked those who had not seen him for a while: his hair and beard were largely white, and when he adjusted his white scarf a reporter thought his wrist looked like that of a skeleton. At this stage, according to an account forwarded to the newspaper the *Saratogian*, "The great malignant looking swelling under his right ear is as big as a man's two fists put together." Grant appeared dazed. Before getting into the carriage, he turned and looked back at the house, his face sad.

At Grand Central the large group making the trip assembled. Accompanying Grant in the Vanderbilt coach were Julia and their daughter, Nellie Sartoris, Frederick and his wife, Ida, their youngest son, Jesse, and his wife, Elizabeth, and three of their five grandchildren. (Their son Buck, whose wife, Fanny, was not well, would later come and go.) Also with them in this car was Dr. Douglas, who was to stay with Grant at Mt. McGregor during the time ahead. Another doctor in the car was George Shrady, who had a summer home at Kingsbridge near the Hudson and had promised Grant he could come to him swiftly at any time in the weeks ahead.

Grant's stenographer Noble Dawson was with him, too, playing a somewhat changed role. Grant sometimes continued to dictate to Dawson, in a whisper, but was losing his voice; in two days Grant would write from Mt. McGregor to Reverend John Newman, "It is just a week to-day since I have spoken. My suffering continuous." Dawson took down Grant's words when he could whisper them, but he was also passing along to others the slips of paper on which Grant had started writing messages of all kinds, often scrawled in pencil. At Mt. McGregor, Dawson would help Frederick Grant check revisions of the book. Completing Grant and Julia's household staff were Harrison Terrell, the "white nurse" Henry McSweeny, and a maid from 3 East Sixty-sixth Street whose discretion in talking to the press had earned her the sobriquet, "the tight-mouthed daughter of the Emerald Isle." Frederick's two children, Julia and Ulysses S. Grant III, were to be in the care of their French nurse Louise.

Others on the train included W. J. Arkell, one of the owners of the Balmoral Hotel, Thomas Cable, the hotel manager, and reporters from the New York newspapers.

Even for Grant to walk to the train from the carriage that brought him to the nearest point at the station was a painful struggle. The *Saratogian* story said, "he trudged forward with the aid of his cane only, his slippers dragging along the walk. The distance from the carriage to the [railroad] car was not more than fifty feet, and his time between them was about four minutes."

It was to be a blazing day, with temperatures as high as 105 degrees reported in towns along the way. The train headed up the line beside the Hudson River, on the same route Grant had taken to visit Alden Goldsmith's racing stables at Goshen the previous November. Grant changed from his top hat and dark coat to one of his skull caps and a long linen duster. The reporter from *Harper's Weekly* wrote this: "At station after station on the route knots of people were waiting to wave greeting and godsend." Grant was dozing when Julia woke him as the train neared West Point. The *Harper's Weekly* story said that Grant then "beckoned to Dr. Douglas and with a smile motioned toward the Military Academy . . . as though the sight were dear to him. Till the last outline of its surroundings had passed his gaze was fixed on the spot." (At the time Grant was a cadet, he was not fond of the academy. He was an indifferent student: in his *Memoirs* he wrote, "A military life had no charms for me, and I had not the faintest idea of staying in the army even if I graduated, which I did not expect.")

Despite all the forethought that had gone into planning this trip, the only way to reduce the sweltering heat in the Vanderbilt car was to open its doors and windows, which brought in cinders, soot, and smoke from the steam engine ahead. To keep this from strangling Grant, Fred and Harrison arranged things so that he could ride backwards.

~ I I ~

At 1:55 the train arrived at Saratoga. Veterans of the town's Wheeler Post of the GAR were lined up on the platform, coming to attention as the train pulled in. The plan had been for Grant to move down the rank in a form of inspection, looking the men up and down and perhaps exchanging words with some of them. Grant had changed back into his dark coat and top hat. He got down from the Vanderbilt coach unassisted, but as soon as the commanders of the Wheeler Post saw this pale, withered figure, they decided that he should be transferred to the smaller train for Mt. McGregor as swiftly as possible. The conductor and brakeman of the Vanderbilt train lifted him the short distance to the steps of the smaller train, and he mounted its steps by himself. As he did, the veterans and other men in the crowd doffed their hats; Grant acknowledged the crowd's silent respectful welcome by raising his cane towards them. Once again, plans went amiss. Unloading Grant's two large armchairs from the big car owned by Webb and getting them aboard a far smaller one would have been difficult at any time, but in the unusually hot sun it required Fred Grant and several other quickly recruited volunteers to wrestle with this heavy furniture, and their sweat made the black leather surfaces slippery to handle. Grant eventually came out onto the coach platform; the man who had commanded a million men started directing the improvised efforts of this squad, and the chairs got aboard.

The smaller train, this time just a locomotive and one car, started off for Mt. McGregor, with the crowd cheering and Grant waving a handkerchief from his place in an armchair by a window. A story in the *World* described the ride: "As the diminutive engine wheezed along the uneven rails up the steep grade she belched out clouds of stifling smoke which filled the car and gave the General much annoyance. Curve followed curve in quick succession and the car pitched from side to side like a boat in a stormy sea." The *Saratogian* called it a "12-mile jolt."

At 2:40 p.m. this second train reached the end of its line, a small platform where guests of the Balmoral would get off and walk the remaining distance up a covered sloping walkway to the hotel, with porters following them with their luggage. A hospital bed was waiting on the little platform for Grant, to be used to take him the shorter distance up the slope to the cottage. He spurned this, and, using his cane, started to make his faltering way up the path. After passing under an arch composed of two poles with an overhead sign between them that welcomed "Our Hero," he began to stagger.

At just this place on the path two strapping men from the Saratoga police department, Detective John Fryer and Constable James Minnick, had positioned themselves on either side of a big wicker chair. Grant collapsed into it. The men carried him up to the steps of the cottage, where he got out of the chair. Using his cane again, he managed to walk up the steps and onto the porch, where Mrs. Drexel stood waiting to greet him. Going inside, he reappeared on the porch fifteen minutes later, after Harrison had changed his clothes and brushed the ashes from the train ride out of his beard and hair. Then, making his first reconnaissance of this new area, he slowly walked along the broad covered porch that ran around three sides of the cottage. He stopped several times, his hands on his hips, and looked at the different views, one of which was of the slope atop which the Balmoral loomed. Once again wearing the black coat and top hat in which he had started the day, he sank into a wicker armchair on which he "sat for hours until the mosquitoes drove him in." In preparing him for the night, Dr. Douglas cleaned some ashy grime from his throat.

Grant had arrived at a place, and a time in his life, when so many things were coming together. Here was the place to do or die, literally, in the writing of his *Personal Memoirs*. Here he would be visited by friends from many periods of his life, and his every move would be reported in the nation's press. Here, on little slips of paper, he would write messages ranging from profound observations to a request that his son Jesse come downstairs and play cards with him. (One contemporary's description of these conversations called them "pencil talk.")

That first night at Mt. McGregor, during which the temperature dropped to 40 degrees, Grant slept for ten hours. He lay comfortably curled up in the combination of the two big leather armchairs brought from New York, while lightning from a mountain thunderstorm flashed in the skies above his new home.

~III~

The next day, the Grants had the chance to inspect more of their surroundings. The Drexel cottage was a structure built in the Queen Anne style. In the swift and thorough renovation that the Drexels had undertaken, the exterior had been painted a golden brown with dark brown trim. Of its dozen rooms, six were upstairs bedrooms, occupied by the family and occasionally by one of Grant's doctors.

The downstairs arrangement was complicated, but proved to be functional. On the northwest corner of the cottage, one entered an office, fifteen feet by twelve in size, where a considerable amount of the writing would be done, and almost all of the editing. This opened onto a room, seventeen feet by fifteen, in which almost all of the space was occupied by Grant's two massive black leather armchairs. As in Manhattan, they were fitted together in such a way that he could curl up in them to sleep and to work. This became known as the sick room, and sometimes the "sick room-office." Three doors opened off this room: one back to the office through which one entered the house, one into what became known as the fifteen-by-twelve "Servants Room" occupied by Harrison Terrell and Henry

McSweeny, and yet another to the parlor, which was thirty feet long, fifteen feet wide, and the largest room in the house. Off the parlor was the dining room, measuring fifteen feet by twelve feet, which proved to be seldom used after Julia decided that the family should eat in a private dining room at the hotel.

There were two doors in the parlor that led directly to the porch; one on the east, and one at the northeast corner, where Grant would find that he loved to sit in a wicker chair and read the newspapers before settling down to work, sometimes in that same wicker chair.

As for the interiors of the rooms that Grant occupied, the walls of the sick room/office had new wallpaper with gold and brown tones, and the downstairs ceilings had gold stars against a blue background. The dining room had a straw mat for a rug.

Having acquainted himself with his new surroundings, Grant, refreshed by his night's sleep and the mountain air, now at 70 degrees, wanted to take a walk. Holding on to Harrison Terrell's arm with one hand and using his cane with the other, he set off on the downward path through the pines, a trail 150 yards long that brought them to the Eastern Outlook. From this clearing one could see a spectacular view, a wide-angled panorama that overlooked the Hudson Valley to the east, with the Saratoga Revolutionary War battlefield less than ten miles away. To the north were the Adirondack Mountains, and the Catskills lay to the south.

Grant rested for a time on a wooden bench in a big gazebo that perched high above green fields. Laboriously making his way back to the cottage on Harrison's arm, he went into his room. Lying exhausted in his combination of armchairs, he thought for a while. Then he had Harrison bring him a pencil and paper. The first thing he wrote was a note to Dr. Douglas, who was up at the hotel.

Dr. Since coming to this beautiful climate and getting a rest of about ten hours, I have watched my pains and compared them with those of the past few weeks. I can feel plainly that my system is preparing for dissolution in three ways; one by hemorrhaging, one by strangulation and the third by exhaustion. The first and second are likely to come at any moment to relieve me of my early sufferings; the time for the arrival of the third can be computed with almost mathematical certainty. With an increase of daily food I have fallen off in weight and strength very rapidly for the last two weeks.

There cannot be a hope of going far beyond this time. All any physician, or any number of them can do for me now is to make my burden of pain as light as possible. I do not want any physician but yourself but I tell you so that if you are unwilling to have me go without consultation with other professional men, you can send for them. I dread them however, knowing that it means another desperate effort to save me, and more suffering.

Next, Grant wrote Fred a note, "Memoranda for my Family," which appears to have been an addition to the "Memorandum" concerning financial affairs he prepared before leaving Manhattan. As with so many things he had written in his life, it was a matter-of-fact treatment of a dramatic matter.

I have given you the directions about all my affairs except my burial. We own a burial lot in the cemetery at St. Louis and I like that city, as it was there I was married and lived for many years and there three of my children were born. We also have a burial lot in Galena, and I am fond of Illinois, from which state I entered the Army at the beginning of the war. I am also much attached to New York, where I have made my home for several years past, and through the generosity of whose citizens I have been enabled to pass my last days without experiencing the pains of pinching want.

Reading this, Frederick told his father that there was a national expectation that he would be buried in Washington. Grant responded by writing on one of the slips of paper he now frequently used. In one of the greatest understatements he ever made, he stated, "It is possible that my funeral may become one of public demonstration." He added that he understood he might have no choice in the matter of where he would be buried. But Julia was always in his heart: he wanted to lie beside her forever. "There is one thing I wish you and the family to insist upon and that is that wherever my tomb may be, a place shall be reserved for your mother."

Frederick felt compelled to share his father's wishes with his mother. The idea of getting down to a choice of a burial place affected Julia as nothing before this had. After that, she seldom if ever left the cottage. When Grant was dozing in his wicker chair on the porch, she often sat beside him, holding his hand. Once, he awoke to see her praying, hands clasped.

During the process of seeing his immediate surroundings, Grant met one of his veterans who would perform a most useful service. This was Sam Willett, who had served as a private in Company A, Sixteenth Heavy Artillery, New York State Volunteers. When he enlisted in 1863 he was forty-three years old, and he served to the end of the war. He may have joined up to keep an eye on his son Ebenezer, who was a private in the same company, and he acted as his unit's unofficial chaplain. A lifelong shoemaker and a member of a GAR post in Albany, Sam, now sixty-five, had read of Grant's coming stay at Mt. McGregor and decided that the Grant party would need someone to shield his old general from the public. Shortly before the Grants arrived, he set up an army tent ten yards away from the southern corner of the cottage, complete with a small wood stove and a washtub for doing his laundry. Wearing his GAR uniform, he took up his post in front of the steps at the top of which Grant would sit in a wicker armchair reading the newspapers or writing his book and waved away sightseers who wished to stop and gaze at Ulysses S. Grant.

Willett also became a figure of great interest to Grant's grand-children. Despite the presence of the French nurse, Louise, that Frederick and Ida employed for their two children, and the close-mouthed Irish maid from 3 East Sixty-sixth Street, the five grand-children (two more would soon arrive) and Dr. Douglas's two daughters, also soon to arrive, made a clubhouse out of Willett's tent. They played with his military equipment and enjoyed various games he taught them and stories he told them when he was not on guard. He would find time to hang some swings from the limbs of nearby trees, set up a croquet ground, and build them a little sum-merhouse whose thatched roof consisted of boughs and leaves. The children also enjoyed splashing around in a good-sized pond not far from Willett's tent; in a note to Dr. Douglas, Grant mentioned that his wife's namesake, Julia, and Douglas's two young daughters en-joyed "their lawn tennis and nice shade" and that they "get along very happily together."

* * *

MILLIONS OF Americans now knew that Grant was in a hilltop re-treat. The support given to Grant by individuals, both nearby and in different parts of the nation, took unusual forms. The *Saratogian* reported this: "Duncan McGregor of Glen's Falls, after whom the mountain was named, purchased a valuable Jersey Cow on Wednes-day, and has sent it to the cottage for the use of the General and family during their sojourn there." As for persons farther away, the *Saratogian* told its readers about something sent to Grant, whose diet now consisted entirely of liquids, three days after he reached Mt. McGregor.

Yesterday morning he received a small box of bovinine, which is said to be a condensed extract of beef and mutton, and is prepared by the J. P. Bush Manufacturing Company of Chicago. Accompanying it were the following instructions: To all trainmen and conductors on the Michigan Central and New York Central roads: This box is for General Grant and contains the food he uses. It is extremely important that the box should arrive there in good shape and at once. Please see that it is forwarded immediately, and that it is kept cool.

Not everyone was so helpful. The *Saratogian* noted an odd communication. "One of the many cranks in the country lives down in Texas. That Lone Star individual yesterday telegraphed General Grant asking him if he had ever used pepper-sauce for cancer, saying it was a sure cure. The Texan called for an answer to his dispatch, and is probably wondering by this time why he does not receive an answer."

~ I V ~

On Sunday, June 21, his fifth morning at Mt. McGregor, Grant got back to his book. He now had on hand the printed page proofs of Volume One, and the handwritten manuscript of Volume Two, some of it done in his own hand, and some in the handwriting of Noble Dawson, to whom he could still sometimes dictate in a whisper.

He had Dawson read to him what he had written earlier, both the printed and handwritten material, and then would indicate in one way or another the changes he wanted, either insertions of new sentences and paragraphs, or the rearrangement of existing sections. The next day, he worked for several hours out on the porch, sitting in the wicker armchair with a writing board that ran across from one of the chair's arms to the other, and using a pencil and a pad of lined yellow paper. Although Grant took no notice of it, fifteen years before this day, on June 22, 1870, he had signed the document creating the Department of Justice. Until then, there had been the office of Attorney-General, which was authorized to hire lawyers, but the new department gave the government greater powers to enforce civil rights legislation.

The next day, a week after arriving at the cottage, Dr. Douglas noted that Grant "spent several hours devoted to dictating in a whisper and writing." A reporter from the *New York Tribune* filed a story of that day's activity in which he said that Grant "dictated enough to add nearly ten printed pages to his history . . . Dr. Douglas asked General Grant after he had finished his work if he could talk in a louder key and he replied that he could, but that he spoke low to economize his strength."

From Manhattan, Mark Twain was trying to stop Grant's practice of making handwritten changes on the printed page proofs. Much as he continued to admire Grant's writing, he saw that this was both expensive and time consuming, and he kept attempting to lock up Volume One. Had Twain succeeded, the public might never have read Grant's 550-word preface, written now and placed at the front of Volume One. "Man proposes, and God disposes," Grant began, and went on to say of his race with death to finish his *Memoirs*, "I would have more hope of satisfying the expectation of the public if I could have allowed myself more time."

* * *

AT THE END of a pain-filled day, Grant and his doctors would strike at his enemy, cancer. "Cocaine Water" was applied to Grant's mouth and tongue to alleviate the pain. The doctors also used brandy and morphine, which dulled the pain but muddled his mind. Then they cleaned out his mouth, which by evening became filled with phlegm and dead skin.

With all this, it was Grant who attempted to raise his family's spirits. For the personal philosophy he hoped to imbue in those closest to him, on one occasion he fished one of his blank slips of paper out of a pocket and scrawled on it: "Do as I do. I take it quietly. I give myself not the least concern. Give yourselves not the least concern. If I knew that the end would be to-morrow I would try and get rest in the meantime. As long as there's no progress [of the disease] there's hope." To Frederick, who often looked grief-stricken and worn as he cared constantly for his father, Grant wrote one of his longer messages, speaking of himself as if he were already dead.

> You ought to feel happy under any circumstances. My expected death called forth expressions of the sincerest kindness from all the people of all the sections of the country. The Confederate soldier vied with the Union soldier in sounding my praise. The Protestant, the Catholic and the Jew appointed days for universal prayer in my behalf . . . All societies passed resolutions of sympathy for me and petitions that I might recover. It looks as if my sickness has had something to do to bring about harmony between the sections . . . Apparently I have accomplished more while apparently dying than it falls to the lot of most men to be able to do.

Up at the hotel, the guests and the staff felt the greatest curiosity about the "Grant Cottage" and its occupants. At the outset, the hotel had sent down meals for all the Grant contingent, but Julia decided that it would be simpler to have everyone but her husband take their meals up there. The hotel set aside a small private dining room for them, but this in no way satisfied the curiosity to see Grant himself. It cost a dollar to make the round trip on the little train that ran between Mt. McGregor and Saratoga Springs. To board or alight from it at Mt. McGregor required the passenger to pass some twenty yards from where Grant was often to be found sitting in a wicker chair on the porch, bundled up and reading the newspapers or working on his book. Some of these passengers came up from Saratoga Springs just to see Grant and then would take a later train back, and there was reason to think that many of the hotel guests came down to the train platform as if intending to board the train, gazed at Grant, and then went back up to the hotel.

Despite GAR veteran Samuel Willett's gestures that all these passersby should keep right on moving, some paused, and occasionally waved to Grant, who would sometimes look up and wave back. On one occasion a pretty young woman wearing a yellow gown and carrying a yellow-and-white parasol stopped and curtsied. Grant, seemingly engrossed in his work, rose, took off his top hat, and bowed.

Once Grant went up to the hotel himself, in an unusual form of transportation. On Thursday evening, June 25, an odd-looking contraption was delivered at Mt. McGregor, something arranged for Grant's use by Dr. Douglas. It was a Bath chair, of the type first developed to pull or push vacationers or invalids along the boardwalk at the English seaside town of that name. It had a slanting wicker chair set inside a matching tublike wicker body, with three small wheels like those of a bicycle. This machine could be pulled from the front by means of a wooden tongue with a crosspiece, and pushed from the rear by a rod that was bolted across its back.

Near noon the next day, Grant settled himself into the chair; with the ladies of the family cheerfully walking along beside him and Harrison Terrell pulling, occasionally helped by others, he set off for the short journey up the slope to the Balmoral. The *Saratogian* carried this eyewitness story.

> When Harrison made a facetious reference to his having become a draught horse, the General smiled, and, drawing forth his pencil wrote the following: "For a man who has been accustomed to

drive fast horses this is a considerable come down in point of speed." Reply was made that though there was less speed there was more safety. Whereupon the General glanced at Harrison and then wrote in response: "My horse will not run away up-hill." The General joined audibly in the laugh.

In one of his unpredictable spurts of energy, Grant got out of his novel form of transportation and walked up the hotel steps by himself. The Bath chair was hauled up behind him, and he was wheeled up and down the covered porches, two hundred feet long and twenty feet wide, which had spectacular views similar to those he had seen from the Eastern Outlook. He then sat in this vehicle, near the hotel's front door, and read the newspapers as he did down at the cottage. Asked later in the day if this had been his best day since arriving at Mt. McGregor, Grant replied, "Decidedly."

Three days after this, Grant wrote what was in effect a letter of farewell to Julia. He could not bear to say this good-bye face-to-face, so in a postscript to what he had to say, he wrote, "This will be found in my coat after my demise." He put with the letter a ring that Julia had given him long in the past, and which was now too loose to stay on his finger because of how thin the cancer had made him. Grant added to that a lock of Julia's hair, mixed with a lock of Buck's when he was a boy, which he had kept with him when he was an officer serving on the West Coast. This is what he had to say.

My Dear Wife;

There are some matters about which I would like to talk but I cannot. The subject would be painful to you and the children, and, by reflex, painful to me also. When I see you and them depressed I join in the feeling.

I have known for a long time that my end was approaching with certainty . . . the end is not far off . . . My will disposes of my property . . . I have left with Fred a memorandum giving some details of how the proceeds of my book are to be drawn from the publisher.

Look after our dear children and direct them in the path of rectitude. It would distress me far more to think that one of them could depart from an honorable, upright and virtuous life than it would to know they were prostrated on a bed of sickness from which they were never to arise alive. They have never given us any cause on their account. I earnestly pray they never will.

With these few injunctions, and the knowledge I have of your love and affections, and of the dutiful affections of all our children, I bid you a final farewell until we meet in another, and I trust better, world.

Grant wrote many notes, on greatly varying topics. To Dr. Shrady he penciled this. "I do not know one tune from another. One time in traveling, when there were brass bands everywhere, and all played, it seems, the same tune, 'Hail to the Chief,' on the arrival of the train or of my party at a reception till I remarked at last, with greatest innocence, that I thought that I had heard that tune before."

Grant handed most of his notes to Douglas, who spent the nights at the Balmoral but was at the cottage many hours of the day. One of them said, "I will have to be careful about my writing. I see ever[y] person I give a piece of paper to puts it in his pocket. Some day they will be coming up against my English."

In regard to grammar, another note to Douglas presented this thought. "The fact is that I am a verb instead of a personal pronoun. A verb is any thing that signifies to be; to do; or to suffer. I signify all three." On yet another topic, another slip to Douglas told him, "I found this a.m. what was the matter with my watch when you had it last night. You got the two parts of the split hand apart and did nok [sic] know how to get them together again. Look and I will shew you."

Evidently the subject arose of the temperature at night in this cottage high in the hills, eliciting this: "I like a cold room to sleep in. Even if water freezes in the room I sleep well. Mrs. Grant also sleeps with a window open the coldest nights." Again concerning sleep, at 10 p.m. on June 29 he wrote Douglas this: "I have been asleep three times since you went out, and once made noise enough to propel a Hudson River boat."

Turning from these matters, Grant occasionally shared his most serious thoughts with Douglas.

> I am thankful for the providential extension of my time to enable me to continue my work. I am further thankful, and in a much greater degree thankful, because it has enabled me to see for myself the happy harmony which has so suddenly sprung up between those engaged but a few short years ago in deadly conflict.
>
> It has been an inestimable blessing to me to hear the kind expression towards me in person from all parts of our country; from people of all nationalities of all religions, and of no religion, of Confederate and National troops alike; of soldiers organizations; of mechanical, scientific and all other societies, embracing almost every citizen in the land. They have brought joy to my heart if they have not effected a cure. To you and your colleagues I acknowledge my indebtedness for having brought me through the "valley of the shadow of death" to enable me to witness these things.

* * *

OVER THE WEEKEND of June 29–30, Grant had a visit from Mark Twain, who was making yet one more effort to carry off a completed version of the *Memoirs*. All he was able to get from Grant was a series of excellent maps of his battles and campaigns, but in time

Twain saw that, even now, the more work Grant continued to do on the manuscript, the better it became. Grant said in a memorandum to Twain, "I have worked harder than if I had been well. I have used my three boys and a stenographer." He had finished his account of Lee's surrender before leaving 3 East Sixty-sixth Street, and was in the process of writing three short chapters and a chapter titled, "Conclusion."

Before returning to New York, Twain spent the afternoon on the porch of Grant's cottage, chatting with him and his sons Buck and Jesse. The day before, Ferdinand Ward's partner, James D. Fish, in jail convicted of bank embezzlement, had finally received his sentence to serve seven years in the Auburn, New York state prison. Twain unleashed some of his choicest curses in talking about Fish and his role in the Grant & Ward swindle, sentiments emphatically echoed by Buck and Jesse. Grant listened to all this, and then pulled out one of his slips of paper and wrote on it in pencil, about Fish, "He was not as bad as the other."

Mixed in with all these encounters and reflections were the painful realities of Grant's condition. In the slips he used to report to Douglas, he mentioned having "spasms"—a term he had not employed before coming to Mt. McGregor. At eight in the morning of Wednesday, July 1, he said, "I feel weak from my exertions last night in throwing up," and days later wrote to Douglas, "About an hour ago I coughed up a piece of stringy matter about the size of a small lizard."

Of all the incoming mail, Grant was most touched by a letter from an A. M. Arnold, writing from Rockbridge Baths, Virginia.

> I hope that you will allow one, who, when but a boy, laid down his arms at Appomattox and gave his allegiance to the Union, to express his warmest sympathy for you in your hour of affliction. Dear General, I have watched your movements from the hour

you gave me my horse and sword and told me to go home and "assist in making a crop"—I have been proud to see the nation do you honor . . .

May the God who overlooked you in battle and who has brought you thus far give you grace to meet whatever He has in store for you. And may He restore you to health & friends is the fervent prayer of one who at 15 years of age entered the lists against you and accepted the magnanimous terms you accorded us at Appomattox.

Grant expressed his intention to answer this letter, but evidently did not have the strength to do so. The book stood foremost in his mind. He wrote this to Fred: "If I should die here make arrangements for embalming my body and retaining it for buryel [sic] until pleasant weather in the fall. In that case you can continue your work [on the book] and insure its being ready as fast as the printers can take it. This is now my great interest in life, to see my work done. . . . Do *not* let the memory of me interfere with the progress of the book."

Hard as Grant was working on the final portion of his *Memoirs*, it was far easier to pull a pencil and a slip of paper out of his pocket and tell Douglas what was on his mind. He did this again notably on July 8.

If I live long enough I will become a sort of specialist in the use of certain medecines [sic]. It seems that one mans destiny in this world is quite as much a mystery as it is likely to be in the next. I never thought of acquiring rank in the profession I was educated for; yet it came with two grades higher prefixed to the rank of General officers for me.

I certainly never had either ambition or taste for political life; yet I was twice president of the United States. If any one had suggested the idea of my becoming an author, as they frequently did, I was not sure whether they were making sport of me or not. I have now written a book which is in the hands of the manufacturers . . . I ask that you keep these notes very private lest I become an authority on the treatment of diseases. I have already to[o] many trades to be proficient in any.

On this same busy day, in a note to Julia signed "Your loving and affectionate husband," he underscored his preoccupation with completing his book. He told her that he was convinced that "my end is approaching rapidly," and that "I am sure I will never leave Mt. McGregor alive. I pray God however that it [my life] may be spared to complete the necessary work upon my book . . . Should my career be closed at an earlyer [sic] day I would be very glad if the boys would make arrangements to retain quarters here and go on with their work."

The next person to appear on the cottage porch that day was a Catholic priest, Father Raymond Didier of St. Vincent's Church in Baltimore. He came to present the good wishes of his archbishop, the famous James Cardinal Gibbons, and said, "We are all praying for you, General Grant." Didier's presence marked yet one more area of reconciliation: in 1875, Grant had made a speech to a veterans' group in which he said, "Leave the matter of religion to the family altar, the Church, and the private school, supported entirely by private contributions. Keep the Church and State forever separate." This became linked to the repeal of the tax exemption enjoyed by religious schools. The principal beneficiaries of this exemption were Catholic educational institutions of all kinds, and the Catholic hierarchy had seen Grant's remarks as bigotry. In the ensuing controversy over the separation of church and state, the exemption for Catholic schools was protected along with that for all other religious schools, and this visit by Gibbons's emissary was an olive branch extended to Grant. When Didier said, "We are all praying for you," Grant penciled this reply:

> Yes, I know; and I feel very grateful to the Christian people of the land for their prayers on my behalf. There is no sect or religion, as shown in the Old or the New Testament, to which this does not apply. Catholics, Protestants, and Jews, and all the good people of the Nation, of all politics as well as religion, and all nationalities seem to have united in wishing or praying for my improvement. I am a great sufferer all the time, but the facts I have related are a compensation for most of it. All that I can do is to pray that the prayers of all those good people may be answered so far as to have us all meet in another and a better world.

Before the afternoon was out, Grant received a group of twenty Mexican journalists and editors. This delegation of the Mexican Associated Press was touring the United States. Stopping at the Balmoral, they conferred with Fred Grant, asking if it might be possible to meet with his father. Grant sent word that he would be happy to see them. Mexico was a country in which he had always taken an interest. As a young officer, he felt that the American invasion of Mexico and the seizure of Texas, New Mexico, and Upper California was "one of the most unjust wars ever waged by a stronger against a weaker nation." During the Civil War, he had shared Lincoln's anger and concern at the actions taken by the French emperor Napoleon III to install the Austrian Duke Maximilian as the puppet ruler of Mexico. After his presidency, Grant made two trips to Mexico as part of his role in the combined American and Mexican effort to push a railroad line south of Mexico City to Guatemala. That had not succeeded, but he liked Mexico and its people and believed in that nation's potential. Tiring as it was, he shook hands with each of the twenty journalists and listened as some awkward speech making began. As Grant described it the next day, one of the Mexicans "delivered a speech in Spanish—that had to be translated and spoken in English—I replied and my speech was made in English then translated and spoken in Spanish. Then there was a second speech and reply. By this time I was nearly exhausted." Grant's speech said in part, "I hope Mexico may soon begin an upward and prosperous departure [course]. She has all the conditions; she has the people; she has the soil; she has the climate; and she has the minerals." Referring to both the Mexican War and the Maximilian adventure, he concluded, "The conquest of Mexico will not be an easy task in the future." The Mexicans were greatly pleased with Grant's words. He urged them to give his statement as wide a distribution as they pleased, and they saw to it that it was printed throughout their nation.

The influx of visitors continued, but Grant took particular pleasure in greeting two that came the next day. The first was Charles Wood of Lansingburgh, New York, the man who sent him $500 within days of learning about Grant's being swindled in May of 1884, and subsequently sent him another $1,000. Fred had invited him to come. Grant received Wood while lying in his armchairs, still tired from his exertions the day before, and wrote him this message: "I feel very thankful to you for the kindness you did me last summer. I am glad to say that while there is much unblushing wickedness in this world yet there is a compensating generosity and grandeur of soul. In my case I have not found that Republics are ungrateful nor are the people."

Later the same day, he had a visit from Robert Underwood Johnson, associate editor of the *Century*. Grant's family had sent many telegrams to friends explaining that Grant's condition was too fragile for him to receive them, but Johnson came to see Fred about the final proofs of Grant's article on the Vicksburg campaign. Nonetheless, when Grant learned of Johnson's presence, he insisted on seeing him and in conveying to him his thanks for, as Fred later put it, the *Century*'s staff always "acting the part of gentlemen," despite his having chosen Twain as his publisher for the *Memoirs*. Johnson wrote that as he rose to leave, Grant "gave me his hand," and added, "I could hardly keep back the tears as I made my farewell to the great soldier who saved the Union for all its people and to the man of warm and courageous heart who had fought his last long battle for those he so tenderly loved."

The parade of figures from Grant's past continued the next day, with a visit from Simon Bolivar Buckner, a Kentuckian who had been a class behind him at West Point. He and Grant had served together in the Mexican War. After the fighting ended in 1848, both Grant and Buckner were among a group of officers who, as Grant put it in Volume One of his *Memoirs*, "obtained leave to visit Popocatapetel [sic], the highest volcano in North America." Grant's descriptive abilities came to the fore in writing of an experience he and Buckner shared. Going up the side of the mountain, heading for a hut where they were to spend the night, they and some heavily laden mules and their owners came to a road that "was very narrow with a yawning precipice on one side, hundreds of feet down to a roaring mountain torrent below, and almost perpendicular walls on the other side." At a particularly hazardous point, this occurred:

> . . . one of our mules loaded with two sacks of barley, one on each side, the two about as big as he was, struck his load against the mountain-side and was precipitated to the bottom. The descent was steep but not perpendicular. The mule rolled over and over until the bottom was reached and we supposed of course that the poor animal was dashed to pieces.
>
> What was our surprise, not long after we had gone into bivouac, to see the lost mule, cargo and owner coming up the ascent. The load had protected the animal from serious injury; and his owner had gone after him and found a way back to the path leading up to the hut where we were to stay.

Grant met Buckner again six years after that. In 1854, Grant was charged with being drunk on duty while paying troops at a remote post on the West Coast. His colonel gave him the choice of resigning from the army, or facing a court-martial. Saying that he would never want Julia to know that he had been drunk on duty, Grant quietly resigned. On his roundabout way back to be reunited with Julia in St. Louis, he ran out of money in New York City after arriving there by ship. He was sustained by money supplied him by his friend Buckner, then stationed in New York as captain of the commissary department of the Regular Army's Sixth Infantry Regiment, until funds sent by his father reached Manhattan.

Grant and Buckner next saw each other eight years later, on February 15, 1862. Buckner was a Confederate general, and Grant was the Union general conducting the attacks on besieged Fort Donelson. The night before, Buckner's three superiors had fled, along with three thousand of the defenders; at dawn Buckner had the responsibility of sending out a messenger carrying a white flag and a letter asking what 'terms of capitulation' Grant would accept.

Grant replied with the sentence that made him famous: "No terms except an unconditional and immediate surrender can be accepted." During the war's inconclusive first year, the North had been waiting to hear those iron words: "unconditional surrender." The nation would know him now as "U. S." (Unconditional Surrender, or United States) Grant. As the day went on, fourteen thousand or more captured Confederates emerged from Fort Donelson. A total of twenty thousand muskets, sixty-five cannon, and a thousand horses also fell into Union hands. The size of the victory became apparent; it was, as Grant wrote Julia during the day, "the largest capture I believe ever made on the continent"—larger than the numbers surrendered by the British at Yorktown.

When it came time for Buckner to board a transport going down the Cumberland River on a route that would carry him into captivity at Cairo, Illinois, Grant accompanied him to the landing. Taking him off to one side, Grant said, "You are separated from your people, and perhaps you need funds. My purse is at your disposal." Buckner declined with thanks, later remarking that they both had in mind the time when Grant was penniless in Manhattan.

Simon Buckner had returned to the Confederate side in a prisoner exchange six months following his surrender of Fort Donelson and had gone on to play an important role in the Southern victory at Chickamauga. Now he was at Mt. McGregor twenty-three years after the fall of Fort Donelson. Having become a widower when his first wife died of tuberculosis in 1857 when he was thirty-four, he was in upstate New York now on his way back to Kentucky from his honeymoon at Niagara Falls with his much younger second wife, who was twenty-eight.

Grant was very pleased to see Buckner, who entered Grant's combination of sick room and office without his bride. He began conversing with Buckner by means of a series of paper slips. "I appreciate your calling very highly," he wrote, and added, "You look very natural, except that your hair has whitened, and you have grown stouter." After a pause during which Buckner apparently spoke, Grant replied on paper, "I am very glad to see you indeed; and allow me to congratulate you. I still read the papers, and saw a full account of your recent marriage." He next wrote, "Is Mrs. Buckner at the house with you? I would be very glad to see Mrs. Buckner, if she can come in and see me as I am now."

The next slip was clearly for the new Mrs. Buckner, Delia Claiborne of Richmond, Kentucky. "I knew your husband long before you did. We were at West Point together, and served together in the Mexican war. I was with him on a visit to the top of Popocatepetl, the highest mountain in North America. Your husband wrote an account of that trip for publication at the time. I have just written my account, which will be published in my forthcoming book."

Before the Buckners left, Grant wrote his old West Point friend, Mexican War comrade, and Civil War opponent something that was close to an essay.

> I have witnessed since my sickness just what I wished to see ever since the war; harmony and good feeling between the sections. I have always contended that if there had been no body left but the soldiers we would have had peace in a year. [Confederate generals] Jubel [sic] Early and [Daniel H.] Hill are the only two that I know of who do not seem to be satisfied on the southern side. We have some on ours who failed to accomplish as much as they wished, or who did not get warmed up to the fight until it was all over, who have not had quite full satisfaction. The great Majority too of those who did not go into the war have long since grown tired of the long controversy.
>
> We may now well look forward to perpetual peace at home, and a national strength that will secure us against any foreign complication. I believe my self that the war was worth all it cost us, fearful as that was.—Since it was over I have visited every state in Europe and a number in the East. I know, as I did not know before, the value of our inheritance.

In what would seem in retrospect an uncanny prediction about his book and his life, on this same day, Friday, July 10, Grant wrote to Douglas: "Buck has brought up [from New York] the last of first vol. in print. In two weeks if they [Buck, Fred, Jesse, Dawson] work hard they can have the second vol. copied ready to go to the printer. I will then feel my work is done."

17

Sunlight and Shadow

O N Saturday, July 11, Grant sat on his porch with Reverend Newman, who was to preach to a congregation of more than two hundred on the porch of the Balmoral the next morning. In the course of their meeting, Grant wrote him on a slip of paper, "I have my book off my mind now. That relieves me of a tax upon my strength which I could not avoid." As had been the case before, Grant was not quite through, but his editorial team led by Fred was tackling the final stage of working on the page proofs of the first volume.

During their meeting, Newman asked Grant to receive communion at his service the next day. There is the possibility that Grant saw that, if he received communion in such a public way, this would cement Newman's ambition to be known as "General Grant's pastor." Perhaps disingenuously, Grant wrote in response: "I would only be too happy to do so if I felt myself fully worthy. I have a feeling in regard to taking the sacriment [sic] that no worse sin can be committed than to take it unworthily. I would prefer therefore not to take it, but to have the funeral services performed when I am gone."

* * *

THE NEXT DAY, Sunday, Grant stayed at the cottage and spent a lot of his diminishing strength in writing a letter to Adam Badeau. His reasons for doing this appear to have been varied. Among other things, Badeau had gone lame since their dispute that ended with Badeau leaving 3 East Sixty-sixth Street in early May. Badeau had also received what Mark Twain called a "foolish letter" from a Judge Albion W. Tourgee of Mayville, New York, proposing that members of the public could buy Grant's book by sending the price of it directly to anyone the Grants named. The book would then be sent straight to the purchaser, those profits to bypass the publisher's sales agents and go to Julia. Badeau swiftly sent this on to Frederick, who shared it with his father.

In any event, Grant saw the communication from Badeau to Frederick as an attempt to profit by getting some good publicity, and to regain the good graces of the Grant family. He began his letter to Badeau with this:

DEAR GENERAL:

Since last night particularly, and for several days before that considerably, I have thought very much about your affairs. It is not possible now that I can be of further assistance to you. My health and other circumstances do not permit it.

Grant then began to list these "other circumstances."

I say since yesterday particularly, &c. My first vol. is now all in print. The last of it was corrected up to be broken in pages yesterday. Fred says that that portion which you had gone over and arranged gave more trouble than all the balance. He changed it entire[ly]. He found also many inaccuracies in it when he came to correct it by the records.

Grant then mentioned another "circumstance."

Before yesterday, I was thinking of your helpless condition without some one with means or influence to help you, and what I had done for you for the last twenty years and could not do for you again if I would.

To be frank with you[,] you are helpless, and filled with a false pride. With $1,500 pr. year you speak of my doctor, my shoemaker, my lawyer &c. &c. as if you owned them and they were beneath you . . . Now General I had been a clerk in a Hardware and leather store, and supported myself and family off of the salary. I felt proud of it too.

Now thoroughly warmed to his task, Grant continued:

Through me you got an appointment on my staff, which was a personal appointment, and from there you got into the regular army which gives you now the little money you have. As a staff officer you did not do me credit while in Washington . . . People remonstrated against your retention in public place. I resisted and retained you. I then sent you as sec. of Legation, and then Consul General, to England . . . On one occasion you were sent to Madrid with very important dispatches, got overcome with liquor and switched off by the wayside and did not turn up in Madrid for some days after you should have been there.

Grant continued with his indictment. "You have managed to get in a broil with every official and every unofficial since Mr. Hayes [President Rutherford B. Hayes] went out of office. With publishers you have had disputes. With the departments of government it is the same thing. You now have two or three suits against the government which, if you win the lawyers will get the bulk of; if you loose [sic] they have your ready cash already and you will probably loose [sic] the $1,500 which you are still receiving."

Grant started in on his summation.

My advice to you now General is that you look upon yourself for a while as you have heretofore looked upon others. Take up your pen and go to work earnestly. Regard yourself as belonging to the publisher who pays for your work, for the time being, and not upon him being "my publisher."

. . . In concluding it is due to myself to say that the more I have thought of what took place just before you left my house the more strongly convinced I become that your nature is not of that unselfish kind I had supposed. I am also satisfied that my book would never have been finished as "my book" if you had been permitted to continue in the capacity you now seem disposed to think you were in. I however never regarded you in any such capacity.

Yours Truly

U. S. GRANT

Below this, Grant wrote: "Note. I do not want this mailed but at your leisure copied and retained so that if advisable it can be sent." Just what Grant had in mind by writing this uncharacteristic letter and then not sending it never became clear. Perhaps he simply wanted to get something off his chest.

Nor is there any suggestion that he saw an irony in the fact that he, a man who had to resign from the army for being drunk while paying off troops on a payday should criticize Badeau for a different form of being drunk while on duty. And his remark about being proud of his prewar job in his father's leather goods store in Galena, Illinois, does not square with a neighboring store owner's comment. The man remembered that "Grant was a very poor businessman, and never liked to wait on customers . . . [He] would go behind the counter very reluctantly, and drag down whatever was wanted; but hardly ever knew the price of it, and, in nine cases out of ten, he charged either too much or too little."

~ II ~

A strange mood settled upon the Grant cottage. Here was Grant, still making changes on Volume Two, with everyone certain that his life was coming to an end, but no one sure when that would be. The Grant and Douglas children continued to laugh as they splashed in the pond near Willett's tent. A clergyman staying at the Balmoral looked down the slope to where Grant sat writing in his wicker armchair on his cottage porch and said that the sight of Grant at work while in pain was the finest sermon at which he had ever been present.

On Thursday, July 16, in a note to Dr. Douglas, Grant wrote, "There never was one more willing to go than I am." Even now, while still working on Volume Two, he said, "There is nothing more I should do to it now, and therefore I am not likely to be more ready to go than at this moment."

In fact, what Grant was "doing to it now" was to rise to heights of eloquence and perception in its final pages. He was saying good-bye to his life and his era and looking forward to the age that was to come. "It is probably well," he wrote, "that we had the war when we did. We are better off now than we would have been without it, and have made more rapid progress than we otherwise should have made." In the moral balance, Grant wrote, "We must conclude, therefore, that wars are not always evils unmixed with good." Grant also recognized the change that the war had brought in the European view of America. He was speaking of national spirit when he said, " . . . our republican institutions were regarded as experiments . . . monarchical Europe generally believed that our republic was a rope of sand that would part the moment the slightest strain was brought upon it."

Not so, Grant told his fellow Americans. The United States "has shown itself capable of dealing with one of the greatest wars ever made, and our people have proven themselves to be the most formidable in war of any nationality." But as for the time ahead, "To maintain peace in the future it is necessary to be prepared for war . . . growing as we are in population, wealth, and military power, we may become the envy of nations which led us in all these particulars only a few years ago; and unless we are prepared for it we may be in danger of a combined movement being made some day to crush us out."

For a general whose campaigns on land would be studied for generations, Grant showed a remarkable appreciation for naval power.

> We should have a good navy, and our sea-coast defences should be put in the finest possible condition. Neither of these cost much when it is considered where the money goes, and what we get in return. Money expended on a fine navy, not only adds to our security and tends to prevent war in the future, but is very material aid to our commerce with foreign nations in the meantime. Money spent upon sea-coast defences is spent among our own people, and all goes back again among the people. The work accomplished, too, like that of the navy, gives a feeling of security.

Abraham Lincoln, whose immortal Second Inaugural Address gave the nation "With malice toward none, with charity for all," would have recognized the spirit of the torch being passed that emanates from the last two pages of Grant's book. Twenty years after the man who grew up in a log cabin was murdered, here were the words of the tanner's son as he completed the work that his wife called "a labor of love."

I feel that we are on the eve of a new era, when there is to be a great harmony between the Federal and Confederate. I cannot stay to be a living witness to the correctness of this prophecy; but I feel within me that it is to be so. The universally kind feeling expressed for me at a time when it was supposed that each day would prove my last, seemed to me to be the beginning of the answer to "Let us have peace."

~III~

AS THIS MARCH through summer continued at Mt. McGregor, the Grant family and the press continued to look forward to the next day, and the next. On Saturday, July 18, a correspondent reported that Dr. Shrady recommended that Grant should "read [Oliver Wendell Holmes's] 'The Autocrat of the Breakfast Table,' which Mrs. Grant promptly ordered." The newspaper story continued, "His mind needs nourishment as much as his body, the doctor thinks, and as the idea of writing has not developed beyond yesterday's suggestion the remedy of reading will be applied as soon as the book comes."

The suggestion referred to had just come in from the *Century*, which was proposing that Grant write a short article on the subject of presidential term limits—an issue not to be decided until well into the twentieth century.

The chronology of events suggests that this time Grant was truly through with his book. Mark Twain was soon to write of July 20, "One day he put aside his pencil and said there was nothing more to do." Grant did more than that. He placed the pencil which he had gripped for so many hours atop a bureau in the room in which he had worked and slept. Then he slipped into the pocket of the coat in which he expected to be buried the letter he wanted Julia to read after his death, and the ring she had given him, and the locks of her and Buck's hair.

The moment marked the end of an amazing effort. He had begun writing his *Memoirs* at the beginning of the previous September and was ending his work almost exactly a year later. The printed two-volume book would contain 1,215 pages of text and 291,000 words. This included a seventy-seven-page appendix consisting of Grant's report written at the end of the war concerning his command of the "Armies of the United States" during 1864 and 1865. In an added instance of symmetry, Grant had submitted that report to Secretary of War Stanton on July 22, 1865—just two days short of twenty years before this day he finished the *Memoirs*. Subtracting those seventy-seven pages, written when he was in good health, in the past year he had written an average of seven hundred and fifty words every painful day.

It may have been that this news that Grant had finally finished working on his book reached the *Century*, and that Associate Editor Johnson, who had bid Grant what he thought was a final farewell ten days before, saw this chance to get Grant to write his thoughts on a third successive presidential term as an opportunity for a coup—the last piece Grant would write. Apparently aware that Frederick was still working on some part of the book, Grant wrote him this.

> FRED. If you feel the least unwell do not work until you feel like it. Your services are to[o] important now to have you break down. I woke up a little while ago dreaming that Ida [Fred's wife] was crying and I supposed it was because you were suddenly taken seriously ill. But this was caused by your saying before you went to sleep that you felt badly and would go and take a walk. Then too your Ma told me that you were feeling badly.

There were in fact extraordinary pressures on Fred Grant. In addition to his involvement with his father's daily care, he was handling the subject of where his father was to be buried. Offers were coming in from West Point, Washington, St. Louis, Galena, Illinois, and Manhattan. Fred had already begun dealing with the officials of these places. At just this time, Philip Sheridan, commanding general of the United States Army, was riding around Washington with Secretary of the Interior Lucius Q. C. Lamar, looking at various government lands that would be suitable burial sites. Their preference was for the Soldiers' Home, a peaceful wooded tract of 270 acres three miles northwest of the White House that had served as a summer retreat for Lincoln and his family during the war. In St. Louis, Sherman continued to hope that city would be chosen, but he had heard nothing from Fred and was ready to take a train that would go to Chicago and then on to New York.

After consulting with Fred, Julia would reach the decision that the best place was one of three offered by New York City—neither one of two large pieces of land in Central Park, which could never be a sanctuary of peaceful rest, but a strip of city land on a cliff high above the Hudson River known as Riverside Park, where a temporary tomb could be built quickly.

During these days, Fred's little daughter, Julia Grant, realized that something was going wrong.

I became conscious one day that the grown-ups on the balcony near which I was playing were worried . . . evidently the speakers were worried about my grandfather; he had ended his book, and was not so well as before. It was true that he had not come out of doors that day, nor dressed as usual. Soon—it may have been a day or two later, or three—my mother came out onto the balcony and called us children. "Quick, papa wants you to come and see dear grandpapa," she said. We joined her, and she took us into the room where my grandfather was more or less reclining in his great chair . . .

My mother came behind me. "Kiss grandpapa," she said, but I could not reach over and up to his cheek. I noticed once more how beautiful his hand was. I looked at my father, who nodded, and who put his arm around me. Then I stood for a moment or two, steadied by his arm, when my mother whispered, "We must go now." With a lump in my throat I leaned down and kissed the beautiful hand, and was led out of the room.

~ I V ~

At four in the afternoon of Monday, July 20—the day he finished his book—Grant wrote to Douglas, "What do you think of my taking the bath wagon and going down to overlook the south view?" Douglas looked him over, found his pulse normal and his color good, and agreed. Off they went to the Eastern Outlook, the place Grant had gone to once, on June 16, thirty-seven days before, on his first full day at Mt. McGregor. Harrison Terrell was pulling the Bath chair, and Douglas, Fred, and others were pushing it by means of the bar bolted across its back. By the time Grant reached this site, he was pale, clearly exhausted, and unable to take in the magnificent view. Dr. Douglas allowed Harrison Terrell a few minutes to rest before returning to the cottage. Having decided to take a route back that they thought would be a shortcut, the group found that this road actually stopped at a platform and some tracks used by the railway for storing tons of coal, and that the road continued on the other side of this obstacle. Grant got out of the Bath chair; using his cane, he struggled around the edges of this irregular pile, occasionally having to go up and down little valleys of coal, and fell back into the chair when it was brought around to the other side. In this state of exhaustion, Grant once again proved himself the gentleman;

in notes that Douglas made of what was becoming a crisis, he wrote, "On the way back, we crossed under the covered way which led to the hotel. Just as we crossed the plank path of this covered way, we met some ladies coming from the hotel, who saluted [greeted] the General. He responded by lifting his hat."

Noticing that Grant "was very pale," Douglas and the others took him around to the side of the cottage, "where the steps were few." With the assistance of Fred and the male nurse Henry Mc-Sweeny, "he entered his own room, sank immediately into his chair, from which he did not again stir that night."

The next morning, Douglas felt that Grant had "had eight hours of at least restful repose." While Grant appeared to be continuing to doze through the rest of the morning, Douglas was eating lunch at the hotel when the family sent him word that Grant appeared to be increasingly weak and confused. By evening of a day when the temperature reached a stifling 85 degrees, the decision was made to move Grant into the larger and cooler living room that lay beyond his combination of office and sick room. Then or soon thereafter, the hotel sent down an ingeniously designed piece of furniture, a long desk that could be opened up and expanded into a bed. This was placed in a corner of the room, where a framed print of Abraham Lincoln hung directly above where Grant, who was still in one of his armchairs, could lie on his back with his head propped up by a pillow. Just to the left of the picture of Lincoln was one of Grant himself. A few feet beyond the foot of the bed was a window, kept open and with a lace curtain moving slightly in whatever night breezes there were.

Rev. Newman's account of that night of Tuesday, July 21, included this: "He was carried into the drawing room & death seemed to seize him. We gathered around him & I prayed for him. At 9 P.M. he revived & wrote three messages to his family, which surprized us." Dr. Douglas examined Grant, and found that his temperature was higher, with his pulse fundamentally out of control and reading between 100 and 120. In his notes, Rev. Newman continued, "At 11 P.M. he sent us word—'There's no earthly reason for you to sit up.'"

At one on the morning of Tuesday, July 22, Dr. Douglas gave an impromptu medical bulletin to reporters who were clustered around the cottage in the night. The man from the *New York Tribune* telegraphed a story to New York from the Balmoral, stating in part that Douglas "said that the patient was in critical condition and he would hazard no prediction, even of the night." During these hours Douglas sent word to Dr. Shrady and another physician, the able surgeon Dr. H. B. Sands, to come as quickly as possible, and they, along with Buck and his wife, Fanny, made plans to arrive at three the next afternoon on a special train. Fred "gave orders that all manuscripts and literary effects at the cottage office should be at once packed up and made safe, as no more work on the General's memoirs would probably be done there."

In New York, readers of the *Times* started the day looking at a headline that pronounced, DEATH COMING VERY NEAR. The *World* did not say that, but printed its front page with a black border. Down in Saratoga Springs, the members of the GAR post loaded up their dress uniforms and equipment, including several tents, in preparation to serve as a guard of honor at the Grant cottage. One of those veterans would be carrying a sword that he wore at the funerals of Lincoln, Admiral Farragut, and President Garfield.

At noon, the boxlike porcelain clock sitting on the mantel in the big parlor began striking. When it had finished, Grant wrote a note to Fred: "Fix the clock right. It only struck eleven."

As planned, doctors Shrady and Sands arrived, along with Buck and his wife. The doctors went up to the hotel to register; when Buck went in to see his father, Douglas remembered that Grant greeted him "with an intelligent look, and a slight movement of the lips, as if he wanted to speak." All the adults in the family were now present; Douglas added that when Shrady and Sands came in, they "saw that professional aid was no longer of any avail." Slipping in and out of his lucid state, Grant realized that he was surrounded by those dearest to him, and that the mood was one of quiet grief. His reaction was this. "He said, in little above a whisper, yet quite distinctly: 'I don't want anybody to feel distressed on my account.'"

Douglas turned his patient over to Shrady and Sands; exhausted himself, he went up to the hotel to rest.

At 7 P.M., while I was seated at the dinner table at the hotel, Harrison came for me, saying that the General had suddenly become weaker. I immediately hastened to the cottage, and found that the General had been transferred from the chair . . . to the bed, which had hastily been prepared for him, and was then lying on his back, a position I had not seen him occupy at any time during his sickness.

Observing that Grant's "pulse was much weaker and faster," Douglas gave him a "hypodermic of brandy," which "in ten minutes I again repeated." In a consultation with Shrady and Sands, "we all recognized that the end was very near. Every one about the cottage remained up, expecting the end at any moment."

Grant being Grant, the end was not "very near." Douglas kept making his observations. "As the hours grew on, the symptoms of dissolution grew. The respiration quickened, the pulse became small and very frequent, the respiration shallower and quicker, the pulse too frequent to be counted. . . . The action of the heart ran up from 80 rapidly to 100, and by degrees higher, until it could not be counted; his respiration from 20 a minute to 30 and 40 and even 60."

Fred asked his father if he were in pain. Quite audibly, Grant said, "No," but his head slumped to one side. Standing next to the bed, Fred put his arm under a pillow, and kept that under his father's head. When Fred asked his father if he wanted anything,

Grant replied, "Water." The nurse Henry McSweeny placed a wet towel against his mouth.

This vigil went on past midnight. Julia sat at her husband's side, mopping his brow, holding his hand, constantly gazing into his face. Rev. Newman said of the scene, "Mrs. Grant has been sitting with the General. When she speaks to him he opens his eyes. She says little and bears up wonderfully." The room remained silent. The Grants were together: Grant, Julia, their three sons and their wives, their daughter, Nellie, who would look down into her father's face and receive a ghostly smile of recognition. Also there were Harrison Tyrrell, Henry McSweeny, and the three doctors. At some time after midnight, Douglas told everyone to go to their rooms, in the cottage or at the hotel. Heading up to the hotel himself, he left Mc-Sweeny with the unconscious Grant.

~ V ~

"At sunrise," Douglas wrote, "I walked up to the brow of the hill in front of the hotel, just as the first rays of the new day shot over the mountains in the East, and illuminated the valley upon which the General had looked when he took the [Bath chair] ride only three days before. After standing there a few moments, looking at the sunrise, and breathing in the pure and delicious air of the early morning, I returned to the cottage . . ." He found Grant in extremis.

> Going to the bedside, I found . . . the rhythm of the heart had been so rapid and irregular that the pulse could not be counted, the impulse too had become so weak that venous stagnation had taken place; the blue discoloration about the nails presaging approaching dissolution . . . About seven, Dr. Sands having come down from the hotel, Dr. Shrady and myself met him upon the piazza, and while we were then discussing the situation, Henry

came hurriedly out from the parlor, and said that a sudden change had come over the General's features; he thought he was dying.

I immediately went in, and confirmed this opinion by my own observations, and sent Henry at once to summon such members of the family as were temporarily absent.

Little Julia saw part of what happened next. When her French nurse, Louise, dressed her and her younger brother, Ulysses, to go up to the hotel for breakfast early the next morning, "she told us how 'le general' had had a bad night . . . so we must creep out of the house without any noise, as now 'le general' was sleeping well, and so were the others." Then this occurred:

As we opened our nursery door and stepped into the hall Harrison rushed across it from my parents to my grandmother's door and knocked there, having left the first door thrown wide open . . . I saw my father throw on his jacket—probably he had been asleep in shirt and trousers, ready for any emergency . . . He rushed out of his bedroom and passed us without seeing us at all, taking the staircase faster than I could imagine his doing. My mother was moving about rapidly, putting on her things, also, and across the hall from grandmamma came a sob, and "I'm coming," in reply to Harrison's quick knock . . .

We children were taken over to the hotel. I was put in my chair and told as usual to eat all the things before me; but I couldn't. I was too frightened by what I had heard.

Of events down at the cottage, a reporter would soon write, "All eyes were intent on the General." On July 10, Grant had told Douglas that if he could have two more weeks, "I will then feel my work is done." After ten days of those two weeks elapsed, on July 20 he had put away his pencil; now, on Thursday, July 23, with thirteen days of the two weeks he had wished for gone, he lay there, his work done. Describing the condition of the man lying in the cottage—author, general, president, loving family man—the reporter continued:

> His breathing had become soft, though quick . . . His bared throat quivered with the quickened breath. The outer air, gently moving, swayed the curtains at an east window. Into the crevice crept a white ray from the sun. It reached across the room like a rod and lighted a picture of Lincoln over the deathbed. The sun did not touch the companion picture, which was of the General . . . [He] made no motion. Only the fluttering throat, white as his sick robe, showed that life remained. The face was one of peace . . . The moments passed in silence. Mrs. Grant still held the General's hand. The Colonel still stroked his brow.
>
> The light on the portrait of Lincoln was still sinking; presently the General opened his eyes and glanced about him, looking into the faces of all. The glance lingered as it met the tender gaze of his companion. A startled, wavering motion at the throat, a few quiet gasps, a sigh, and the appearance of falling into a gentle sleep followed. The eyes of affection were still upon him. He lay without a motion. At that instant the window curtain swayed back in place, shutting out the sunbeam.

Ulysses S. Grant was dead. The end of his life had been so quiet and graceful that, Dr. Douglas said, "to be sure it had terminated, we waited a minute. Then looking at my watch, I found it was precisely eight."

The account in the *New York Times* described the minutes just after Grant's death. "Mrs. Grant could not believe it until the Colonel, realizing the truth, kneeled at the bedside clasping his father's hand. Then she buried her face in her handkerchief. There was not a sound in the room, no sobbing, no unrestrained show of grief. The example set by him who had gone so quietly kept grief in check at that moment."

As everyone began to disperse to their rooms, Colonel Frederick Grant walked over to the clock on the mantel, whose face gave the time as 8:08. He stopped the clock. A hundred and twenty-five years later, its hands remained fixed at that time.

* * *

UP AT THE HOTEL, granddaughter Julia remembered, "Breakfast dragged; then one of those serving it suddenly said: 'It is all over there at the cottage.'"

When her nurse, Louise, replied that was not so, the waiter answered, "Yes, yes, a telegram has just been brought over to forward from the hotel office, and the messenger said that General Grant had just died."

That telegram was the bulletin to the world: six minutes after Fred Grant stopped the hands of the clock at the cottage, the *New York Times* had the news on a blackboard in its window in Manhattan. By nine every flag in New York City was at half-mast, and by four in the afternoon Bloomingdale's department store had sold over six miles of black crepe.

And at the breakfast table at the Balmoral, little Julia Grant experienced this: "I felt stunned, could not swallow another mouthful and would have cried out there and then, had it not been that Nurse Louise, with good-hearted tact, undid the small brother's bib and said: 'Come.'" Within minutes, Julia was walking in the woods by herself.

I think this was the first time in my life I had felt heavy with sorrow . . . It was not just a relative who had passed out of my small world, but a friend and comrade from whom I had always had both understanding and sympathy, together with a strong, gentle, protective affection, which I was too young to analyze yet old enough to appreciate deeply.

Julia began to cry. Then, "The storm passed. I dried my eyes . . . I seemed without resources for usefulness. Then I remembered [that] one made wreaths for dead people . . . Perhaps I could make a wreath. Often we had done so in play, with nurse's help." Looking about her, she picked some flat oak leaves. In half an hour she had fashioned a wreath of broad, shining leaves.

The next thing was to get it to my grandfather. Once on the balcony I went and looked in the window of the death-chamber . . . in the centre of the room stood a coffin, a thing I had never seen before; and moving about, two men, strangers to me, were setting out a few chairs, probably for use at the service soon to be held. I was recognized at once by the elder of the two men, who came to the door and inquired what I wanted.

"I've brought grandpapa a wreath . . ." I replied. He said, after a little hesitation: "Sure, miss, and your papa is just after going up and getting a little sleep, and I wouldn't disturb him if I was you. Suppose you give me the wreath to lay on the general. It's a mighty fine wreath: and I think there's no harm your coming in to help me yourself." In I went with the undertaker [who later recorded that Grant's corpse weighed less than 100 pounds], and he laid the wreath carefully in a circle on the casket. Then he left me standing there, gazing down at the familiar face under the glass, while he went off about his business of tidying up. It seemed heartbreaking that my grandfather should be so still and so dead.

Julia was not sure of how others might react to her little wreath, but came to this conclusion: "However, later, I was very proud, because with carloads of flowers coming in by every train, and florists bringing special great set pieces which filled the house with their beauty and fragrance, my wreath was the only one on the casket." When the leaves began to curl and the wreath started to fade, her father put her mind to rest, saying, "Never mind, pet, my little girl's wreath is going to be varnished so it will keep, and then it shall be buried with grandpapa. I know he would have liked to keep it with him always."

That cheered Julia. "I was glad to have it so. Somehow my deepest sentiment had gone into the little, silly contribution to the offerings brought him."

Upon her grandfather's death, her grandmother had retreated upstairs; she remained there day after day, comforted by her daughter and daughters-in-law and announcing that she would not attend any public funeral services. Baskets of telegrams and letters were carried down to the cottage from the hotel, and Fred read them to his mother. Julia Grant soon received Cleveland's representative, the army's adjutant-general, Brigadier Richard C. Drum. He handed her President Grover Cleveland's message of condolence and told her that the government stood ready to do for her and her family anything that they wanted to have done.

Julia remained fully in touch with what she knew the wishes of her Ulyss would be. When she learned that President Cleveland had named a number of former Union generals and wartime federal officials, led by Sherman, as honorary pallbearers, Julia asked that Confederate generals Simon Buckner and Robert E. Lee's West Point classmate Joseph E. Johnston be added to the list.

~ VI ~

Things went into motion everywhere. In Washington, hundreds of messages from the world's leaders, including Queen Victoria and the Chinese viceroy Li Hung-chang, poured in to the office of the nation's Chief of Protocol at the State Department. In England, planning began for a memorial service in Westminster Abbey, to be attended by notables including William Gladstone, who had been prime minister twice and would soon hold that office for the third of five times. Grant's friend the Mexican envoy Matias Romero arrived at Mt. McGregor the day after his death. Mark Twain, two hundred miles away at his Quarry Farm on a hill above Elmira, New York, learned of Grant's death two hours after it occurred. He wrote in his notebook, "I think his book kept him alive several months. He was a very great man and superlatively good." Referring to the tremendous volume of telegrams the news of Grant's death was generating, the *New York Tribune* put out this statement: "Such a flood of world-wide sympathy has probably never before been told by the electric spark to suffering hearts, and the family is profoundly grateful."

Tributes came from the South as well as the North: the legislatures of former Confederate states passed resolutions paying tribute to Grant, and Confederate general T. J. Churchill said of a "Grant memorial meeting" to be held in Atlanta, "I think it is the especial duty of every ex-Confederate to participate in those ceremonies on account of the terms accorded to Gen. Lee and his army at Appomattox. General Grant was a great soldier and deserves this last compliment at our hands." The Charleston *News and Courier* told its readers this:

> . . . had his life ended but a few years since, the mourning for the great leader would have been more or less sectional in its manifestations. Dying as he now dies, the grief is as widespread as the Union, and the sorrow is as National as his fame . . . The good will of all, whether heretofore friends or not, was his in his agony and will abide with his name forever.

* * *

THE DAY AFTER Grant's death, the *New York Times* appeared with a remarkable sixty-eight-page obituary. Some of it had been in preparation for months, but in the past twenty hours the paper's reporters had made several swift visits to figures of importance in Grant's life. One of them found Confederate general James Longstreet, Julia's cousin who had been best man at their wedding, in the garden at his house three miles from Gainesville, Georgia. The reporter's story filed from Gainesville began with, "'He was the truest as well as the bravest man who ever lived,' was the remark made by Gen. James Longstreet when he recovered today from the emotion caused by the sad news of Gen. Grant's death."

Longstreet was quoted as adding, "Grant was a modest man, a simple man, a man believing in the honesty of his fellows, true to his friends, faithful to traditions, and of great personal honor. When the United States District Court in Richmond was about to indict Gen. Lee and myself for treason, Gen. Grant interposed and stopped the wholesale indictments of ex-Confederate officers which would have followed."

During the course of the interview, Longstreet mentioned both Grant's idealism and his practical side. He told the reporter that when Grant as president had put his name forward for the post of Surveyor of the Port of New Orleans, a move that encountered opposition in the Senate, Grant had reassured him about his nomination. According to Longstreet, Grant said at the time, "Give yourself no uneasiness about that. The Senators have as many favors to ask of me as I have of them, and I will see that you are confirmed." Longstreet summed up his reaction to the death of his friend whom he called "the soul of honor," saying that he "was the highest type of manhood America has produced."

* * *

HAVING ARRIVED in Manhattan from St. Louis, Sherman learned that it would be only a few days before Grant's body would be transported to be viewed by crowds in Albany, and then taken on to lie in state at New York's City Hall, before what would be an enormous funeral procession to the temporary tomb in Riverside Park. He headed for Mt. McGregor and later wrote this to Julia:

> May you continue for many years to receive tokens of love and affection and then rest at that majestic spot on the Banks of the Hudson made sacred by the presence of the mortal part of the Great and Good General, to whom you were as true as the needle to the thread, in poverty and in health, in adversity as in exaltation.

~VII~

At Mt. McGregor, the shock wore off. Grant's body remained at the cottage; the obvious change was the presence of two large military tents. They housed two Grand Army of the Republic units, each with attached cooking facilities. The first to arrive had been the Wheeler Post from Saratoga: twenty years before, one of its now middle-aged members, H. M. Knight, had assisted in carrying the mortally wounded Abraham Lincoln from Ford's Theater to the nearby house in which he died.

These two companies, sent as a guard of honor, soon proved to be necessary for protecting the cottage. The American passion for collecting souvenirs was on display. Most guests from the hotel and people who came up on the train from Saratoga contented themselves with gazing at the cottage, but a good number started chipping off pieces of its shingles. When it was announced that a special open-sided observation car would be used to take Grant's remains down to Saratoga, with the coffin in full view, lady guests at the hotel began making black rosettes and sashes of black bunting to decorate the train. *Leslie's Illustrated* reported that "Every speck of black cloth which was trimmed off [in the making of] these rosettes was eagerly picked up by the visitors and carried off."

Real violence struck the long funeral car itself. Although guarded by two soldiers while it stood in a siding at Mt. McGregor, during the night vandals managed to cut off some of its permanent ornamentation and a part of a side of the car. The next morning it was taken down to Saratoga and put under heavier guard.

* * *

UNTIL WEDNESDAY, July 29, Grant's body rested in a temporary coffin in the room in which he died, and Julia remained in her room upstairs. On that day the permanent coffin arrived. Made of polished oak and lined with copper, it was covered with dark purple velvet. Silver handles ran the length of the coffin, and a gold nameplate read, "U. S. Grant." The body was transferred to it from the temporary coffin, and Harrison Terrell and Henry McSweeny helped the undertakers. They dressed Grant in a black broadcloth suit, with a white shirt that had a black silk scarf knotted as a bow around its neck. Fred slipped around his father's shrunken finger the ring Julia had given him years before.

The next morning Fred brought Julia down from her room. The GAR guards posted at attention around Grant's coffin withdrew, and Julia had her last close look at her Ulyss. Neither she nor Fred ever spoke of that moment of parting.

That night of July 30th, a violent mountain thunderstorm struck, flashing through the evening sky the way it had the day that Grant had arrived at Mt. McGregor. A bolt of lightning struck the hotel, blazing down the wires to the station and to the cottage. In the nursery room, a lot of plaster was knocked from the ceiling, and a charred hole made in the floor. Little Julia's younger brother, four-year-old Ulysses S. Grant III, was walking across the floor when the thunderbolt hit. He remained unharmed, but the French nurse, Louise, went into hysterics, and could not be calmed for hours. Three soldiers were also shocked and burned. The next morning's light revealed the reason for the near-fatal damage. One more souvenir hunter had cut off part of the lightning rod on the back of the cottage, allowing the bolt to pass right through.

During the last days of July, Colonel Roger Jones of the Regular Army arrived at Mt. McGregor, sent there by his superior Major General Winfield Scott Hancock, who was then in command at Governor's Island in New York Harbor. President Cleveland had named Hancock as the project officer for the government's participation in all the funeral arrangements. Hancock and his staff would arrive at Mt. McGregor on Monday, August 3, and the first of the funeral services for Grant was to be held at the cottage at ten the following morning.

A classmate of Grant's at West Point, Hancock was eager to honor his Civil War commander. Receiving reports from Colonel Jones, Hancock began sending small Regular Army contingents, including artillery batteries, to Mt. McGregor, to augment the GAR units already there.

Hancock, an imposing man with a black handlebar moustache, knew that he would be leading the gigantic funeral parade in Manhattan, but he intended to make his and the army's presence felt at Mt. McGregor as well. When Hancock and his staff arrived on the morning of Monday, August 3rd, his deputy Colonel Roger Jones led him and his staff up to the cottage. Julia had come downstairs; her son presented the visiting officers, including General Rufus Ingalls, who had been Grant's roommate at West Point.

That evening, the family discussed with Julia their hope that she would leave Mt. McGregor the next day after the funeral service and accompany them to New York City. All of them knew that there would be sixty thousand participants in the six-mile long parade, and a million or more spectators, but Julia had a better sense of what it would be like for her to ride in a carriage through all that. She told them that "what she would see there could only wound her sorrow, while it would have no compensating comfort." It was agreed that she would stay on for a time at Mt. McGregor, accompanied by Reverend Newman's wife.

At nine thirty the next morning the cottage was opened to visitors, who passed through the parlor, gazing at Grant in his coffin. Julia and her family sat in chairs in a corner. Rev. Newman seated a group of clergymen in chairs in front of the eastern porch, near where Grant had read his newspapers and written many pages of his book. Hancock's deputy Colonel Jones led them past two companies of regulars, lined up at attention, to the side porch, where Grant's son Fred had chairs placed for them. Behind them were seated General Sherman, General Horace Porter, Mexico's Minister Matias Romero, and several members of the combined Regular Army–GAR guard of honor.

At ten, the Reverend Dr. Benjamin L. Agnew of Philadelphia read the Ninetieth Psalm—"A thousand years in thy sight are but as yesterday"—followed by a prayer led by the Methodist Episcopal bishop W. L. Harris of New York. After the congregation recited the Lord's Prayer, a small group of singers drawn from GAR posts in Boston, Brooklyn, and Manhattan came forward on the porch. Led by Comrade Henry Camp of Brooklyn's Ulysses S. Grant GAR post, they led everyone in singing the hymn, "My Faith Looks Up to Thee."

Then it was Rev. Newman's turn. For an hour and twenty-five minutes, he read from a manuscript on the text, "Well done, thy

good and faithful servant, enter thou into the joy of thy Lord."
Other than praising Grant in every possible way, he saved for the
last yet one more effort to claim that he had converted Grant to active spiritual life. Mark Twain, who was already on record as saying
that Newman's stories of leading Grant in private prayer were "rot,"
commented that "Colonel Fred Grant told me that his father . . .
was *not* a praying man." Twain added that "most of Newman's daily
reports originated in his own imagination." Nonetheless, preaching
for an hour and a half near the body of Ulysses S. Grant, who had
said that he did not care how much praying went on at 3 East Sixty-
sixth Street as long as it kept Julia happy, Newman invoked an image
of a man of mute devotion. He concluded with this: "More than all
things else, he was taciturn touching his religious faith and experience. The keenest, closest, broadest of all observers, he was the most
silent of men. He loved within himself." After that, to the mourn-
ful sounds of a trumpet dirge and the booming of the twenty-one-
gun salute honoring a president, a group of GAR pallbearers carried
their old commander down to the observation car. The family and
some of the honored guests boarded passenger cars behind it, heading down the slope to Saratoga, where the coffin was transferred to
a train for Albany.

Good-bye, Ulyss.
And Thank You.

As the funeral train made its way to Albany for the brief public viewing of Grant's body there on Wednesday, August 5th, preparations in Manhattan accelerated for the massive final tributes to be paid him there on Saturday the 8th. At the site selected for the temporary tomb on the cliffs above the Hudson River, New York's city architect J. Wrey Mould had sketched out its plan in twenty minutes. It was a brick vault with a semicircular roof, in appearance similar to powder magazines at the forts of the day. At its entrance stood a gate with vertical bars, under an arch of bluestone with a metalwork "G" in its center. Inside were two blocks of marble, side by side, with two steel beams running between them. Grant's coffin would be placed across them; when Julia died seventeen years later, a widow who had become wealthy from the sales of her husband's *Personal Memoirs*, she would lie beside him in the massive Grant's Tomb the next generation would know. As the masons worked with what should have been an ample supply of bricks, they sold some of them off as souvenirs, and visitors to the site carried off other bricks. Carpenters built wooden stands covering half an acre to be occupied by guests of honor.

* * *

THE PLANNING for the parade required that several thousand carriages be used. The military escort commander had commandeered every horse and every carriage available from the stables of Manhattan. When the need for additional horses and carriages was announced, many well-off citizens volunteered the services of their horses, carriages, and coachmen. General Henry Shaler of the New York Militia had the massive task of organizing many details of the line of march. In what could be likened to a feat of military choreography, Shaler had come up with the solution of how to feed more than forty thousand troops into the line of march. From City Hall up to Thirty-sixth Street, there were fifty side streets on the east and west sides of Broadway. As General Hancock passed each street, the unit waiting there would turn into the line of march, followed by the troops that would emerge from the next street to the north. When the last of these regiments swung into place, the enormous column would proceed the miles up to Riverside Park, marching in step to the music of a total of two hundred bands and fife and drum corps.

One constituency required special care. In the midst of what would be in a sense a celebration of the Union victory twenty years before, there would be many wounded veterans, some missing limbs, in a visible and moving reminder of the cost of that war. Shaler had their carriages ready to be placed in an area southeast and west of City Hall, with doctors and nurses ready to attend them. They would be part of eighteen thousand members of the GAR; every post in the nation was to be represented, and they would be led on horseback by the flamboyant Major General Dan Sickles, who lost a leg in the Peach Orchard at Gettysburg.

~ II ~

On Thursday, August 6th, Grant's funeral train left Albany and headed down the Hudson on the final leg of its trip to Manhattan. Going up to Mt. McGregor Grant's train had traveled on the east side of the Hudson, but now, coming down on the west bank, directly in front of West Point, the funeral train slowed as it passed beneath the walls of the academy. The Corps of Cadets, all wearing black armbands on their uniforms, was turned out alongside the track at attention. As the car bearing Grant's body slowly rolled by, the Corps brought their weapons to "Present Arms." The cadet who gave that order was First Captain John J. Pershing, who would command the American Expeditionary Force when it fought the Germans in France during the First World War. Soon after the train passed, lightning, high winds, and lashing rain slammed down on the academy from Storm King Mountain.

* * *

ON FRIDAY, the day before the parade, young Julia Grant looked out the windows of the Fifth Avenue Hotel, where she and most of her family were staying. "I remember vast crowds of men's hatless heads," she recalled, "and of women in black . . . Clothes, all black, were brought in, and each member of our party bought something to complete [our funeral] wardrobes."

On this day before the funeral, the Governor's Room at New York's City Hall where Grant's body lay in an open coffin was opened at 8 a.m., and in the next seventeen hours a quarter of a million people filed past in respectful silence. Inside and outside City Hall, which was draped in black, three hundred and twenty policemen kept the endless lines moving. Every sort of citizen came through the line: manual laborers in overalls on their way to construction jobs, students, women in threadbare dresses, other women wearing "Grant" medallions sold by Bloomingdale's, and parents and grand-parents bringing children who could later say they were there. The *New York Times* caught the spirit of the day.

> The outward manifestations of common sorrow are by no means confined to the costly decorations of the houses of the rich and to the abundance of material festooned and draped with all the care. In the narrow streets and the tall crowded buildings where the poor make their homes the sign of grief is on nearly every door post. In many cases it is nothing but a narrow strip of cheap black cambric fluttering in the breeze from the topmost story of some tenement house or a small flag bordered with a piece of folded crepe from a wornout bonnet.

Looking forward to the next day, the railroads that serviced Manhattan—the Pennsylvania, the Central, the New Haven, and the Harlem River Lines—were planning on crowds so large that every train coming into the city would have to be pulled by two lo-comotives. The elevated trains prepared to carry six hundred thou-sand passengers. The ferries from Hoboken and Jersey City, which would be carrying people from Philadelphia, Washington, and be-yond, would be assisted by extra police officers from Jersey City. Along the march route, owners of warehouses had moved obsta-cles away from their big windows so spectators could look down on the parade.

At one in the morning of this day of the funeral, Regular Army soldiers and GAR veterans at City Hall closed Grant's coffin for the last time, sealing within it the ring Julia had given her Ulyss so long ago. They draped the American flag over the coffin. Until later in the day, Grant's body would remain in the custody of William Murry, New York City's Superintendent of Public Works.

During the hours after midnight, lower Manhattan took on a dreamlike appearance. Its streets and buildings were bathed in moonlight. Ferries began arriving at Battery Park, disembarking soldiers from Governor's Island. The ghostly grey walls echoed to the sounds of men marching in step, accompanied by the clatter of horses' hooves. When the sun rose, with rays of light striking the brass buttons of military uniforms, the city's electric streetlights went off.

In these same hours before first light, the waters of the Hudson River became transformed. Hundreds of privately owned sailboats had dropped anchor opposite the cliffs of Riverside Park. Nearest the Manhattan shore lay five of the navy's warships, including the *Powhatan*, which had entered Nagasaki harbor in 1853 when Commodore Matthew Perry "opened" Japan in 1853. At the end of the flotilla was the revenue cutter *U. S. Grant*. As the sun rose, the American flags aboard the ships were first raised, and then lowered to half-mast. The men who were to fire cannon salutes prepared to stand by their guns.

Since first light, crowds had been walking across the Brooklyn Bridge to Manhattan. As various military units began to assemble in their assigned streets, some found themselves placed next to regiments that had fought on opposite sides in the war. These ranks were now filled with young men, but they knew their military history. Far downtown at Broome Street, men of the Virginia State Guard lined up beside the First Massachusetts Infantry. Their forebears had clashed bloodily at the first and second Bull Run, but in the dawn's light each unit restricted itself to cheerfully disparaging the other's military appearance and bearing.

At 8:30 a.m., General Hancock took custody of Grant's coffin at City Hall. An honor guard from Brooklyn's GAR Ulysses S. Grant Post carried it out of the building and rested it on the steps. Reverend Newman, Bishop Harris, and eight other clergymen waited there. Next to them stood Grant's doctors Douglas, Shrady, and Sands, in mourning clothes complete with wide black-and-white sashes. As New York's German-American Liederkranz Society sang pieces by Schubert and Wagner, the large hearse rolled up to the steps. It was drawn by an enormously long team of twenty-four black horses, harnessed as twelve pairs of two. On the right-hand horse of each pair rode a slender black groom dressed in a uniform of black boots, light breeches, black short jacket trimmed with gold braid, and a black silk jockey's cap. The black coachman, Albert Hawkins, had driven Grant around Washington when he served as secretary of war and as president and had remained a driver for the White House. He had asked President Cleveland for the privilege of driving Grant on this last ride.

The GAR pallbearers carried the flag-draped coffin down to the hearse and placed it on the catafalque, which had black plumes at each of its corners. Hancock, mounted on a splendid black charger, rode to the front of the twenty generals on horses acting as escort at the head of the parade. The generals presented a colorful picture: riding spirited horses as they maneuvered themselves into line in order of seniority, they were in a sense a military fashion show. The army was experimenting with new uniforms, some officers wearing fore 'n' aft gold-trimmed hats like those worn by admirals, and others wearing German-influenced helmets topped by spikes or plumes.

Hancock raised a white-gauntleted hand and thrust it to the north, his strong voice crying out, "Forward March!" Behind the escort, the David's Island Military Band stepped off, playing Beethoven's "Marche funebre." After them came the West Point Corps of Cadets, clergymen, and the hearse. In the custom of the most formal military funerals, a soldier marched beside the coffin, leading a riderless horse with boots reversed in the stirrups.

As each band in the parade came to the Fifth Avenue Hotel, it struck up "Hail to the Chief" in tribute to President Cleveland

and the Grant family's presence there, but they had already gone downstairs and were in carriages waiting their turn to wheel into the line of march behind the hearse. Little Julia remembered the moment. "Even my childish brain was awed by the immensity of the demonstration. From 23rd Street to 116th Street a five-mile stretch of sympathetic people covered sidewalks and fences, windows and doors, and every face was sad and some of them were even weeping."

Behind the Grant family came a carriage drawn by six bay horses, carrying President Grover Cleveland and his secretary of state Thomas Francis Bayard, followed by a carriage occupied by former presidents Rutherford B. Hayes and Chester A. Arthur. Next came the justices of the Supreme Court. After them the crowds saw a procession of carriages holding a galaxy of honorary pallbearers, including the chief pallbearer Sherman, the army's present general in chief Philip Sheridan, Admiral David Porter, who had worked so well with Grant during the Vicksburg campaign, and Joseph E. Johnston and Simon Buckner, the Confederate generals that Julia had asked to have named to that list. From his publishing office at Fourteenth Street, Mark Twain watched his friend Grant go by, followed by so many famous Americans he knew. He had decided not to go to Riverside Park, but had arranged to meet Sherman that evening uptown at the Lotos Club at Fortieth Street and Fifth Avenue, where they would talk of the man each of them cared so much about.

As the parade passed, the crowds contrived every way of seeing as much as they could. Men sat on rooftops, and boys roosted in the branches of trees. At one place two men made three-legged stools, and sold them for a quarter to spectators who used them to see above the crowd. Food vendors offered everything from apples and pretzels to lemonade and cider. The August day was turning hot. A spectator described the spectacle.

Broadway moved like a river, a river into which many tributaries were poured. There was one living mass choking the thoroughfare . . . to the grim gates at Riverside open to receive him [Grant]. From 14th Street to the top of the hill—pavements, windows, curbs, balcony and housetop teeming. All walls and doorways were a sweep of black.

In addition to the many thousands of soldiers passing by, there were civilian officials. Every governor passed by, his carriage in line in the order in which his state entered the Union. Mayor William Grace of New York City brought up the last massive contingent, eight thousand civil and municipal officials from around the nation. Realistic estimates of the number of spectators ran as high as one and a half million; the crowd was certainly the largest ever to gather on the North American continent. The combination of military strength and constitutional law would have pleased Grant, who believed so firmly in the prosperous future he saw for his nation.

Amidst all this, little Julia was less than comfortable in the funeral carriage on this August day.

With both my parents and my Aunt Nelly we were shut into intense heat and semi-darkness. Some sandwiches, the long silences, and now and then a question asked and answered; my weary body and my own wet eyes I only felt occasionally, but I remember well my father's white, set face and his strained, hoarse voice. My young brother gave my mother some difficulty, for his movements were not always easy to control. I think she must have had great trouble keeping both of us children in order.

* * *

HANCOCK HAD started off from City Hall at eight thirty in the morning. By two thirty, allowing rest stops and the chance to eat sandwiches, he had brought more than sixty thousand people to Grant's tomb. Two hours later, after ceremonies, singing, and prayer, he ushered the honorary pallbearers into the brick structure. (In an example of the future's inscrutability, the vigorous Hancock would die seven months later of unknown causes, and Grant's friend William H. Vanderbilt, then the richest man in the world with a net worth of $194 million, would die five months after this day of Grant's funeral.)

In the brick vault, Sherman stood at the head of Grant's casket, wearing his dress uniform. The burial detail folded the American flag that had been on Grant's coffin into a triangle, and an officer presented it to Colonel Frederick Grant. Then an enlisted man placed little Julia's wreath on top of her grandfather's coffin. Everyone filed out of the tomb, and the metal gates were locked.

A bugler came to the center of the area in front of the tomb, pivoted to face Sherman, raised his bugle, and began to play "Taps." As the notes rang out above the Hudson and the cannon from the warships boomed above the water, the guests around the tomb saw Sherman, standing at rigid attention, convulsively sobbing.

Driving back to the hotel in the family carriage, little Julia experienced "a feeling of unutterable weariness and loss."

NOTES

In citing works in the notes, short titles have generally been used. Works frequently cited have been identified by the following abbreviations. The full citation appears in the bibliography, under the name of the author or editor.

NYT *New York Times*

PUSG Simon, John Y., ed. *The Papers of Ulysses S. Grant*

Chapter One: A Change in Fortune

1   Most photographed person: "Photo Gallery," Ulysses S. Grant Homepage.

1   Three days a week: PUSG 31, 135n.

1   Mexican Southern Railroad Company: Badeau, *Grant in Peace*, 351–353, 395–397; Pitkin, 3; McFeely, 486–489; Smith, *Grant*, 618–619.

2   Trip around the world: Smith, 606–614. Details of, also in Goldhurst, 101–102. Buck's money enabling them to continue, Smith, *Grant*, 607, Goldhurst, 102, and Pitkin, 1. Background on Jerome Chaffee, McFeely, 489.

2   "He is no doubt": Ross, 266.

3   "I saw at once": Church, 449.

3   "Father and mother": Grant, Jesse, *In the Days of my Father*, 317.

4   "not possessed of the backbone": Smith, *Grant*, 618.

4   $100,000 to help the couple settle in New York: Goldhurst, 12.

4   to receive $15,000 a year: Pitkin, 9; Wabash failure, Goldhurst, 21.

6   To become a partner: Background of Grant &Ward situation, Smith, *Grant*, 618–620; McFeely, 489–490. For the sum of $400,000, NYT, May 19, 1984, consistent with Smith, *Grant*, 619, citing Garland, *Ulysses S. Grant*, 490n. The Smith citation makes the distinction between the $200,000 in cash put down by Grant and his son and the

pledging of $200,000 in securities done by Ward and Fish. In an interview with Ward that appeared in the *New York Herald* magazine section on December 19, 1909, he details how Grant raised his $100,000. Figures vary, in different sources, concerning both the investments made by various individuals and the losses they suffered. Where there are such differences, I chose to use the figures that appeared in the NYT, May 8–June 24, as the story unfolded.

6　They valued at $100,000: Goldhurst, 3–4 et seq.

7　"These deposits": Fish, *Memories of Early Business Life*, 7.

7　Ward's investments: Goldhurst, 14.

7　Henry Clews: Clews, 215.

8　Grant knew little: For the sum of $350,000, see Smith, *Grant*, 618. The figure of $98,000 is from Badeau, *Grant in Peace*, 420; in Badeau, principally 420–422. Badeau sets forth in detail his understanding of the facts of Grant's financial situation.

8　$750,000 in his personal account: Perry, *Grant and Twain*, xx.

8　Capitalization of $16 million: Goldhurst, 19. Johnson and Willing, *Remembered Yesterdays*, 209, say "Grant believed his fortune amounted to a million dollars." PUSG 31, 323, quotes Grant as saying he believed his net worth at that time was "nigh to a million."

8　Twenty-five Havana cigars: Interview with Ferdinand Ward, in *New York Herald* magazine section, December 19, 1909. Other things about USG's cigar smoking, playing poker, Ward's evenings with USG, country house in Stamford, CT, etc., all in the interview, "The topics of the day" Home Page, Ferdinand Ward, 1 of 23; this is from the *Herald* interview of December 19, 1909. Havana cigars: Goldhurst, 14.

9　George Spencer, and documents: Goldhurst, 19.

9　"how regally New York entertains": Grant, Julia Dent, *Memoirs*, 324.

10　to give Julia $1,000 a month: Goldhurst, 4.

10　pedestal on which The Statue of Liberty: Pitkin, 2, says, "Early in 1884 the general felt affluent enough to start a round robin Subscription toward the Statue of Liberty pedestal fund, offering $5,000 on Condition that nineteen other prominent men did the same." The citation in Pitkin is: Ulysses S. Grant, William M. Evarts, and Joseph Drexel to George Jones, January 1884, George E. Jones Papers, New York Public Library.

10　Bonds worth $2,500: PUSG 31, xvii.

10 "Julia, you need not trouble": Grant, Julia Dent, *Memoirs*, 327–328.
10 a severe accident: Headley, 388; Grant's orthopedic condition: *Orthopedic Review*, 78–80.
11 "I have not been able": PUSG 31, 101.
11 "I think the injury": USG to Badeau, February 27, 1884, in Badeau, *Grant in Peace*, 555.
11 Pleurisy: PUSG 31, 109.
11 "laden with curios": Ulysses S. Grant Homepage.
11 Ward quickly revealed: Smith, *Grant*, 620.
12 "I care nothing": Ibid.
13 "The Marine Bank closed this morning": Goldhurst, 6.
13 "Father, everything is bursted": PUSG 31, 144n.

Chapter Two: The Man Waiting for More Bad News

15 knocked him to the ground: Fleming, 102.
15 "Ulysses Grant had": Ulysses S. Grant Homepage, entry under "Mrs. Orvil Grant," citing the New York state *Troy Intelligencer*, April 17, 1892.
16 "Our spirits rose": Porter, *Campaigning*, 79.
17 "When General Grant": Williams, 100.
17 "When Grant once gets possession": Porter, *Campaigning*, 223.
18 the firm was "all right": PUSG 31, 138n.
19 "The whole thing is suspicious": Perry, *xxiii*.
19 Other members of the Grant family: Goldhurst, 21; NYT, May 9, 1864. Goldhurst has Frederick putting in only $7,000.
20 had sent in $95,000: PUSG 31, 141n, quotes Fish as saying that Jesse Grant was "allowed to come in" for $50,000. In a letter from USG to Governor Leland Stanford of California dated June 4, 1884, USG stated, "He [Jesse] deposited with the firm on the 2d of May $86,000.00." PUSG 31, 157.
20 counting up that loss: NYT, July 5, 1884, reprinting the *San Francisco Alta* article of June 26, 1884.
20 Frederick owed $25,000: PUSG 31, 140–141n.
20 "Spencer, how is it": Smith, *Grant*, 621.
20 Grant bury his head in his hands: Goldhurst, 8.
21 Whiskey Ring: Grossman, 364–365.
21 Thirty-seven investigations: Grossman, 404.

Chapter Three: The Lady at 3 East Sixty-sixth Street

23 "I was nearing my seventh birthday": Casey, 11–12. All quotations from Emma Dent Casey are from this recollection. It should be noted that in the full sentence beginning, "I was nearing my seventh birthday," I have changed "that bright spring afternoon in 1843" to read "that bright . . . afternoon." I do so because other evidence suggests that Grant did not in fact arrive at Jefferson Barracks until the autumn of that year. It is also possible that his first visit to the White House did not occur until the spring of 1844.

24 "a darling little lieutenant": Ulysses S. Grant Homepage, interview with Julia Dent Grant.

24 An academy record: Green, 12. A vivid account of Grant's equestrian skill while at West Point is in Garland, *Ulysses S. Grant*, 52.

25 "serious the matter with me": Grant, *Memoirs and Selected Letters*, 37–39.

25 Lieutenant Grant behaved with distinguished gallantry: Headley, 23; Lee adds more praise on 24.

25 "In the thickest of it": PUSG 1, 86.

25 "One of those beautiful" through "hand to glove": See note in Flood, *Grant and Sherman*, 404. "I enjoyed sitting": Grant, Julia Dent, 56. Work cited under John Y. Simon, ed., in Flood, *Grant and Sherman*.

26 "a sharp, quick, nervous rap": Grant, Julia Dent, 137.

27 "They would seek a quiet corner": Porter, *Campaigning*, 284.

27 "The ninth day of battle": PUSG 10, 443–444.

28 "We have taken in battle": PUSG 10, 444n.

28 Julia consulted a specialist: Grant, Julia Dent, 126–127. In PUSG 10: 126–127, in a letter dated February 4, 1864, Grant says, "Mrs. G. is in St. Louis and very much afflicted with her eyes."

29 "The art of war is simple enough": Ulysses S. Grant Quotes, from Brainy Quotes, http://www.brainyquote.com/quotes/authors/u/Ulysses _s_Grant.html.

30 "When I gave my hand": McFeely, 471.

30 On May 22, 1875: McFeely, 404, citing PUSG, which at that time had eight volumes. When expanded, volume 26 does not have that exchange for the date of May 22, 1875.

31 "Grandmama was delightful": Cantacuzene, 11.

32 "The failure of Grant and Ward": Grant, Julia Dent, 327.

32 "Imagine the shock": Ibid., 328.

33 GIVING NO EXPLANATIONS: NYT, May 8, 1884.

35 "hopelessly insolvent": NYT, May 11, 1884.

35 "One of the expert accountants": NYT, May 29, 1884. Figures continued to climb: NYT, May 19, 1884. Final accounting: Pitkin, 19.

35 Owed its investors: NYT, July 8, 1884.

35 Cheating the Grants and Senator Chaffee: Goldhurst, 13–14.

36 "Ward invented": NYT, May 19, 1884.

36 Cases against Ward and Fish: Smith, *Grant*, 620–621.

38 Paroled after six and a half: NYT, April 6, 1909.

38 state prison at Auburn: Smith, *Autobiography of Mark Twain, Vol. 1.*, 487, citing NYT, June 28, 1885.

38 "Is Grant Guilty?": McFeely, 492. McFeely attributes the "Is Grant Guilty?" to the *New York World*, but Pitkin, 6, cites this as being in the New York *Sun*, and says, "The New York *Sun*, long his [Grant's] bitter opponent, led the attack."

38 "The conclusion is irresistible": Perry, *xxix*.

39 "The opinion on the Street": McFeely, 492.

39 "Look at *Grant* now": PUSG 31, 142n.

39 "no soldier": PUSG 31, 182n.

40 Bill was introduced: NYT, May 8, 1884; Smith, *Grant*, 622. NYT editorial in support: May 9, 1884. Opposition in the House: NYT, May 24, 1884.

41 "on account of my share": Perry, 160.

41 "General, I owe you this": Grant, Julia Dent, 328.

41 "that his timely thoughtfulness": NYT, August 5, 1892.

41 Romero had worked closely: Badeau, *Grant in Peace*, 351–353, 395–397; McFeely, 486–489; Smith, *Grant*, 618–619; Pitkin, 2, 3, 99, 109.

42 Situations of Frederick and Buck: Goldhurst, 21.

42 Their son Buck: Ulysses S. Grant, Jr., in Westchester County. PUSG 31, 213.

43 Black valet named Harrison Terrell: PUSG 31, 370n.

43 "personal loan" of $150,000: Smith, *Grant*, 622.

43 Details of the Grants' finances at the time: Goldhurst, 21–25.

43 Ward had managed: *Grant in Peace*, 420. 43 a mortgage for $48,000: Grant, Julia Dent, 324.

43 Background of gift to the Smithsonian: Ross, 285–286.

43 With Vanderbilt's approval: But regarding what was in fact given to the government, see Ward, *Herald* interview, 22.

44   large collection of books: Headley, 384. It should be noted that other
     accounts of the Grants' crisis and disposition of property have differ-
     ing details; for example, Smith, *Grant*, 622, states that Vanderbilt did
     in fact take title to the Sixty-sixth Street house.

44   "No one will ever know": PUSG 31, 161–162n.

Chapter Four: Retreat to New Jersey

45   "my little villa": Grant, Julia Dent, 328.

45   private beach: Ross, 288.

46   "At Elberon, New Jersey": Mende, 140, 139.

47   "We decided at first": Grant, Julia Dent, 328.

49   "one spectacle of flags and streamers": All quoted descriptions, and
     quotations from those involved in this event, are from the NYT, June
     12, 1884. The statement about bullet holes being in some of the flags
     is based on the assumption that they were the same regimental battle
     flags carried in the Union Army's Grand Review at the end of the war,
     in Washington, May 3–5, 1865. Contemporary accounts of that parade
     describe many of those faded banners as being burnt with powder
     smoke and torn by enemy musket and cannon fire.

52   This gathering attracted: McFeely, 495–496; Goldhurst, 110.

53   "vast congregation" through "I was one of a million": McFeely, 496;
     "No Combination of Wall Street sharpers": Goldhurst, 110; "after say-
     ing a few words": McFeely, 49.

Chapter Five: An Opportunity

55   Alfred D. Worthington: PUSG 31, 162 and 163n.

56   Well-regarded *Century Magazine*: Johnson and Willing, 209–213;
     Pitkin, 10–11.

57   *Scribner's Monthly:* Johnson and Willing, 82.

57   Sore throat: Goldhurst, 113.

57   "began to open his heart to me" through "almost penniless": Johnson
     and Willing, 211–213.

58   "[Grant] asked me": Ibid., 213.

58   "The South never smiled again": Flood, *Grant and Sherman*, 120, 140n,
     citing Brooks, *Grant*, 144.

58   great success: Perry, *xviii*.

58 "Grant is my man, and I am his": Flood, *Grant and Sherman*, 188, 415n, citing Smith, *Grant*, 259.

58 The battle of Chattanooga: PUSG 31, 187.

59 "substantially a copy" through "he revealed the human side": Johnson and Willing, 213–215.

60 "I told him that what was desirable": Ibid., 215.

62 "If we take it": Perry, 62.

62 "probably will publish": PUSG 31, 186.

62 "My Dear Little Pet": Ibid., 199.

62 "When the book is ready": Pitkin, 16.

63 "His manner is clear and terse": Smith, *Grant*, 611–612, citing Young, 416.

64 "The whole thing reminded me": PUSG 3, 132.

64 "'Yes,' said the General": Young, 385.

64 The oath that Lee: Flood, *Lee: The Last Years*, 9.

65 "I was angry at this" through "The matter was allowed to die out": Young, 385.

66 General Adam Badeau: Badeau, *Grant in Peace*, 12, 16, et seq., this work upon his new book: PUSG 31, 347.

66 McFeely, 498, citing Adams, Henry, *Education of Henry Adams*, 263–264.

66 "exceedingly social": Adams, *Education of Henry Adams*, 263–264.

67 "some charge of Grant's unofficial letters": Badeau, *Grant in Peace*, 161.

67 Grant's aide-de-camp: Grant, Julia Dent, 202, 225n; "culpable frauds": Badeau, *Grant in Peace*, 556. Badeau's suit against the government: Badeau, *Grant in Peace*, 550.

68 A military person: See PUSG 31, 51n. and 430.

68 "London accounts": Badeau, *Grant in Peace*, 561.

68 "[he] soon after sent for me" through "seized the idea": Badeau, *Grant in Peace*, 424–425.

68 "a duplicate set": Johnson, 216. The one note at the bottom of that page reads, "Badeau's relationship to the writing of . . . [Grant's] 'Memoirs' is a subject in much dispute. He was with Grant both at Long Branch late in August and later in New York." Some perspective on this is to be found in Pitkin, 10, 16–17. On 16, Pitkin writes of Badeau's work with and for Grant during 1884 and 1885, "How much this assistance amounted to eventually became a matter of bitter controversy."

70 Memorandum that Grant wrote: PUSG 31, 271, has a text including these terms and signed by Grant. It is dated New York City, February 7th, 1885.

On March 2, 1884, Badeau endorsed this memorandum, and on October 15, 1884, in a letter to Julia Grant, Badeau refers to "the agreement made with me by General Grant in August 1884," PUSG 31, 271n.

70 "filled up my time": USG to Dent, February 16, 1885, PUSG 31, 291.

70 "My family is American": Grant, *Personal Memoirs of U.S. Grant*, 17.

71 Battle of Belmont: The best source on Belmont is from Grant, who commanded there. Grant, *Personal Memoirs*, vol. 1, 270–281. This includes all quotations.

Chapter Six: To Eat a Peach, and Soldier On

73 "There was a plate of delicious peaches": Grant, Julia Dent, 329.

74 "He habitually wears": Smith, *Grant*, 300.

74 "So it continued for weeks" through "writing for bread": Grant, Julia Dent, 328–329.

75 Purrington prepare will: PUSG 31, 199n.

75 "I make this my last Will": PUSG 31, 195–198, 199n.

76 S Panic of 1873: Adams, *The Epic of America*, 221.

76 14 percent: *American Experience*, "The Panic of 1873."

77 "when it came time to leave": Johnson and Willing, 52–55.

77 "It was my fortune": A draft text of Grant's eighth and final Annual Message to Congress, dated December 5, 1876, is to be found in PUSG 28, 62–69.

Chapter Seven: Grant Puts on his Armor

81 "I herewith resign": PUSG 31, 211.

82 As if it were not enough: PUSG 31, 219, 226, with background on 226n. See also NYT October 10, 1884, p. 8. Background on William Magear ("Boss") Tweed and the "Tweed Ring": Mandelbaum, 66–86 et seq., and Lynch, 67 et seq.

82 "Tweed Ring": Grossman, 320–321, 335–337.

83 "At this time": Badeau, *Grant in Peace*, 427.

83 "he complained constantly": Ibid., 426.

84 "Is it cancer?": For this and the following description and dialogue concerning Grant's diagnosis and initial treatment, see Goldhurst, 143–146.

85 "General Grant has just been in": Perry, 68.

85 "complaint with a cancerous tendency": Ross, 291.

85 "I asked again and again": Grant, Julia Dent, 329.

86 "As you are aware": PUSG 31, 52.

86 "This specimen comes from": Goldhurst, 145–146.

87 Three cigars a day: Ibid., 148.

87 As November went on: Perry, 74.

88 "Grant's fortitude": Badeau, *Grant in Peace*, 427.

89 "The doctor will not allow me": Perry, 71. In PUSG 31, 266, the sentence following the one ending "swallowing water" is absent.

90 "Pretend you are a boy again": Perry, 81.

90 "There is not the slightest danger of that": Ibid.

90 "literary tutor": Johnson and Willing, 215.

Chapter Eight: Mark Twain Strides onto the Stage

92 "General Grant got slowly": Harnsberger, 227–228.

93 "General Grant was looking": ibid.

93 "the embodiment of": Jones, 269, citing O'Connor, 356–357.

93 " I'll step back": Powers, 426.

94 "Imagine what": Goldhurst, 124.

94 "Grant seated himself": Powers, 428.

95 "The Babies": Fatout, *Mark Twain on the Lecture Circuit*, 201.

95 "We have not all had the good fortune" through "Gen. Grant sat through fourteen speeches": Powers, 429–431.

97 "I had been": This and the subsequent scenes involving Twain starting to acquire the publishing rights to Grant's memoirs are based on Perry, 82–90. There is a discrepancy between Twain's account of the date, which he places as being "in the first week of November," and Perry's statement (Perry, 116), that Twain finished his first two conversations with Grant about publishing his book on November 20. Online there is a study by Barbara Schmidt, "Chronology of Known Mark Twain Speeches, Public Readings, and Lectures" (http://www.twain quotes.com/SpeechIndex.html). According to this, Twain's only appearances at Chickering Hall were on November 18 and 19 and by some point on November 20 he was speaking at Newburgh, New York, up the Hudson River from Manhattan.

98 William Dean Howells: Smith, *Autobiography*, 70.

99 "sitting down to baked beans": Powers, 452.

99 Kaolatype: Powers, 435, et seq.

101 "I didn't know whether": Pitkin, 20.

102 "I wanted the General's book": Ibid.

102 "On re-examining": PUSG 31, 237. For what Childs' lawyer, Joseph G. Rosengarten, called "papers in reference to the proposed Contract for the publication of Genl Grants [sic] Memoirs," see PUSG 31, 237n.

103 "It was a shameful thing": Perry, 119.

104 "If these chickens": Ibid., 118, citing on 260 Webster, 302; Goldhurst, 166.

105 "One visitor frightened me": Cantacuzene, 41.

Chapter Nine: Horses, and a Last Cigar

107 "I learned that": C. E. Meade, in Post, 106, et seq.

108 "ordinary, scrubby-looking": Green, 116, quoting Richard Henry Dana, author of *Two Years Before the Mast*.

108 "My father was the best horseman": "Grant the Equestrian," at Ulysses S. Grant Homepage.

108 Grant and a horse named York set a record: Flood, *Grant and Sherman*, 11.

109 "crossed at such a flying rate": Grant, *Memoirs*, vol. 1, 116.

109 "appeared to look upon": Grant the Equestrian," at Ulysses S. Grant Homepage.

109 "that had never been ridden": Smith, *Grant*, 28n.

110 "Gentlemen," he said: C. E. Meade in Post, 110.

110 "something the matter": Supra, 133, citing Neider.

111 "he smoked a pipe" and "he chewed tobacco": Mary Robinson's account, *St. Louis Republican*, July 24, 1885.

111 "I had been a very light smoker": Porter, *Campaigning*, 381.

113 "horse-back ride of fifty miles": PUSG 9, 317.

113 "General Grant sat for some time": Porter, *Campaigning*, 4.

114 "As I entered": Ibid., 6.

115 Grant confided: This is made clear by Porter's saying that "I sat by his death-bed." Ibid., 70.

115 Twenty cigars: Ibid., 70.

115 "The general, after having given": Ibid., 70–71.

116 "The cannon did it!" and "It seemed to me as though": Perry, 121.

Chapter Ten: A Bittersweet Christmas

117 "In December": Badeau, *Grant in Peace*, 427.

117 "[He] often sat": Ibid., 428.

118 "I am not going to commit suicide": Ibid., 429.

118 "Daily about one o'clock": Ibid., 429–430.

118 "had always promised": ms., supra, 88.

119 "No one, indeed": Badeau, 430.

119 "I found him in his shirt-sleeves": Porter, *Campaigning*, 283.

120 "We were as brothers": Ward, 14.

121 "I knew": PUSG 10, 186.

121 "set of honor": NYT, June 17, 1869.

122 "Grant says my visits": Lewis, *Sherman* 638.

122 "I made him two long visits": PUSG 31, 249n.

123 "I appreciate both the motive": Ibid., 251.

123 Sent $1,000 to Charles Wood: Goldhurst, 171.

123 "I wish to state": PUSG 31, 250.

123 "a remittance of $100": Ibid., 249.

124 "generous and princely": Ibid., 257n.

124 "The whole world honors and respects you": Ibid., 258n.

124 "I conversed with him to-day": Ibid.

125 "from an association": Ibid., 261–262.

125 "It is the nearly unanimous": Ibid., 262n.

126 "now improving": Ibid., 266.

126 "The sore throat which you recollect": Ibid., 293–294.

127 Containing his article on Shiloh: Ibid., 270 and 270n.

128 "I always admired the South": Grant, *Personal Memoirs*, 444.

129 "I have made up my mind": PUSG 31, 295.

129 he signed the contract with Grant for his *Personal Memoirs*, signed February 27, 1885: Ibid., 296.

129 "As I understand it": Pitkin, 31, citing on 144, Hill, *Mark Twain's Letters to his Publishers*, 184–185.

130 "General Grant dictated": Perry, 162, citing "Grant's Last Stand," a piece by Dawson in the *Philadelphia Enquirer*, February 4, 1984, 4.

130 "the same high merits": Ulysses S. Grant Homepage, GRANT THE AUTHOR, quoting from observations about the *Personal Memoirs of Ulysses S. Grant* that appeared in the *Saturday Review*, July 9, 1955. A somewhat differently worded version of Twain's praise is in Perry, 175–176, citing Smith.

131 He designed a new letterhead: Perry, 141–142.

131 On March 1, the *New York Times*: This and several other examples of the interest in Grant's illness are to be found in Goldhurst, 172–174; and Pitkin, 25–27, et seq.

132   "bulletin boys": Pitkin, 34.
132   Three thousand unanswered letters: PUSG 31, 337n.
132   Hansfelt declared: Goldhurst, 176.
133   "He's my old commander": Goldhurst, 176–177.
133   skating cap: Ibid., 183.
133   Several newspapers a day: Ibid., 174.
133   "You would think": According to Frederick Grant, his father weighed 135 pounds in April of 1861, and 142 pounds in June in 1865. NYT, Oct. 12, 1885.
133   Balanced at 146: Ibid., 183.
134   "General Grant is dying": Ibid., 180.
134   "I am very glad": Ibid.
134   "He was a far greater man": Ibid.
134   NOT CANCER AFTER ALL: Ibid., 184.

Chapter Eleven: Things Come Together

135   "You know during the last day": Goldhurst, 169.
135   Randall's actions in getting the legislation for Grant passed, and reaction at the Grants' house in Manhattan: Perry, 156–159.
136   Reaction of passage of bill at Grant household: Perry, 159.
136   "the effect upon him": Pitkin, 30.
137   "It *insures* a sudden sale": Pitkin, 31. Timing of first and second volumes: Goldhurst, 203.
137   "close at hand": Pitkin, 30.
139   Begin his second volume with The Battle of Chattanooga: Perry, 164–165.
138   Twain put it to Smith: Ibid., 165.
138   Grant had yet to finish: Ibid., 163. Goldhurst, 193n., claims that in his first volume, Grant wrote about Chattanooga before he wrote about Vicksburg, and in the second volume he wrote about Appomattox—an idea subsequently abandoned—before he wrote about Sherman's March to the Sea. No other account of Grant's negotiations and arrangement with the Century Company mentions an article on Sherman's March to the Sea.
139   Rise in subscriptions to the *Century* Magazine: Perry, 191.
139   $500 to $2000 per article: Century Company payments to Grant for his articles. Ibid., 164.

139 Possibility of a pirated publication: Goldhurst, 163. For readers wishing to learn more about Twain's publication arrangements for Grant's *Personal Memoirs*, the principal sources used here are: Goldhurst, 157–163, et seq.; Perry, 162–165, et seq.; Pitkin, 27–31.

140 Gerhardt now showed this little statue: Ibid., 166–169, and Goldhurst, 164–166.

140 "That's the General": Goldhurst, 165.

141 He and Nellie would go for a ride: Pitkin, 33.

142 "There's been a good deal of nonsense" and Grant's view on prayer being fine if it made his wife feel better: Goldhurst, 191.

142 "This piece of reporting": Ibid., 191.

143 "I have never been": PUSG 31, 327.

143 "any mistrust": Ibid., 332.

144 "There is nothing wrong": Ibid., 327.

144 "had a pleasant talk": Ibid., 323–336.

144 "very sick"; Grant's relapse in the days before March 31 and his condition that night: Perry, 170–172.

144 "The truth is": Ibid., 170.

144 "It is doubtful": Goldhurst, 181.

145 "Many a person": Ibid.; Perry, 171–172.

145 At some time after midnight on April 1, 1885: Ibid., 171–172.

145 Julia sat beside him, weeping: Perry, 172.

145 "I said, 'I will baptize him'": Goldhurst, 190.

146 "As the pulse did not respond": Ibid. Goldhurst, 181–182, has him "hobbling back and forth in his room on the arm of Fred."

146 "May I ask you to favor": PUSG 31, 336 and 336n.

147 Masonic organization: Goldhurst, 183.

148 Substitute to "prayerful": Ibid., 184.

148 Three political parties in America: Ibid., 189.

148 Grant's life had been saved: Ibid., 191.

Chapter Twelve: Twenty Years After The Nation's Great Redemptive Moment

150 A telegram came for Julia: The telegram was sent from Aix-les-Bains, France, on April 8, and Frederick Grant replied on April 9. PUSG 31, 342n.

151 "one or two puffs": Perry, 172.

151 "I now feel like ending": PUSG 14, 253; "with reference to the surrender of this army": Ibid., 371n.

152 "I am delighted and amazed": Ibid., 353n.

152 "I think you had better return home": Ibid., 366. It should be noted that the date of April 7 is in brackets, representing the best effort to fit this into the chronology of correspondence.

152 "I did not obey": Ibid., 367n.

Chapter Thirteen: Reactions to a Sick Hero

161 "Sometimes I go": PUSG 31, 343–343n.

162 ASTONISHING HIS FAMILY: NYT, April 17, 1885, 1.

162 GEN. GRANT'S IMPROVEMENT: NYT, April 22, 1885, 4.

163 "Gilt trimmings": NYT, April 22, 1885. Veterans Association of the Seventy-First. 4.

164 "Toward the end of spring": Cantacuzene, 47.

164 "My chances, I think": PUSG 31, *xxxi*.

164 "Speaking of his disease": The excerpted piece from the *Philadelphia Times* appeared in the NYT of April 26, 1885.

166 Of course you do not know me: This and the subsequent letters are from PUSG 31, 344–345.

168 "Spring flowers": NYT, April 28, 1885. PUSG 31, 346n.

168 "The population of Kansas": Ibid.

168 "Twenty thousand citizens": NYT, April 28, 1885.

168 Grant on his birthday, and birthday dinner: Goldhurst, 187; Ross, 299.

169 "Remembering him now as the generous victor": PUSG 31, 346n.

169 Guests included Mark Twain: Ross, 299.

170 "To the various army posts": NYT, April 28, 1885.

171 "The work upon . . . his [Grant's] new book": Perry, 197; Pitkin, 37, says that this appeared in a column, "National Capital Gossip," compiled by the *World's* Washington correspondent.

171 "Composition is entirely my own": Perry, 199.

172 "I must efface myself": PUSG 31, 358n.

172 There was a suggestion of blackmail: Powers, 501. Perry, 199, makes a stronger statement, "This was blackmail, pure and simple."

172 "I have concluded": PUSG 31, 350–351, et seq. The entire correspondence, and later letters relating to it, is set forth between pages 350 and 362.

173 "an old staff officer": Grant, Julia Dent, 330.
173 "had not seen": Smith, *Autobiography*, 493.
174 Paid Badeau his $10,000: Ibid., 487.

Chapter Fourteen: Unmarked Anniversaries

175 "I wish my health": PUSG 31, 362.
176 "General Grant wishes to take this occasion": Ibid., 364n.
176 "Tell the boys": Ibid., 363–364.
177 "the first two persons": Lewis, *Captain Sam Grant*, 251.
177 "found a church": Grant, *Personal Memoirs*, 106.
178 "The shots from our little gun": Ibid., 109.
178 "saying that every shot": Ibid.
178 "I could not tell the General": Ibid.
179 "a man of iron": Garland, *Ulysses S. Grant*, 1920.

Chapter Fifteen: The "Man of Iron" Keeps Going

181 "so much broken down": This scene is based on the account in Green, 305.
182 "malarious condition" through "and at times became a mere whisper": NYT obituary, "The Career of a Soldier," July 24, 1885, 41.
182 Family had declared to sell it: Pitkin, 58.
182 "It is a great deal better": PUSG 31, 410, 410n.
183 "authorized to receive": Ibid., 367.
184 Drexel and his wife set about renovating: Pitkin, 59.
184 "That is just the place": Ibid., citing Clarke, O. P., 11–12. For additional background on Mr. McGregor, the Hotel Balmoral, Drexel, and this cottage, see Pitkin, 46–59. Details concerning Mt. McGregor, the Hotel Balmoral, the Grant's Cottage, and the arrival there. Pitkin, 55–64; Goldhurst, 209–212: Clark, O. P.
184 "I give this letter to you now": PUSG 31, 370.
185 Veterans' organization: The account of Horace Porter, referring to the "heavy measured steps of moving columns," suggests large bodies of men. Ibid., 365n, quotes the *New York Tribune* as saying of the GAR contingent, "After the 400 men had passed out of sight. . . ." Considering the number of Union Civil War veterans living in Manhattan at that time, this number may be low.

185 "Now he heard the sound of martial music": "Tribute to General Grant" speech made by Horace Porter at the inauguration of the Grant Equestrian Statue in Chicago, October 8, 1891, p. 949.

186 " . . . the old warrior": PUSG 31, 365n, quoting from the *New York Tribune*, May 31, 1885.

Chapter Sixteen: Another Loan from Vanderbilt

187 "fitted up most luxuriously": This and the details of Grant's trip from New York to Mt. McGregor are from Pitkin, 62–64.

187 Grant came out the door of 3 East Sixty-sixth Street: Goldhurst, 205.

188 Promised Grant he could come: Goldhurst, 204–205.

188 "It is just a week to-day": PUSG 31, 376; Dawson's expanded duties: Pitkin, 66–67.

189 At station after station: Green, 307, citing *Harper's Weekly* of June 27, 1885.

189 Details of this trip: Pitkin, 62–64; and Goldhurst, 204–209.

190 "In an arm chair facing": Porter, *Campaigning*, 1.

191 Fryer and Constable James Minnick: Goldhurst, 210.

192 "pencil talk": Pitkin, 69.

193 "Dr. Since coming to this beautiful climate": PUSG 31, 374–375.

194 "Memoranda for my Family": See Pitkin, 64–65; Goldhurst, 213–214. The text of the financial memorandum referred to is in PUSG 31, 367–369. The text there deals exclusively with family financial arrangements.

195 When Grant was dozing: Goldhurst, 214, has Grant handing this to Julia; PUSG 31, 389n, says of this, "On June 29, USG wrote a note, presumably for his family."

195 This was Sam Willett: *Saratogian*, June 17, 1885; Goldhurst, 212, 216; Pitkin, 64, 65, 106.

196 Took unusual forms: *Saratogian*, June 25, 1885.

197 "One of the many cranks:" Undated photostat copy of a *Saratogian* article, from Grant Cottage Archives.

198 "spent several hours": PUSG 31, 383; Grant's writing: Goldhurst, 216–217.

199 "Do as I do": Goldhurst, 214, has Grant handing this to Julia; PUSG 31, 389n, says of this, "On June 29, USG wrote a note, presumably for his family."

201 "This will be found": Objects placed along with the letter of farewell, Goldhurst, 231.

202 "The fact is that": PUSG 31, 441n.

202 "I found this a.m.": Ibid., 393n.

204 "I have worked harder": Ibid., 391n.

204 State Prison: Smith, *Autobiography*, 487.

204 "About an hour ago": PUSG 31, 409n.

205 "If I live long enough": Ibid., 415.

206 "my end is approaching rapidly": Ibid., 416.

207 "We are all praying for you": Pitkin, 79; Goldhurst, 223.

207 "Yes, I know": PUSG 31, 144 and 114n.

207 "one of the most unjust wars": Grant, *Personal Memoirs*, facsimile edition, 53.

208 "delivered a speech in Spanish—": PUSG 31, 419.

208 "I hope Mexico may soon begin": Ibid., 417.

208 "I feel very thankful": Ibid., 419.

208 "acting the part of gentlemen": Ibid., 436n.

209 "gave me his hand": Goldhurst, 221.

209 one of our mules: Grant, *Memoirs*, facsimile, vol. 1, 182–183.

210 He ran out of money: The overall situation and arrangement is in Goldhurst, 59–60.

211 "You are separated from your people": Smith, *Grant*, 165.

211 Conversing with Buckner: PUSG 31, 424.

212 "I have witnessed": Ibid., 423–424.

212 "Buck has brought": Ibid., 425. The majority of Grant's notes to Douglas are to be found in Ibid., 383–440.

Chapter Seventeen: Sunlight and Shadow

213 "I have my book off my mind now": PUSG 31, 129.

213 "I would only be too happy": Ibid., 429n.

214 "foolish letter": Ibid., 432n.

214 "corrected up": Ibid., 429.

216 "the $1,500": Ibid., 430n., and supra, 50–51 and 51n.

216 "Grant was a very poor businessman": Lewis, *Captain Sam Grant*, 377.

217 "It is probably well": Grant, *Personal Memoirs* 2, facsimile edition, 547–553.

219 "I feel that we are on the eve of a new era": Grant, *Personal Memoirs* 2, 553.

219 Summer continued: PUSG 31, 423–442n.

219 "One day he put aside": Goldhurst, 230.

220   "Fred. If you feel the least unwell": PUSG 31, 441.
221   Julia would reach the decision: Pitkin, 96.
223   "On the way back": Ibid., 134, quoting from Douglas's account in the appendix, 133–139.
223   "three messages to his family": These are not readily identifiable.
224   "There's no earthly reason": Ibid., 441n.
224   "said that the patient": Ibid.
224   "gave orders": Ibid.
224   "July 22": details of newspapers and preparations Goldhurst, 228–229.
224   "Fix the clock right": Pitkin, 137.
224   "with an intelligent look": Ibid.
225   "I don't want anybody": NYT, July 24, 2; also, for nearly the same quote, Goldhurst, 138.
225   At 7 p.m.: Douglas, in Pitkin, 137.
225   Fred put his arm: Goldhurst, 229.
226   "Water"" Ibid.
226   "Mrs. Grant has been sitting": NYT, July 24, 1885. It should be repeated that the chronology of these days is complicated; certain quotations could apply to events of either July 23 or 24.
226   "At sunrise": Pitkin, 138–139.
227   "she told us how": Cantacuzene, 53.
227   July 20 he had put away: Grant, Twain to Henry Ward Beecher, re "three days later": Goldhurst, 220.
228   "His breathing had become soft": NYT, July 24, 1885.
229   "Breakfast dragged": This and other quotations involving Julia that morning and her wreath are from Cantacuzene, 54–56.
229   Examples of news traveling, and signs of mourning in Manhattan: Goldhurst, 230.
231   Richard C. Drum: Pitkin, 99, and Goldhurst, 232.
231   Things went into motion: Goldhurst, 238–239, 241.
232   "I think his book": Ibid., 230.
231   Messages from the world's leaders: Ibid., 238–239, 241.
232   "Such a flood": Pitkin, 99.
232   Tributes came from the South: Ibid., 98. "Grant memorial meeting," NYT, August 12, 1885.
232   " . . . had his life ended": Pitkin, 98.
233   Confederate General James Longstreet: NYT, July 24, 1885.
234   Headed for Mt. McGregor: The only source I find that places Sherman at Mt. McGregor is Ross, 312.

234 "May you continue": Pitkin, 112, citing Ross, 313–316.

234 Grand Army of the Republic units: Goldhurst, 233.

234 Passion for collecting souvenirs: Pitkin, 106.

237 "what she would see there": Ibid., 108.

238 Twain, who was already on record: Concerning Newman: Smith, *Autobiography* 1, 99–100.

238 "More than all things else": Goldhurst, 237.

Chapter Eighteen: Good-bye, Ulysses. And Thank You.

239 It was a brick vault: Goldhurst, 234.

240 Planning for arriving crowds: Goldhurst, 238–239, 241.

241 John J. Pershing: Ibid., 237.

241 "I remember vast crowds": Cantacuzene, 56–57.

243 Five of the Navy's warships: Ibid., 239.

245 "Even my childish brain": Cantacuzene, 57–58.

246 "Broadway moved like a river": Goldhurst, 241.

246 "With both my parents": Cantacuzene, 58.

247 "a feeling of unutterable weariness and loss": Ibid.

BIBLIOGRAPHY

Adams, Henry. *The Education of Henry Adams: An Autobiography*. Boston: Houghton Mifflin, 1974.

Adams, James Truslow. *The Epic of America*. New York: Garden City Books, 1931, 1933.

Allison, Jim. "*President U. S. Grant's Speech*," *New York Tribune*, October 1, 1875.

American Experience. "The Panic of 1873." http://www.pbs.org/wgbh/americanexperience/features/general-article/grant-panic/.

Badeau, Adam. *Grant in Peace. From Appomattox to Mount McGregor; a Personal Memoir*. Freeport, NY: Books for Libraries Press, 1971.

———. *Military History of Ulysses S. Grant: From April, 1861, to April, 1865*. 3 vols. New York: D. Appleton, 1868–1881.

Badeau, General Adam, "The Last Days of General Grant." *Century* 30(6): 919–939.

Barber, James, and John Y. Simon. *U. S. Grant, The Man and the Image: An Exhibition at the National Portrait Gallery . . . 1985, and the Lyndon Baines Johnson Library and Museum . . . 1986*. Washington: The Gallery; Carbondale: Southern Illinois University Press, 1985.

Bradley, Joseph P. *Miscellaneous Writings of the Late Hon. Joseph P. Bradley. . . .* Reprint. Newark, NJ: L. J. Hardman, 1901.

Brown, Francis. *Raymond of the Times*. New York: Norton, 1951.

Buell, General D. C. "Memoranda on the Civil War," *Century* 30(6): 956–957.

Calhoun, Charles W., ed. *The Gilded Age: Essays on the Origins of Modern America*. Wilmington, DE: Scholarly Resources, 1996.

Cantacuzene, Princess Julia. *My Life Here and There*. New York: Scribner's Sons, 1921.

Casey, Emma Dent. "When Grant Went A-Courtin'" Pt.1–2. *The Circle: A Modern Department Magazine for All People*. 1909(Jan.): 11–12, 63; 1909(Feb.): 80–81, 108.

Cashman, Sean Dennis. *America in the Gilded Age: From the Death of Lincoln to the Rise of Theodore Roosevelt*. New York: New York University Press, 1988.

Clark, Judith Freeman. *America's Gilded Age: An Eyewitness History*. New York: Facts on File, 1992.

Clarke, Martha J. "General Grant and Mount McGregor." Transcribed by Marie Kelsey, June–July, 2002, from a document in the Grant Cottage Archives. Available at http://faculty.css.edu/mkelsey/usgrant/MarthaClarke.html.

Clarke, O. P. *General Grant at Mount MacGregor*. Saratoga Springs, NY: The Saratogian Print, 1906. Reprinted August 2009 by Velocity Print Solutions, Scotia, NY.

Chidsey, Donald Barr. *The Gentleman from New York: A Life of Roscoe Conkling*. New Haven: Yale University Press, 1935.

Church, William Conant. *Ulysses S. Grant and the Period of National Preservation and Reconstruction*. New York: G. P. Putnam's Sons, 1897.

Clews, Henry. *Twenty-eight Years in Wall Street*. 1908. Reprint. New York: Arno Press, 1973.

Coolidge, Louis Arthur. *Ulysses S. Grant*. 2 vols. Boston, New York: Houghton Mifflin Co., 1924.

Dodge, Grenville Mellen. *Personal Recollections of President Abraham Lincoln, General Ulysses S. Grant and General William T. Sherman*. Council Bluffs, IA: The Monarch Printing Co., 1914.

Eldridge, Charles W. "Memoranda on the Civil War." *Century* 30(6): 957–958.

Ellington, Charles G. *The Trial of U. S. Grant: The Pacific Coast Years, 1852–1854*. Glendale, CA: A. H. Clark Co., 1987.

Fatout, Paul. *Mark Twain on the Lecture Circuit*. Bloomington, IN: Indiana University Press, 1960.

Fish, James D. *Memories of Early Business Life and Associates*. New York, 1907.

Fleming, Thomas J. *West Point: The Men and Times of the United Military Academy*. New York: Morrow, 1969.

Flood, Charles Bracelen. *Grant and Sherman: The Friendship that Won the Civil War*. New York: Farrar, Straus and Giroux, 2005.

———. *Lee: The Last Years*. New York: Houghton Mifflin, 1981.

Ford, Worthington Chauncey, ed. *Cycle of Adams Letters, 1861–1865*. Boston: Houghton Mifflin, 1920.

Frost, Lawrence A. *U. S. Grant Album; A Pictorial Biography of Ulysses S. Grant from Leather Clerk to the White House*. New York: Bonanza Books, 1966.

Garland, Hamlin. "Ulysses Grant—His Last Year." *McClure's Magazine* 11(May 1898): 86–96.

————. *Ulysses S. Grant; His Life and Character*. New York: Macmillan, 1920.

Glatthaar, Joseph T. *Partners in Command: The Relationships Between Leaders in the Civil War*. New York: Free Press, 1994.

Goldhurst, Richard. *Many Are the Hearts: The Agony and the Triumph of Ulysses S. Grant*. New York: Reader's Digest Press, 1975.

Grant, Jesse Root. *In the Days of My Father, General Grant*. New York, London: Harper & Brothers, 1925.

Grant, Julia Dent. *The Personal Memoirs of Julia Dent Grant (Mrs. Ulysses S. Grant)*. New York: Putnam, 1975.

Grant, Ulysses S. "Battles and Leaders of the Civil War: The Battle of Shiloh." *Century* 29, no. 4 (1886).

————. *Memoirs and Selected Letters. New York:* Library of America edition, 1990.

————. *Personal Memoirs of U. S. Grant*. 2 vols. New York: Charles L. Webster & Company, 1885.

————. "Preparing for the Wilderness Campaign." *Century* 31, no. 5 (March 1886).

————. *Ulysses S. Grant; Warrior and Statesman*. New York: Morrow, 1969.

Green, Horace. *General Grant's Last Stand; a Biography*. New York: C. Scribner's Sons, 1936.

Gressley, Gene. *West by East; the American West in the Gilded Age*. Provo, UT: Brigham Young University Press, 1972.

Grodinsky, Julius. *Transcontinental Railway Strategy, 1869–1893; a Study of Businessmen*. Philadelphia: University of Pennsylvania Press, 1962.

Grossman, Mark. *Political Corruption in America: An Encyclopedia of Scandals, Power, and Greed*. Santa Barbara, CA: ABC-CLIO, 2003.

Guare, John. *A Few Stout Individuals: A Play in Two Acts*. New York: Grove Press, 2003.

Harmon, Mark D. "The *New York Times* and the Theft of the 1876 Presidential Election." *Journal of American Culture* (Summer 1987): 35–41.

Harnsberger, Caroline. *Everyone's Mark Twain*. South Brunswick, NJ: A. S. Barnes, 1972.

————. *The Gilded Age*. New York: Oxford University Press, 1996.

Headley, P. C. *The Life and Deeds of Gen. U. S. Grant*. Boston: B. B. Russell, 1885.

Hesseltine, William Best. *Ulysses S. Grant, Politician*. New York: F. Ungar Pub. Co., 1957.

Hill, Hamlin Lewis. *Mark Twain's Letters to his Publishers: 1867–1889*. Berkeley: University of California Press, 1967.

Hoogenboom, Ari Arthur. *The Gilded Age*. Englewood Cliffs, NJ: Prentice-Hall, 1967.

———. *Outlawing the Spoils: A History of the Civil Service Reform Movement 1865–1883*. Urbana: University of Illinois Press, 1961.

Johnson, Robert Underwood, and Clarence Clough Buel. *Battles and Leaders of the Civil War: Being for the Most Part Contributions by Union and Confederate Officers*. 1887. Reprint, Secaucus, NJ: Castle 182.

Johnson, Robert Underwood, and Margaret Woodbridge McFadon Willing. *Remembered Yesterdays*. Colt Kipling Collection (Library of Congress). Boston: Little, Brown, and Co., 1923.

Jones, James Pickett. *John A. Logan, Stalwart Republican from Illinois*. Tallahassee: University Presses of Florida, 1982.

Jones, Wilmer L. *Generals in Blue and Gray*. 2 vols. Westport, CT: Praeger, 2004.

Jordan, David M. *Roscoe Conkling of New York: Voice in the Senate*. Ithaca, NY: Cornell University Press, 1971.

Kaplan, Justin. *Mark Twain, A Profile*. New York: Hill and Wang, 1967.

———. *Mark Twain and His World*. New York: Crescent Books, 1982.

———. *Mr. Clemens and Mark Twain, A Biography*. New York: Simon and Schuster, 1966.

Krout, John A. *United States to 1877 with Mid-Term and Final Examinations*. 7th ed. New York: Barnes & Noble, 1971.

Larsen, Reif. *The Selected Works of T. S. Spivet*. New York: Penguin Press, 2009.

Lewis, G. B. "General Ulysses S. Grant's Hip Fracture." *Orthopedic Review* 16, no. 11 (November 1987): 78–80.

Lewis, Lloyd. *Captain Sam Grant*. Boston: Little, Brown, 1950.

———. *Sherman: Fighting Prophet*. New York: Harcourt Brace, 1932.

Lyman, Theodore. *Meade's Headquarters, 1863–1865; Letters of Colonel Theodore Lyman from the Wilderness to Appomattox*. Boston: Atlantic Monthly Press, 1922.

Lynch, Denis Tilden. *"Boss" Tweed: The Story of a Grim Generation*. New York: Boni and Liveright, 1927.

Mandelbaum, Seymour. *Boss Tweed's New York*. New York: John Wiley & Sons, 1965.

Maverick, Augustus. *Henry J. Raymond and the New York Press*. Reprint. New York: Arno Press, Inc., 1970.

McFeely, William S. *Grant: A Biography*. New York: Norton, 1981.

McFeely, William S. and Neil Giordano. *Ulysses S. Grant: An Album: Warrior, Husband, Traveler, Emancipator, Writer*. New York: W. W. Norton, 2003.

Mende, Elsie Porter. *An American Soldier and Diplomat: Horace Porter*. New York: Frederick A. Stokes Company, 1927.

Misa, Thomas J. *A Nation of Steel: The Making of Modern America, 1865–1925*. Baltimore: Johns Hopkins University Press, 1995.

Morgan, H. Wayne. *The Gilded Age: A Reappraisal*. Syracuse, NY: Syracuse University Press, 1963.

Morris, Roy. *Fraud of the Century: Rutherford B. Hayes, Samuel Tilden, and the Stolen Election of 1876*. New York: Simon & Schuster, 2003.

Nagle, John Copeland. "How Not to Count Votes." *Columbia Law Review* 104, no. 6 (October 2004): 1732–1764.

Neider, Charles, ed. *The Selected Letters of Mark Twain*. New York: Cooper Square Press, 1999.

———. *The Autobiography of Mark Twain*. New York: Harper, 1959.

Nevins, Allan. *Hamilton Fish, The Inner History of the Grant Administration*. 2 vols. New York: Dodd, Mead & Co., 1937.

Newton, F. M. "Taps." *Century* 30(6): 956.

O'Connor, Richard. *Sheridan the Inevitable*. Indianapolis: Bobbs Merrill, 1953.

Packard, J. F. *Grant's Tour Around the World; with Incidents of his journey through England, Ireland, Scotland, etc.,* . . . Cincinnati, OH: Forshee & McMakin, 1880.

Perry, Mark. *Grant and Twain: the Story of a Friendship that Changed America*. New York: Random House, 2004.

Pitkin, Thomas M. *The Captain Departs; Ulysses S. Grant's Last Campaign*. Carbondale, IL: Southern Illinois Press, 1973.

Porter, General Horace. *Campaigning with Grant*. Edited with an introduction by Wayne C. Temple. New York: Bonanza Books, 1961.

———. "Lincoln and Grant." *Century* 30(6): 934–947.

Post, J. L., ed. *Reminiscences by Personal Friends of Gen. U.S. Grant and the History of Grant's Log Cabin*. St. Louis, 1904.

Powers, Ron. *Mark Twain: A Life*. New York: Free Press, 2006.

Reed, Thomas B. *Modern Eloquence*. Vol. 3. Philadelphia: John D. Morris and Company, 1900.

Rhea, Gordon C. *To the North Anna River: Grant and Lee, May 13–25, 1864*. Baton Rouge, LA: Louisiana State University Press, 2000.

Ross, Ishbel. *The General's Wife*. New York: Dodd, Mead, 1959.

Scaturro, Frank. *President Grant Reconsidered*. Lanham, MD: University Press of America, 1998.

Seawell, M. E. "General Grant's Premonition." *Century* 30(6): 958.

Sherman, William T., Ulysses S. Grant, William M. McPherson, William K. Bixby. *Two Letters from General William Techumseh Sherman to General Ulysses S. Grant & William T. [sic] McPherson in the Collection of W. K. Bixby of Saint Louis*. Boston: Privately printed by the Merrymount Press, 1919.

Shrady, George. "General Grant's Last Days; With a Short Biographical Sketch of Dr. Shrady." *Century Magazine* 76 (May–July 1908): 102–113, 411–429.

Simon, John Y., ed. *The Papers of Ulysses S. Grant*. 31 vols. Carbondale, IL: Southern Illinois University Press, 1967–2009.

Simpson, Brooks D. *Ulysses S. Grant: Triumph Over Adversity, 1822–1865*. Boston: Houghton Mifflin, 2000.

Smith, Harriet Elinor, ed., *Autobiography of Mark Twain, Vol. 1*. Berkeley: University of California Press, 2010.

Smith, Jean Edward. *Grant*. New York: Simon & Schuster, 2001.

Stein, Gertrude, and Thornton Wilder. *Four in America*. New Haven, CT: Yale University Press, 1947.

Tilden, S. J. *The New York City "Ring": Its Origin, Maturity and Fall, Discussed in a Reply to the New York Times*. College Park, MD: McGrath Publishing Co., 1969.

Ulysses S. Grant Homepage from the Keya Morgan Collection. http://www.empirenet.com/~ulysses/index.htm.

Ward, Geoffrey C., "We were as brothers." *American Heritage*, November 1990, 14.

Webster, Samuel C., ed. *Mark Twain, Business Man*. Boston: Little, Brown, 1946.

Williams, T. Harry. *McClellan, Sherman, and Grant*. New Brunswick, NJ: Rutgers University Press, 1962.

Wilson, Edmund. *Patriotic Gore; Studies in the Literature of the American Civil War*. New York: Oxford University Press, 1962.

Wilson, James Grant. *Great Commanders: General Grant*. New York: Baker and Taylor, 2007.

Wilson, Gen. James Harrison. "Reminiscences of General Grant." *Century* 30(6): 947–955.

Wister, Owen. *Ulysses S. Grant*. Boston: Small, Maynard, 1900.

Young, John Russell. *Around the World with General Grant*. Baltimore, MD: John Hopkins University Press, 2002.

INDEX